The
GO ON GIRL!
BOOK CLUB Guide
for Reading Groups

The
GO ON GIRL!
BOOK CLUB Guide
for Reading Groups

· Works worth reading

· Chats with our favorite authors

· Tips for starting and sustaining a literary circle

· Questions and topics to get you talking ... and more!

Monique Greenwood, Lynda Johnson and Tracy Mitchell-Brown

Founders of the largest national reading group for Black women

HYPERION

New York

Dedicated to the memory of Earl N. Garrett, Jr.,
the sisters in our literary circle,
and the men in our lives—Glenn and Darrell—
who respect the sanctity of the second Sunday
of every month.

Library of Congress Cataloging-in-Publication Data
Greenwood, Monique.
    The Go on Girl! Book Club guide for reading groups / by Monique
Greenwood, Lynda Johnson, and Tracy Mitchell-Brown
        p. cm.
    Includes bibliographical references.
    ISBN 0-7868-8350-2
    1. Go on Girl Book Club.   2. Group reading—United States—
Handbooks, manuals, etc.   3. Book clubs—United States—
Handbooks, manuals, etc.   4. Afro-American women—Books and
reading—Handbooks, manuals, etc.   I. Johnson, Lynda.
II. Mitchell-Brown, Tracy.   III. Title.
LC6651.G74   1999
374'.22—dc21   98–40564
                                                                      CIP

FIRST EDITION

Designed by Robin Arzt

10 9 8 7 6 5 4 3 2 1

The authors gratefully acknowledge the following for their cooperation in reprinting the following excerpts:
Excerpt from *Easier to Kill* by Valerie Wilson Wesley. Copyright © 1999
   by Valerie Wilson Wesley. Reprinted by permission of the author.
From *Blanche Cleans Up* by barbaraneely. Copyright © 1998 by Barbara Neely.
   Used by permission of Viking Penguin, a division of Penguin Putnam Inc.
Reprinted by permission of The Putnam Publishing Group from *Straight, No
   Chaser* by Jill Nelson. Copyright © 1997 by Jill Nelson.
Excerpt from *Nouvelle Soul* by Barbara Summers. Copyright © 1992
   by Barbara Summers. Reprinted with permission from Amistad Press.
From *The Isis Papers* by Dr. Frances Cress Welsing. Copyright © 1991
   by Dr. Frances Cress Welsing, reprinted by permission of Third World
   Press, Inc., Chicago, Illinois.
Copyright © 1997 by Virginia DeBerry and Donna Grant. From *Tryin' to Sleep in
   the Bed You Made* by Virginia DeBerry and Donna Grant. Reprinted by permission of St. Martin's Press, Incorporated.
Excerpt from *Tempest Rising* by Diane McKinney-Whetstone. Copyright © 1998
   by Dianne McKinney-Whetstone. By permission of William Morrow &
   Company, Inc.
Excerpt from *The Itch* by Benilde Little. Copyright © 1998 by Benilde Little.
   Reprinted with permission from the author.
From *The Men of Brewster Place* by Gloria Naylor. Copyright © 1998
   by Gloria Naylor. Reprinted with permission of Hyperion.
Excerpt from *Big Girls Don't Cry* by Connie Briscoe. Copyright © 1996
   by Connie Briscoe. Reprinted by permission of HarperCollins Publishers, Inc.
Reprinted by permission of G.P. Putnam's Sons, a division of The Putnam
   Publishing Group from *Singing in the Comeback Choir* by Bebe Moore
   Campbell. Copyright © 1998 by ELMA, Inc.
From *Ain't Gonna Be the Same Fool Twice* by April Sinclair. Copyright © 1996
   April Sinclair. Reprinted with permission from Hyperion.
Excerpt from *Chesapeake Song* by Brenda Lane Richardson. Copyright © 1993
   by Brenda Lane Richardson. Reprinted with permission from Amistad Press.
Excerpt beginning page 253 from *Parable of Talents* by Octavia E. Butler
   reprinted by arrangement with Octavia E. Butler and Writer's House as agent
   for the author. Copyright © 1999 Octavia E. Butler.
Excerpt from Chapter 2 from *Dust Tracks on a Road* by Zora Neale Hurston.
   Copyright © 1942 by Zora Neale Hurston. Copyright renewed 1970
   by John C. Hurston. Reprinted by permission of HarperCollins Publishers, Inc.

Contents

Contents

Contents

Contents

Contents

Part 1

How It All Began

CHAPTER ONE

Book Clubs Now and Then
An Introduction

Don't even bother to call or drop by in the afternoon on the second Sunday of the month. This is sacred time, sister-bonding time. It's when the 12 women of the founding Go On Girl! Book Club chapter push back the rest of the world and get together with each other to talk—sometimes shout; reflect—sometimes emotionally cleanse; listen—sometimes strategize; eat—sometimes gorge; but always renew. At the center of the exchange is a single book . . . just sheets of paper bound by a cover, but with words that touch the very core of who we are as diverse, dynamic Black women.

All across the country this same powerful scenario is taking place among sisters, from the Imani-Nia Book Study Group in Denver, Colorado, to the Bibliophiles, a literary sister-circle in Essex County, New Jersey. We are following through on our culture's long-standing tradition of coming together around a sustained and sustaining interest in literature. While it is commonly accepted that we are an oral people—some of our most memorable stories were told to us by our elders—it is also true that we have always placed a value on books and the collective reading experience (perhaps because our very right to read was so long denied).

Since the beginning of the nineteenth century, Black women have gotten together to read, discuss, enlighten and bond.

Free women of color in the early 1800s called their book clubs literary societies, and in addition to self-enrichment, their agenda almost always included furthering abolitionist causes.

Although books were not readily accessible, nor easily attainable, in nonfree states prior to the Civil War, free Blacks met to discuss whatever was available. Often it was the Bible or personal essays. Our literary foremothers were generally professional-class women—beauticians, dressmakers, teachers—or wives of men of professional status. Their meetings were run much as ours are today. They provided members with intellectual stimulation, and frequently inspired them to adopt projects that benefited the race, such as fund-raising to support local colored schools. In this way, Black women developed leadership skills unhampered by either male or White dominance long before the suffragette movement of the early 1900s.

While such literary societies proliferated across the country—even in the South—before the abolition of slavery, Northern cities, especially Philadelphia, had the largest share of reading and discussion groups; Philadelphia also holds the distinction of being home to the first Black women's literary society—The Female and Literary Society of Philadelphia. This group was founded around 1831 with some twenty members who met every Tuesday evening with the goal of "mental improvement in moral and literary pursuits." Members wrote original plays, short stories and essays that were anonymously placed in a box and later critiqued by the group.

The Harlem Renaissance period also turned out to be a time of resurgence for Black reading groups. In the early 1900s, the Works Project Administration, instituted by President Franklin Delano Roosevelt, provided funds for promising artists and writers, freeing talents like Langston Hughes and Zora Neale Hurston to create without financial worry. The public—Black and White—devoured the works of the "Black Literati," which used Harlem as its spiritual home base and creative playground. Not surprisingly, one of the most popular reading and discussion groups throughout the 1920s was held at the New York Public Library's Harlem Branch, now the site of the Schomburg Center for Research in Black Culture.

Now, as we approach a new millennium, Black literature and organized reading clubs are again at the height of popularity. Some attribute this third wave of interest in our literature to Terry McMillan. In the summer of 1992, there was hardly a sister around who didn't have her nose buried in *Waiting to Exhale*. On city subways, perfect strangers greeted each other with "Girl, isn't this book the bomb!" On suburban playgrounds, mothers kept one eye on the kids, the other on the book, as they talked about Robin and her friends with any sister who happened to sit beside them on the park bench. Terry's storytelling touched Black women of all ages, socioeconomic backgrounds and beliefs, landing her on the prestigious *New York Times* best-seller list for 35 weeks. Others suggest that the current boom began even earlier, in 1982, with Alice Walker's Pulitzer prize–winning *The Color Purple*. One thing, however, is beyond dispute: Both women have given us hours of reading pleasure, and the mega-sales of their books, followed by the successes of their big-screen versions, have prompted the publishing world to give us more of what we crave—our own stories in our own voices.

It's difficult to say just how many Black reading groups exist today, though clearly the popularity of TV talk show diva Oprah Winfrey's Book Club has sent the numbers soaring. The Go On Girl! Book Club predates Winfrey's by about five years. We began humbly during the summer of 1991 when the three of us—best friends who were working together in NYC at the time—decided to turn our spontaneous lunchtime book conversations into an organized discussion group. We started meeting monthly with nine of our other sister-friends, and in less than one year, we expanded our network with a chapter in Washington, D.C. Through word of mouth, our presence at literary events and national publicity ranging from articles in *Essence, Ladies' Home Journal* and *Quarterly Black Review* to television news broadcasts, our numbers swelled. To date, there are 32 Go On Girl! chapters around the country, from Memphis, Tennessee, to Seattle, Washington, with nearly 400 sisters all reading the same book at the same time. That's a potent psychic connection if ever there was one!

Through our many trials and triumphs, we have learned volumes about what it takes to start and sustain a book club. But, more importantly, we have arrived at deep truths about ourselves. This book is our gift to those looking to get a reading group up and running and to those hoping to keep one afloat. Part I tells more about the unique Go On Girl! sisterhood—the nation's largest Black women's reading group—while Part III offers precise, practical and easy-to-follow steps for organizing a book club, selecting the books, keeping the interest high and finessing the operating procedures. Our basic premise is: this is not work, it's fun—but there *is* work involved.

That leaves Part II of the book—our pride, and, we trust, your joy. It's where we say "Go On Girl!" to the many writers of the African Diaspora who have touched and changed our lives by simply putting pen to paper in a powerful way. Though we read our brothers too, every winner of our prestigious Go On Girl! award, which we first presented in 1993, just happens to have been a woman. Some of these winners you will know; others you will meet here for the first time and be pleased to make their acquaintance. We also include excerpts of the latest works from these award-winning authors—a treasure in itself! Each entry is followed by provocative questions specifically crafted to jump-start your discussions after completing the entire book. What's more, intimate chats with our favorite authors will help you get to know them even better. These women inspire us, but who inspires them? What "real-life" experiences have shaped their fictional works? How do they master the discipline to write, and what about their journey to literary success?

Finally, in Part II, we also give you an understanding of genres from science fiction to social commentary, while uncovering the impact Black writers have had on each of these literary forms. We may know mystery writer Walter Mosley, but do we know of his forefather, Rudolph Fisher? The Go On Girls read broadly; for the first time, we make public in this book our rich and varied reading list since our inception almost a decade ago. Let it be a valuable resource for you and your reading group with a guarantee attached to it from us (with thanks to Gladys Knight): You'll be there between each line of pain and glory.

ters are hosting. So far Brooklyn, NY; Washington, D.C.; St. Louis; Philadelphia; Newark, NJ; and Prince Georges County, Maryland, are cities that don't owe us a thing when it comes to fun.

Each annual gathering starts on a Friday night with a board meeting followed by a cocktail mixer for all members. The next morning, there's a general membership meeting over breakfast. That's when we get to hear what individual chapters have done throughout the year. One chapter, for example, may tell how it launched a junior Go On Girl! group for high-school teens, donated books to their local women's jail or went on a group visit to Monticello the month it read Barbara Chase-Riboud's *Sally Hemings*, the historical fiction work about the affair between Thomas Jefferson and his slave on his Virginia plantation. On the other hand, another chapter might share that it read the books and met to discuss them. Period. Both would receive rave applause, because Go On Girl! chapters can do as much as they like—or as little. The only required activity: read and meet once a month.

Of course, the highlight of the annual weekend is the awards banquet. While each month the Go On Girls support authors of African descent by purchasing their books and sending encouraging letters to them and to their publishers, we vote to specially honor two writers: one with our Author of the Year Award and the other with our Best New Author Award. Since the first affair in 1993, every author has attended—from Gloria Naylor to Bebe Moore Campbell—to personally receive her honor and to delight the audiences of 400 or more with a reading and a book signing. Special recognition awards have gone to poetry legend Sonia Sanchez and

Harlem Renaissance writer Dorothy West; and to pioneering publisher Beacon Press for its aggressive stance on publishing authors of color, Black-owned Noble Press for making strides in publishing first-time Black authors, Time-Life Books for its inspiring historical series "Voices of Triumph," and Jubilee Year Books, a one-woman publishing company that produced the children's book *Birth of Christ*, which tells the Christmas story in our voice and with our images.

Almost unanimously, our winning authors say it's the book club's whimsical name and creative logo that grab their attention when we write to announce their selection. If you think back to the hottest Black comedy show at the start of the '90s, you'll probably immediately know the genesis of our name. It was *In Living Color*, and a weekly skit during the show featured an Oprah-like talk-show host who punctuated just about every statement her guest made with the phrase, "Go on, girl!" That saying of the moment clearly communicated the positive attitude the book-club members have about themselves and about the proliferation of writers telling our stories in bold new ways. Lynda's now-deceased husband, artist Earl N. Garrett, Jr., kept the name in mind when creating our logo: a sassy, dreadlock-wearing sister with eyes glued to a good read. The Go On Girl! signature sister now appears on the custom-made awards plate presented to the Author of the Year, as well as on a full line of merchandise, including bookmarks, coffee mugs, cooking aprons, T-shirts, magnets, note cards and pins. She also greets members on a quarterly basis in our newsletter, and it's her face the world sees on our Web site, www.goongirl.org.

We're not exactly sure what's next for the Go On Girl!

Book Club (more chapters for girls, the first chapter for women behind bars and a scholarship for budding literary talent are all in formation), but one thing we're certain of—we'll leave no page unturned when it comes to making time to read and to revel in the company of our sisters.

Part II

The Literary Work

Murder They Wrote
The Mystery Genre

When Denzel Washington was cast to play the title role in 1995's *Devil in a Blue Dress*, female fans of Walter Mosley's detective novel, on which the movie was based, gave an approving nod. While reading *Devil*, *A Red Death*, *White Butterfly* and *Black Betty*, we had always imagined this smooth sleuth as easy on the eyes. Proving popular with more than just African-American women, the "Easy Rawlins" series catapulted Mosley to the top of his genre and earned him worldwide fame and honors, including the Private Eye Writers of America's coveted Shamus Award.

But while 1990 marked the debut of "Easy," the mid-'90s may best be remembered as the time Black female private eyes strutted onto the scene—Valerie Wilson Wesley's Tamara Hayle, barbaraneely's self-appointed PI Blanche White and Eleanor Taylor Bland's Marti MacAlister leading the way. Their savvy, sassy and sister-affirming ways have turned Black women by the droves onto sleuthing, a genre that had been largely the domain of men, my dear Watson.

Whether featuring a female or male protagonist, the Black detective novel's roots can be traced all the way back to 1937, when Rudolph Fisher published *The Conjure Man Dies: A Mystery Tale of Dark Harlem*. While Fisher was the first African-American to spin a sleuth story, Chester Himes is per-

BOOK PRAISE FROM GO ON GIRLS

"I love it when a writer expertly weaves issues worth thinking about into a story. barbaraneely never comes off as preachy in her Blanche mysteries. Like in the latest, Blanche Cleans Up, *it wasn't until I had finished the book that I realized she had touched upon so many points. From homophobia in the Black community, to so-called Black leaders selling out, to the supposed indifference in our communities when it comes to environmental issues—it's all in there."*

Jacqueline Contee
Harlem, New York

"Valerie Wilson Wesley's Tamara Hayle character fits me. I could play the hell out of the role, if Angela Bassett isn't available! Tamara's wit, style and way of viewing people; that's me. But the excitement she finds as a private investigator, unfortunately, is not my reality on a daily basis."

Kitwanda Reeves
Brooklyn, New York

"I love reading mysteries, especially Walter Mosley's books. They're easy to read and follow, yet they keep you guessing. Besides, it's hard not to like the characters Easy and Mouse."

Tracey White
Richmond, Virginia

Easier to Kill
by Valerie Wilson Wesley

Valerie Wilson Wesley has become one of the hottest names on the female crime-writing scene. Her mysteries, starring the tough but vulnerable Tamara Hayle, captivate and excite while tackling some of the more disturbing social issues of our time. In the fifth book of her successful series, Wesley poignantly illustrates the dangers of keeping secrets.

It was the most elegant office I'd ever seen, but the flowers on the desk made me think about death. They were the same white lilies that hovered on the edge of every funeral I'd ever been to, and their sweet, sickening smell seemed to hit me no matter where I turned my head. I pushed them out of my mind and tried to focus on the woman in the red Chanel suit who sat across from me.

Her name was Mandy Magic, at least that was what she called herself these days, and she'd clawed her way out of the projects where we both grew up to become the best known radio personality in Essex County. She had a pretty face the color of Kenyan coffee, hair as black and straight as a wig, and a ruby on her finger that was too big *not* to be real. When she'd called last Friday and requested a Monday morning meeting about a "delicate matter," I couldn't believe my good luck. I still didn't believe it.

"I know you're supposed to be a top-notch private eye but

"What were the lyrics?"

"Movin' on up. Movin' on up. To the big time. To that deluxe apartment in the sky. Movin' on up . . . something like that." She shook her head in frustration. I added the words for her.

"We finally got a piece of the pie?"

"Yeah. A piece of the pie." She said it as if it embarrassed her, which made me wonder just how much her slice had cost her.

And if you were talking hard, cold cash, this suite of offices had obviously cost her a chunk. There were two other offices besides the one we were in, a modest reception area, and what looked like a small gym in a far corner. This office was, as she emphasized when I came in, her "personal" rather than professional space, which I assumed could be found in one of the radio stations she owned. I couldn't identify the dark rich wood of the furniture, but every stick matched, and that was more than I could say for the secondhand junk I own. I'd be lying if I didn't admit to a twinge of serious envy when I walked in.

When Newark had been a center of finance and commerce in the early part of the century this address had been the place to be. But that reputation, like everything else after the 1967 riots, had faded even though things were beginning to look up, and thanks to its proximity to NJPAC, the newly built performing arts center, the building was enjoying renewed popularity. But even during its hardest days, there had been a grandness about it—in the stylishly high ceilings, polished parquet floors and leaded windows big enough to let in a lot of sun, which put a golden glint on everything this morning, from the red brocade on the seats of the chairs to the ruby in Mandy Magic's ring. She studied that ring for a moment, turning it around on her finger as if she had something heavy on her mind.

"So when did the note come?"

"Last week."

"Is this the first strange letter you've gotten in the mail? You have a lot of listeners, surely some of them are—" She cut me off.

"I didn't get it through the mail. It was left at the front door of this office. But there have been small acts of vandalism, too. Obscene graffiti cut into my door. The tires of my car slashed when it's parked on the street. Small annoying things that grate on my nerves."

"It may be linked to someone you know." I chose my words carefully.

She gave me a worried look, and rushed her answer, as if she were convincing herself. "Many people have access to this building."

"From the tone of the note, the person who left it is probably resentful of your success," I continued, stating the obvious.

"I really doubt that," she snapped and took a sip of her coffee.

"Then what do you think it means?"

"Why do you think I hired you?" she said with a bitchy twist, and I took a sip of *my* coffee.

"Why not call the police, Ms. Magic? Don't you think this may be a matter for them, especially if you really think there is some kind of a—"

"Threat?" she interrupted me. "And please call me Mandy. I didn't call the cops because I don't want my business in the street. You never know where it will go from there, who will overhear you talking to them. There is no threat. The vandalism could have been a kid. It's really just the note, that's all."

"Just the note?" I tossed her words back at her, not quite mocking her but saying I knew she wasn't saying all there was to say. She thrust out her chin with a toughness that told me she didn't give a damn what I thought and that she was still the kid who had fought her way out of the ghetto. But she finally gave me the whole story. Or some of it anyway.

"My stylist was stabbed to death in Lotus Park about a week ago. His name was Tyrone Mason. They said he was the victim of one of several robberies that have turned violent recently, but this note came the day after he was killed."

"So you don't think his death was random?" She didn't answer me.

"Actually, he was more than just my stylist. He was my cousin's son. A second cousin, I guess I'd have to call him. Actually, he was closer to my daughter. My adopted daughter Taniqua. Much closer. He had only been working for me for about six months." The lack of expression on her face as she explained his death and her connection to him told me more about the state of their relationship than her words did.

"And this note came?"

"The day after he died, I told you that."

"So you think this note means that he was murdered by someone who has something against you, and that he or she is moving on up, from your second cousin to you?" I put it bluntly, and the way she cringed told me I was right. I picked the note up and examined it for some clue that I knew probably wasn't there. "It could still mean nothing," I said, placing the thing back on the edge of her desk, yet handling it too carefully for it to mean nothing. "It could just be some cruel prank from somebody who knew about the death of your cousin and wanted to get your attention or scare you for some reason. It could even be from someone who feels you owe them something. A message, maybe, from somebody who knew you back when."

"There is nobody left who knew me back when," she said with dead certainty.

"Do you think it could be from someone close to you? Somebody you trust and rely on? And could you be afraid that a person who would write a vague, nasty note like that right after your cousin's death is probably capable of other kinds of betrayals?" I was pushing it, and I knew it, but the way she wouldn't look at me told me that fear was part of it, too.

"I'd like to take this with me," I said, picking up the note again. Without saying anything, she reached in her desk and handed me an envelope to put it into. I handled it carefully even though I was sure there were no fingerprints or anything else that would warrant special precaution. "I'd also like to talk to the people on your staff if I could, assistants, secretaries, driver—"

"All I have is family," she said with surprising sadness.

There was an abrupt knock, and three people filed in as if they'd been listening at the door or silently beckoned. A thin woman dressed in a dull brown suit led the group. She was followed by a younger light-skinned man, who could have passed for white or Latino, and finally a startlingly pretty young woman, who brought up the rear. The man pulled over three chairs from corners in the large room, and they all sat down.

"I told you, Starmanda, what I thought about this idea. There is too much to risk here. Too much could get out. We can get to the bottom of this by ourselves. We don't need some woman nobody knows poking her nose around in your business." The woman spit out the words, and her eyes bore into me. But I hardly heard her. I was struck by the name she'd just said.

Starmanda. It was an old-fashioned name I hadn't heard since I was a kid, and it had belonged to my grandmother's sister who had died as a child. But she had lived for me through my grandmother's stories—through the games they played and the toys they made—paper dolls cut from newspapers, jacks made from nutshells, rhymes and hand-claps and foot-stomps that brought back her childhood and made mine richer. I could glimpse Starmanda's presence when my grandmother laughed, and I'd grown up loving that name as much as my grandmother did. Star-man-dah. A mother's way of hanging her daughter's spirit on a star.

So Mandy Magic and I had common roots after all. They were in that name and the star that somebody had dreamed for her once, too. She may have tacked that Magic business on to make some money, but she had kept enough of "Starmanda" to bind her to her past, and I liked her better for it.

"You've decided then," the thin woman said, bringing me back to her presence and that she was clearly one person who knew about that past.

"Obviously, I have."

"You're asking for trouble, Starmanda. I'm telling you that. Digging up shit, spreading it around."

"Asking for trouble, Pauline? I already have it."

"You're making too much of this whole damn thing. It's a goddamn note, for Christ's sake," said the man in a voice with

26

a bored, rough edge to it that made him sound older than he probably was. He looked to be in his early thirties and had a placid, pretty boy face that was too soft to be fine. He was shorter than I like men to be, but built like a wrestler, his biceps straining against the seams of his brown and gray Harris tweed sports coat. A gold watch—a Movado, I figured—peeked delicately from his sleeve. His fingernails were buffed and neatly manicured.

"Mind your own goddamn business, Kenton." Pauline's eyes were hard, and her voice was high and sharp. He gave a loud, rude snort showing her what he thought of her.

"This is my own goddamn business, Pauline, don't you get that yet?" His face looked familiar when he walked in, but it wasn't until she said his name that I realized who he was. Kenton Daniels III was the only son of Dr. Kenton Daniels, Jr., a revered Newark doctor and a member of a wealthy family who had founded and supported one of the first free clinics for pregnant teenagers in the city. Although the son had inherited his father's name and money, the good doctor's soul had clearly gone the way of his corpse. Kenton Daniels was a spoiled and lazy spendthrift, who traded on his family's reputation and had gone through nearly all of their small fortune in less than ten years. But his grey eyes, what they used to call "good" hair and "old-Negro-money" contacts, kept him in nice clothes and in the presence of women foolish enough to pay for his company and color-struck enough to think he represented a life they thought they had missed. It saddened me that Mandy Magic had fallen into his trap.

"Will you'all talk to her, tell her everything you can about everything she asks? About Tyrone?" Mandy asked, her voice a pleading whine. Pauline sucked her teeth. Kenton leaned back in his chair, his disapproval written in the smirk on his face.

"Will she find out what happened to him?" The last member of the party spoke, and everyone shifted uncomfortably in their seats. I turned toward the woman, curious about the reaction her words had evoked. I could see the child who peeked through the tight black jersey dress and flash of cheap gold jewelry. Her face was perfectly oval, and the hair that fell in ringlets to her chin was the kind that some folks buy. Her full lips were outlined in a jarring dark maroon lipliner and her large eyes were ringed in black. Except for the gaudy makeup and her haunted, wounded look, she could have passed for a young Lena Horne or Dorothy Dandridge. I assumed she was Taniqua, the homeless teen-age girl Mandy Magic had adopted. But whatever age she was trying to be, she was much younger than she tried to look. She threw Kenton a sly, sideways glance. He dropped his eyes with a grimace that looked like shame.

"I'll do the best I can," I answered in a matter-of-fact, take-charge voice that I hoped was convincing. "I'd like to start right away. I'll have to talk to you further, Ms. Magic— Mandy—as soon as I can." I glanced at her for approval, but she had stiffened like an animal does when it senses danger, her eyes questioning mine as if they were searching for an answer in my soul. "Will tomorrow afternoon be too soon? I'll call you to confirm?" My question stayed unanswered so long I wasn't sure she'd heard it. She nodded finally and stood up, handing me a sealed envelope that I assumed contained my retainer, then she shook my hand to seal our agreement. Her fingers were cold and trembling.

"Thank you," she said.

"Hey, don't thank me yet. You don't know *what* I'm going to find out," I spoke casually, too lightly and regretted the remark the moment I'd said it. *What in God's name had made me say something so dumb and indiscreet?* Embarrassed, I mumbled an overly formal good-bye, grabbed my bag and headed for the door. But something made me turn around for one last look before I left them. They hovered around her like vultures before a kill.

The Literary Work

DISCUSSION GUIDE

1. What things in the first chapter make you suspect that Mandy Magic is hiding something? When, if ever, do you know what it is?

2. What does Mandy Magic's real name tell you about her background? Why does her name have an impact on Tamara, and what does this say about Tamara Hayle's family history?

3. What do you think about Jake Richard's fall from grace? Will he have to pay? Should he?

4. Tamara is begining to see hints of the man her son Jamal will become. How does she handle his emerging sexuality? Is coping with a son's manhood a difficult issue for single mothers?

5. How do you feel about Mandy Magic by the end of the book? What if anything does her situation and the choices she made tell you about the lives of black women raised in poverty?

VALERIE WILSON WESLEY, SISTER SLEUTH #1

Published Works: *When Death Comes Stealing*, 1994; *Devil's Gonna Get Him*, 1995; *Where Evil Sleeps*, 1996; *No Hiding Place*, 1997; *Easier to Kill*, 1998

Home Base: Montclair, New Jersey

Literary Hero: Toni Morrison

Claim to Fame: The highly acclaimed Tamara Hayle mystery series is also published in Great Britain, France and Germany, and has been optioned for a television series.

Tamara Hayle doesn't fit the sleuth image that typifies the hard-boiled mystery genre. How would you describe the likable heroine of your hugely successful series?

She's very independent, and she's a woman who is deeply connected and committed to her past, her present, her future, her son, the people around her and also to seeing justice done. I enjoy writing her because, like all PIs, she's kind of like a knight riding into the darkness of chaos to set things straight. She fights for those who can't fight. I wanted Tamara to be a single mother, because single parenting is so hard to do. I wanted to create a character that pays my respect to all those single mothers who do it well. I gave her a son, instead of a daughter, to be able to explore some of the issues that affect

Black men. Maybe down the line, she'll adopt a daughter. Tamara is also funny, and I try to write the books with a lot of humor—it's simply the wit of women, the way we talk to each other, the way we share.

You are a prolific journalist, who has served as an editor at *Essence* magazine and who has written for publications like *Family Circle, Ms.* and the *New York Times* on a number of topics. Why did you choose to make your mark in books with mysteries?

I've always loved mysteries. I read Agatha Christie as a child, and I got my first introduction to the macabre of life through the short stories of Edgar Allen Poe. I'm pretty broad in my reading of mysteries; I love Walter Mosley and a couple of English writers like Ruth Rendell. It's the kind of thing where once you've read a lot of something, you want to try it yourself. Plus, mysteries are so appealing because they're like morality plays. They're a good way to talk about social issues, where you're addressing them but not obsessed with them.

What's the issue or underlying message you address in your newest work, *Easier to Kill*, the fifth book in the Tamara Hayle series?

The underlying message would be that you can't lie. They never do any good. You can't ever live a lie, and if you try to, ultimately it's going to catch up with you. This is a story about secrets and what happens when a person has so many of them that she can't tell. Tamara's client is a very popular radio talk-show host who hires her to find out who's been writing her threatening notes. As the story unfolds, so do the secrets that could lead to any number of people wanting to kill her.

What is the greatest mystery in your life that you've solved or that you're working on cracking?

I don't know. You're always discovering and rediscovering parts of yourself, and writing makes you do that. You realize that the older you get, the less you know. Life is always full of surprises.

Why have you set your mysteries in Newark?

Newark is a working person's city. Like a lot of other cities, it has known hard times and is trying to find its way. It's a city of immigrants with broad shoulders and even bigger dreams, a city of hope and of despair. But remember, while Tamara is based in Newark, *Devil's Gonna Get Him* actually takes place in Jamaica, where she goes to vacation. And book number six in the series, which should be out in the year 2000, will be set in Atlantic City. The character Basil Dupree will be big in the book.

So far, you've had a book a year in the Hayle mystery series. Is there a title for 1999?

I will have a non-genre book this year. It's a love story called *Charmed*, to be published by Avon. I'm very excited about this project. It's about a couple in their forties who break up; she falls in love with her daughter's ex-boyfriend, and he falls in love with his best friend's wife. Ultimately, it's about passion and how our lives are sometimes taken by it.

Is this your first book outside the mystery genre?

Oh, no. I've published two children's books that have been quite successful. *Freedom's Gifts* (1997) is a picture book about the celebration Juneteenth, and *Where Do I Go From Here* (1993) is a young adult coming-of-age novel about two Black teenagers, a boy and a girl, who attend a predominantly White private school and are confronted with class and race issues. *Where Do I Go* won an American Library Association citation for "Best Book for Reluctant Readers." I'm currently working on a children's book series for girls ages six to nine. Writing for kids and writing mysteries are two totally different kinds of writing. With children's books, the language is very simple, but you try to be as eloquent as possible. You draw from your child part and remember what it was like to be a kid.

For more than a quarter of a century, you've been married to noted screenwriter and playwright Richard Wesley (*Uptown Saturday Night, Let's Do It Again* and the Showtime movie "Mandela and DeKlerk"). What's it like sharing your life with another creative type? Is it a benefit or a challenge when a couple shares a similar professional passion?

We're a lot more sympathetic to each other and the writing process. We need the same amount of privacy to work, and we both have immediate respect for that. It also helps to be married to someone who knows and understands the pressures and the depressions that can occur when the character or the words just won't come right or when your work is undervalued when you're trying to sell it or when critics don't speak favorably about your work. There's no competition between Richard and I, though, because we write for two different worlds; he's a screenwriter and playwright and I'm a novelist. He has a very good eye for detail, and I really respect his opinions. He's one of the first people I share my work with for feedback.

How do you deal with the pressures and depressions that you say writers often face?

I walk. I also read a lot. And I love good movies, but I'm not a big TV watcher. The only exception is *General Hospital*. It comes on when I break from writing to have lunch.

Valerie Wilson Wesley is the 1996 Go On Girl! Book Club Author of the Year

Blanche Cleans Up
by barbaraneely

The smart and sassy sister snoop Blanche White is back. In Blanche Cleans Up, *the third Blanche mystery, barbaraneely takes us into the Brookline and Roxbury neighborhoods of Boston, where she herself resides. This time out, Blanche is filling in as a cook-house-keeper to a wealthy Boston politician and his wife when she becomes embroiled in a scandal that moves from the Brindles' home to the center of her own Black community.*

DAY ONE—THURSDAY

Blanche climbed out of the cab by the mailbox that read 1020. She ignored the sharp little wind that smacked at the backs of her legs—a reminder that spring in Boston could often pass for winter—and walked down the sloping drive-way. She stopped halfway to the house. Her hand automatically rose to her hip as she gave the Brindle place a good looking over.

The place reminded Blanche of her mother's friend, Miz Alicemae, who still wore lace-up corsets and knee-length cotton bloomers as though the year were 1902. It was an old-fashioned brick house, with shutters and trim in richest green. It rose up from the ground like a grand diva reaching her full height. "Vain like Miz Alicemae, too," Blanche muttered. She adjusted the strap of her slip and continued down the drive.

Understanding houses was part of how she made her living. Just like a good surgeon didn't open up a patient without an examination, she didn't clean or cook in a house until she'd done the same. She couldn't remember when she'd first understood how much houses had to say about themselves, but it was information she'd come to depend upon.

She had an uneasy feeling about this place but wasn't sure if it was due to the house itself, the job she'd promised to do here, the people who lived inside, or all of the above. She wondered if the house had a secret, like those nips of Beefeater gin Miz Alicemae kept hidden all around her house.

This was not the sort of job Blanche liked. Being house-keeper-cook was the kind of position you woke up worrying about in the middle of the night. She wasn't scared of it. There was no type of domestic work that she hadn't aced in the twenty-six years since she'd taken up the profession. It was her ability to cook, sew, clean, launder, wait table, and all the rest that made it possible for her to make her way in the world and feed and clothe her dead sister's two children. Part of the problem with this job was that she never liked supervising folks—too much like being an overseer. She hoped that Carrie, the housemaid she'd met yesterday, and Wanda, the cleaning woman, didn't need somebody looking over their shoulders, because she already had two kids at home.

She had Cousin Charlotte to thank for this job. Charlotte'd showed up at Blanche's house first thing last Saturday morning, one of her ever-present hats cocked on the left side of her head. (Did she sleep in those things?) That day she'd had on her what-to-do-with-old-dishes hat: two overlapping, grungy, gray, felt-covered saucers turned face-to-face with a long, nervous, iridescent feather poking out to the side. That feather had danced a jig while Cousin Charlotte explained that she expected Blanche to stand in for Miz Inez, Cousin Charlotte's friend, so Miz Inez and Cousin Charlotte could travel down home to Farleigh, North Carolina, together.

"Are you sure you can't get somebody else?" Blanche had asked. She'd been smart enough not to add how badly Miz Inez got on her nerves with all that tiresome talk about her wonderful white employers and best-in-the-world son.

"Blanche, I ain't got no time to be foolin' with you," Cousin Charlotte had told her. "If you ain't got the common decency to help out my oldest and dearest friend, a poor woman who ain't never had a real vacation in her life, as a favor to me, your own mama's first cousin, then I . . ."

Blanche had tuned Cousin Charlotte out. It was all over but the shouting, and she was the loser—not that she'd gotten a bit of thank-you from Cousin Charlotte. Of course, Cousin Charlotte didn't need to thank her: She'd taken Blanche and the kids in when they'd moved to Boston in a hurry three years ago. And then there was Mama. She'd tongue-lash Blanche up one side and down the other if Blanche refused to help Mama's favorite cousin.

Blanche just hoped her usual day customers got good service from Cousin Charlotte's niece, Larissa. Cousin Charlotte said Larissa used to work for a housecleaning service, but that didn't mean she knew what she was doing. Blanche had called her clients and warned them that she'd had to replace herself for a week. She'd made note of which ones complained so she could replace *them*. Any employer who couldn't understand an emergency would likely be a problem before long. One of the major reasons she chose to do day work was being able to pick up and drop clients as she saw fit. This meant she didn't have to take no mess from nobody, her preferred way of living.

Now she let herself into the Brindle house with the key Miz Inez had given her. She'd gotten here early so she'd have some time to get a feel for the place. She stashed her bag and jacket on a hook in the utility closet Miz Inez had shown her when they'd toured the house the day before. The house felt like sleep was still in charge, but she walked through the downstairs, looking into each room, making sure the Brindles were still upstairs.

It was a good-sized house: Five bedrooms with baths, two master suites, and another bathroom occupied the two upper floors. A living room, breakfast room with sunroom, dining room, library, an office, two bathrooms, the kitchen, and the laundry room took up the first floor. Each of the major rooms was nearly the size of a small apartment in Blanche's neighborhood. The house was furnished in what Blanche called undeclared rich: gleaming wood chests and tables with the kind of detail that said handmade, sofas and chairs that looked like they'd grown up in the rooms, Oriental carpets older than her grandmama, and pictures so ugly they had to be expensive originals. Light streamed down from a larger window over the stairs to the second floor. The library, with its battered hassocks and mashed throw cushions, looked like the most used room. The office smelled of smoke and men.

Blanche went back to the kitchen to make a cup of tea. While the water boiled, she looked around the room where she'd be spending most of her working hours for the next week. It wasn't the most modern, the largest, or the best appointed kitchen she'd ever worked in. There was a microwave but no convection oven. There was enough work space on the counter between sink and stove, but Blanche was partial to a butcher-block station in the middle of the floor, especially one with wheels. The appliances were on the older side, too. It had been a while since she'd used an oven she had to bend over to reach, and the dishwasher looked to be in its teens. What did impress her about the kitchen was how well Miz Inez had organized it: the bottles and cans arranged by size, the spices alphabetized, and labels on the shelves so you didn't waste time looking for beans where only canned fruit lived. From the looks of what the shelves contained, not a lot of fancy eating went on here, which was fine with Blanche. Less work.

She carried her tea and the note from Miz Inez to her already favorite spot: the sunroom off the breakfast room. She always liked to use the front of the house if she was going to be working in a place for a week or more, a way of reminding herself of her equality with her employers. She took a deep breath and felt her pores soak up some of the moisture. There were palms and rubber plants nearly touching the curved glass ceiling; Boston ferns on narrow columns drooped to the ground. A spleenwort with leaves wider than her hand took up a whole corner. A huge anthurium with what she could think of only as an erect penis in the middle of its flat red flower shared a five-tiered stand with a spider plant, a piggy-back plant, and several others she didn't recognize. Another circular stand held at least twenty plump African violets in every possible color. The white sailcloth-covered chairs seemed to float among the plants. She leaned back in an arm-chair and kicked off her shoes. The tile floor felt warm beneath her feet.

She sipped her tea and looked over the four-page note from

Miz Inez. It included mealtimes: eight-thirty for breakfast (she checked her watch; she had over an hour to get that together), one o'clock for lunch, drinks in the library at four-thirty, dinner at seven. Next came the list of meals for the week and the name of the grocer to call, if necessary. Inez reminded her that Mr. Ted Sadowski, who worked for Mr. Brindle, usually arrived for breakfast (he had his own key) and would take lunch if he was in the house. Allister Brindle himself took care of the plants in the sunroom.

The Brindles' schedules followed, including lots of lunches and dinners out, Blanche was pleased to see. This job was looking up.

As for the staff, Carrie had Sunday off and a half day on Wednesday; Wanda Jackson, the cleaning lady, came on Tuesdays to do the downstairs and Thursdays to do the upstairs, which meant she'd be working upstairs today. Blanche got Inez's regular days off—Saturday afternoon and all day Tuesday. Felicia Brindle's personal trainer was due today, too, and her masseuse tomorrow. Friday was payday for Blanche and Carrie; Wanda's check got mailed to her.

Blanche didn't have much information on the family, except that there were just two of them, a man and wife. She'd met the woman, Felicia Brindle, yesterday when Miz Inez had brought her in to show her around.

"Inez says they're real nice people," Cousin Charlotte had said when Blanche asked her about the Brindles. "They even hired her son, but it didn't last. He didn't used to be so—You'd think he'd spend some time with his mama, stop by and— But don't get me started on Ray-Ray. What was I sayin? Oh yeah. Inez been with these Brindles since Jesus was a child. I know she told you how they just love her."

Exactly. In Blanche's experience, the more a person believed love was a part of what they got from their employer, the more likely it was that the person was being asked to do things that only love could justify. Who knows what all Inez did for these people? Blanche thought about the woman down in Farleigh who routinely told her maid how much she loved her and insisted the maid call her Auntie—things the young maid had bragged about. But the woman also emptied her bowels in a slop pot so the maid could keep a written description of its contents. Blanche doubted Inez went anywhere near that far—and like it or not, this was the job she was stuck with, but only for a week, she reminded herself. She drank the last of her tea and sighed. It was time to get to work.

Blanche was cutting the biscuits when Carrie arrived, breathless and grumbling about the bus being late.

"I'll serve breakfast this morning, Carrie. I haven't seen Allister Brindle yet. I want to check him out. And this Ted who works for him, too."

"Do anything you wanna do. You the boss," Carrie said, but didn't sound like she meant it. Great! A sister with an attitude, Blanche thought. Thank you, Cousin Charlotte; thank you, Miz Inez. She gave Carrie a sharp look. Carrie was a plain-faced, dark brown–skinned woman—nowhere near as dark as Blanche—with permanent frown lines in her forehead and a chin round as a Ping-Pong ball. Her deep-set black eyes peered suspiciously out at Blanche from behind dinky little metal-framed glasses. Who could tell her age? Anywhere from fifty to eighty, Blanche figured. Straightened, gray-streaked hair was visible through the thin black hair net that covered her hair, the tops of her ears, and her upper forehead. She held her mouth as though she'd just had a vinegar cocktail.

42

Blanche had never seen a grumpier-looking woman. Probably constipated, she thought.

She set the biscuit cutter down. "Am I stepping on your toes by serving breakfast?"

"Ain't got nothin' to do wit me."

Blanche waited, sure this lie wasn't all Carrie had to say on the subject.

"It ain't no job of mine, noway. It's Ricardo's job," Carrie said.

"Who's Ricardo?"

Carrie blinked at her. "He works here."

Okay, it's like that, Blanche thought. If I don't ask, she won't tell. Is she mad because a stranger's come in to tell her what to do? Or does she have a constipated personality, too?

"So where's Ricardo?"

"Mr. B sent him and Elena home to Argentina."

"Because . . ."

"Till after the election. That's why Inez said I could wait table and get the door. It don't make me no never mind."

"Why'd he send them home?"

" 'Cause Mr. Ted said it wasn't right for somebody running for governor to have personal servants like that in these times."

"Who's running for governor?" Blanche wanted to know.

"Mr. Brindle." Carrie's tone said everyone in the world knew this but Blanche.

"So Elena is Felicia's personal maid, and Ricardo is his valet and the butler?"

Carrie barely nodded. "That's right."

"What about Elena's work?"

"I'm s'posed to help Mrs. B with her toilet, but she don't

seem to need me much, so I just wait table and . . . I'm just doin' what Inez said for me to do. It ain't no big thing."

"Yeah, right." Blanche folded her arms and stared at Carrie.

Carrie tossed her head. "Well, it do make a change."

That's better, Blanche thought.

"Well, honey, you can keep on waiting table, but not this morning. This morning I wanna check out the household, like I said. After that, you got it."

Carrie gave her a barely visible nod. She didn't look happy but she went off to set the table without further comment.

Sweet Ancestors! If she'd known she was going to have to arm wrestle the housemaid, she'd have gotten more rest. And what a hypocrite this Brindle character was, sending off their personal servants! As if anybody would mistake somebody who lived in this kind of house for just your average Joe.

Murder They Wrote

DISCUSSION GUIDE

1. The high regard in which Miz Inez holds her employers exemplifies the attitude we typically associate with Black domestics. It's a stereotype that has caused many to look down on the profession. barbaraneely has created Blanche from a different mold. What clues does she give to let you know that while Blanche works in a position of service, she is no submissive servant?

2. Speaking of stereotypes, Blanche falls into that game herself after meeting the Brindles' cleaning woman, Wanda Jackson. What do you think Wanda meant when she responds to Blanche's compliment with, "And are you that taken with yer own good sense, darlin'?"

3. With Shaquita, Pookie and Blanche's sister's children, Taifa and Malik, barbaraneely gives us fleshed-out portrayals of Black teenagers, something we rarely see anywhere today, be it TV, movies or literature. How does seeing these multi-dimensional depictions alter your perception of Black teens? Discuss Blanche's relationship with her niece and nephew and her own view of herself as a mother.

4. Discuss the commonly held misconceptions about the Black community that barbaraneely challenges in *Blanche Cleans Up*.

5. *Blanche Cleans Up* is a relatively short work, but there are several characters and storylines featured. How does barbaraneely's writing style accommodate these layers?

BARBARANEELY, A WRITER ON THE CASE

Published Works: *Blanche on the Lam*, 1992; *Blanche Among the Talented Tenth*, 1994; *Blanche Cleans Up*, 1998

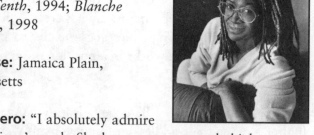

Home Base: Jamaica Plain, Massachusetts

Literary Hero: "I absolutely admire Toni Morrison's work. She has set an extremely high standard under which lots of us [African-American women authors] can fall. Her *Beloved* was particularly special to me because I have always felt that our social and psychological problems will never be resolved until we come to terms with slavery. *Beloved* can be a cathartic reading experience. I think of Toni as *our* psychiatrist."

Claim to Fame: The Agatha, Anthony and Macavity mystery awards for the first two Blanche books and the Massachusetts National Council of Negro Women's Women of Conviction Award for Literature

---

What is it about writing mysteries that appeals to you?

I realized that if I wanted to draw people into thinking about serious subjects, a mystery would be a great way to do it. I once had someone tell me, "I wouldn't go out and buy a book on race and class, but I read *Blanche on the Lam* and I got it." I can use the genre like a magician—dazzle the reader with the left hand while using my right to deal with issues.

To what do you attribute today's popularity of the sister sleuth?

Well, there is always going to be a flavor of the month. I think with the arrival of Walter Mosley's Easy [Rawlins] series and the advance of the Blanche books, a new opportunity presented itself. And as with everything, if a door is opened, Black women will rush right through it.

What did you have in mind when you christened your character Blanche White?

I knew I wanted *Blanche on the Lam* to address race and class in America and how ridiculous it was, so I figured people would immediately have an idea of what this book was about when they saw that name. I also have always had a fascination about Black women with names like Blanche and Magnolia. I've never asked anyone outright what they thought the person who named them was thinking when they came up with it, but I've always heard that Blacks felt that maybe if they gave their daughters names like these, some of the privilege usually associated with a name like this would rub off.

When readers meet Blanche for the first time, they're often surprised to see a modern-day Black woman making her living as a domestic. Why this line of work for your character?

It may be unusual now in the U.S., but if you look at Black women throughout the Diaspora, what you discover is that it is still a major profession. I suppose I wanted to pay homage to a profession that was a tradition in our communities. It was the profession that put food on the table and paid for the college educations of the people who don't want to talk about it now and who pretend that something is wrong with it. In paying homage, I also wanted to bring to light the discrepancy in the notion employers held—"They ['the help'] are too dumb to know they are being cheated by us but smart enough to be our psychiatrists."

Would you say there's a lot of barbara in Blanche or perhaps the other way around?

I don't think it's possible to develop characters that don't have some part of you in them, so I suppose there are some specific personality traits that irascible women like Blanche and I do have in common. But I always say I plan on becoming Blanche when I grow up. She has it together ever so much more than I could ever expect to.

You're very good at keeping it real. Blanche's witticisms and keen observations are right-on.

I really did try to create an everyday Black woman in Blanche. She's not book smart, but she's life smart. She has so many ways of knowing things. She can look at one situation and see how it is similar to another. Like thinking about how her drunken aunt behaves and making a connection to politics in America. Black women—and Black men—are masters at using humor and sarcasm to make a point and to get us past the indignities served upon us almost daily. You can't stay on top without the humor.

With *Blanche Cleans Up* you tackle a number of social issues and you challenge a lot of stereotypes. Do you think writers of color have a responsibility to erase negative notions about their community in their work?

Absolutely not! I think like any other writer[s], we should be free to write whatever comes. We just have a responsibility to tell the truth about whatever it is we are writing about. I was trying to give a glimpse of a Black community that was larger and deeper than the crime reports or the sociological statistics. I wanted to present us in a much rounder way. Teenagers, for example, are not all bad or all evil. No one believes this about the people they know. And we are all people we know. I suppose with the lead paint storyline, I did want to address certain elements within the environmental movement that don't believe these issues have an impact on poor communities. Like Blanche says, if we don't pay attention to the environment, everything else is moot.

Do you have a favorite among your three published Blanche stories?

I guess my favorite is always the one I'm working on. The next Blanche book has Blanche spending the summer in her hometown of Farleigh, North Carolina, which is celebrating its bicentennial. [Her best girlfriend] Ardell asks her to come down and start a catering business with her to handle all the Farleigh celebrations. Blanche decides to try it out for the summer to see if it's something she'd like to do once the kids get out on their own. There's a new boyfriend for Blanche in this one too.

Will you ever write outside the mystery genre?

I'm excited about the non-Blanche novel I'm working on right now. Called *Gideon*, the name of a small town in upstate New York, it's set in the '50s and is about the folks who live on what's considered the wrong side of the tracks. I published short stories before the Blanche series, and I am currently working on a collection. I'm always delighted when someone shows up at a reading with a short story of mine. Several have been published in various magazines, journals and anthologies.

barbaraneely is the 1992 Go On Girl! New Author of the Year

CHAPTER TWO

Life Forces
The Autobiography Genre

Autobiographies—a person's recounting of his or her own life story—represent the earliest form of African-American literature. It was, in fact, slave narratives that were the first African-American works to be published and widely accepted. Typically sponsored by an abolitionist, these early writings usually outlined the author's experience as a slave and his or her eventual escape to freedom. While the life circumstances detailed in most contemporary memoirs are not nearly as horrific, these modern-day stories of pleasure, pain and perseverance are no less interesting or inspiring. Autobiographies of note from well-known figures include Maya Angelou's series, which begins with the classic *I Know Why the Caged Bird Sings* (1970), and the highly influential *Autobiography of Malcolm X* (1965).

Also worth noting are the many novels that adopt an autobiographical form by having fictitious characters describe their lives in first-person narratives. These tales are often so well written and convincing that most readers believe they are true. James Weldon Johnson, who anonymously penned the novel *The Autobiography of an Ex-Colored Man* in 1912 and reissued it more than a decade later using his own name as the author, had to publish his own life story in 1933 to clear up the misconception that he was the "Ex-Colored Man" and that the book was a true account. Other important fictitious autobiographies include Ralph Ellison's *Invisible Man* (1952) and Ernest J. Gaines' *Autobiography of Miss Jane Pittman* (1971).

In recent years, regular folk have felt compelled to share their stories, especially if they are ones of trial and triumph. *Makes Me Wanna Holler* (1994) by Nathan McCall and *Laughing in the Dark* (1994) by Patrice Gaines are two best-selling examples. This trend of tell-all tomes seems only fitting for a nation compelled to discover its own truths by purging, whether on a therapist's couch or on the pages of a book. And stars like Patti LaBelle and Gladys Knight, who we look up to with a twinkle in our eyes, likewise share their personal sagas—which proves that life can throw you a curveball no matter who you are.

THE GO ON GIRL!
Autobiography Reading List

Black Ice / Lorene Cary

Heart of a Woman / Maya Angelou

Autobiography of Jim Brown / Jim Brown

A Taste of Power / Elaine Brown

Volunteer Slavery / Jill Nelson

Having Our Say: The Delany Sisters' First 100 Years / The Delany sisters with Amy Hearth

Makes Me Wanna Holler / Nathan McCall

The Sweeter the Juice / Shirlee Taylor Haizlip

Laughing in the Dark / Patrice Gaines

Why Should White Guys Have All the Fun? / Reginald Lewis with Blair Walker

The Literary Work

Don't Block the Blessings / Patti LaBelle

Nappy / Ailona Gibson

Straight, No Chaser: How I Became a Grown-Up Black Woman / Jill Nelson

Between Each Line of Pain and Glory / Gladys Knight

Dorothy Dandridge: A Biography / Donald Bogle

BOOK PRAISE FROM GO ON GIRLS

*"**B**arcardi 151 straight up could not have been more potent or challenged one's sensibilities more than Jill Nelson's* Straight, No Chaser. *Definitely not a nightcap, Nelson's eloquent views have left me on a constant inquest into how any given incident has contributed to the marginalization, invisibility and erasure of women in general, Black females, in particular and me, specifically. And as for the culprits, no one is too famed or untouchable for Nelson to demand accountability. The fruit of Nelson's rage is an inebriating cocktail that allows one to walk away with her dignity intact. Toast."*

S. Warren Harris
Chicago, Illinois

*"**W**hile Elaine Brown's book* A Taste of Power *is an autobiography, it's really a social commentary on the Black Power Movement that gives us a rare perspective—women in the Black Panther Party. We've heard so much about the men and very little about the important role women played. Had I not been in the book club, I would not have read this historical work. I'm glad I did, because I'm wiser for it."*

Colleen Lee
Washington, D.C.

*"**I** really loved the frankness and openness of the Delany sisters' book* Having Our Say. *All that life experience rolled up into two professional women with wonderful strong family values. What an inspiration! They reached out to people in their communities, and they spoke out about racism. That was a courageous thing to do back then. What a beautiful life story!"*

Shirley Harper
Seattle, Washington

Straight, No Chaser
by Jill Nelson

With revolutionary courage and frank honesty, Nelson reveals her life and gives voice and visibility to Black women who struggle daily to form a positive identity in a hostile culture.

THE NIGGERBITCHFIT

There is between black women a language all our own, sometimes spoken, oftentimes not. We communicate with each other through a tilt of our head, a quick cutting of eyes, a heartfelt exhalation of breath as we pass in the street, a quiet sucking of teeth, a fleeting smile that can absolutely transform the tenor of a bad day.

It is a feminine, coded, unwritten language that cuts many ways. It is complex in its simplicity, as were the languages created by slaves denied the use of their native tongue but compelled to communicate. Black women's language grows out of our particular experience of oppression because of our race and our gender. Each gesture and word has multiple, sometimes contradictory meanings. It is a language that transcends class, age, skin tone, attitude, cuts to the essential chase of our femaleness.

Some of this language black men share with us. That is the part that has to do with racism and white people. We are skilled at saying what is acceptable to the dominant group while at the same time saying what we mean to one another. We have had centuries to practice dissembling, shucking, and jiving, making white people feel comfortable and unthreatened even as we deceive, laugh at, and conspire against them. But there is a part of the language that only black women speak and understand, and it is that part which is inextricable from our being women. We use this language to discuss what is our business: our bodies, minds, hearts, dreams, children, rage, and joy. That business often involves men, the wonderful and heartbreaking quality of our interaction with them, the ways in which we are treated at home, in the streets, in the bedroom, in our communities, in the world.

Most of the time no one but us hears or notices when we speak our language, it is a surreptitious, quiet dialect, this dialogue among women. Crossing a street on the way to work early in the morning, a man in a four wheel-drive vehicle wants to turn right, but we are crossing the street, black women, some with children in tow, dropping them off at school on our way to the job. He does not allow us the right of way, but turns rapidly in front of us so that we must stop or be run over. A sister turns toward me and cuts her eyes, I suck my teeth, behind me a woman mutters, "Typical!" In seconds the eight of us in the crosswalk connect, acknowledge the man's lack of courtesy, pass judgment. All the while we keep stepping toward the curb, reach it, and scatter in various directions. "You all have a nice day," a woman singsongs, and each of us laughs, nods, briefly united by her affirmation of his blindness and of our visibility, her positive wish.

We speak this language numerous times each day, casually, without thinking, noticing, never having to fumble for the right word or syntax as we do with languages consciously learned. I do not know if we were born knowing this language, but do know that it is absorbed early in the company of mothers, sisters, aunts, grandmothers, other women. Heard as a little girl in the shift of lap or shoulder when men, or white people, or those who are not like us come around, seen in the movement of eyes, heads, legs, the two- or three-word comments that elicit that black woman's head-tilting thing, or smiles or frowns or gales of womanly laughter when they exit.

Created out of a need to communicate rapidly and secretly, mostly this language is abbreviated, quiet, its words and gestures so rich that a few suffice. This is as it must be, because most of the time black women are too busy taking care of others to take time to care for ourselves and one another. We communicate in passing, on the way someplace more important than where we are, about events great and small. The body language and movements of my sisters tell me what they feel about the night before, the weather, the everyday violence we all encounter, local and national politics, their own lives.

Sometimes, usually under extreme and negative circumstances, our women's language mutates, a woman's voice expands, grows loud, broadens so that everyone who hears her knows, if not exactly what she's talking about, then at least her rage. In these moments, we tell our secrets, let the cat out of the bag. Mostly, this happens individually, when one woman has reached her end, has had enough of violence, or dishonesty, or being demonized, or being invisible, and breaks out, goes off. It is a powerful thing when this happens. Imagine how much power we'd have as black women if we could figure out how to do this collectively.

One day I'm talking to my friend the writer Thulani Davis on the telephone, we are both nearing the end of the rope in our work, that point at which we either cut ourselves down like Marie Thompson or hang, and Thulani drawls, "I think maybe it's time to go into my editor's office and have a nigger-bitchfit."

And I say, laughing, "A what?"

"Nigger. Bitch. Fit." She enunciates slowly and clearly, so that I will make no mistake. She explains that a niggerbitchfit is what happens when a nice colored girl, having exhausted all possibility of compromise, communication, and peaceful conflict resolution, turns into everyone's worst nightmare, a visible grown-up black woman mad as hell and with nothing to lose, and opens her mouth. When she breaks it down, I am a happy African-American woman. The coining of "nigger-bitchfit" does two things. It gives name and context to the feelings of anger and rage that for much of my life I'd been taught to deny as antithetical to my conditioning as both a woman and a black woman. If there is one thing women learn early on, it is that anger is unattractive, unladylike, and unacceptable. As black people we are also told early that our rage is always inappropriate. To embrace the concept of the nigger-bitchfit shatters a lifetime of conditioning as all-suffering-salt-of-the-earth-stoic-black-woman. It allows me to shed years of explanation and dismissal of my rage as simply being out of control, a manifestation of my penchant for high drama, or just another annoying example of black people's collective chip on our shoulders. With the articulation of the word niggerbitchfit, Thulani let me know not only that my rage was acceptable, but, most important, that I was not alone.

D I S C U S S I O N   G U I D E

1. Jill states that Black women struggle to form a positive identity. Do you believe this to be the case? How can we best make ourselves visible and seize power?

2. The book's subtitle is "How I Became a Grown-up Black Woman." What life experiences helped Jill grow up? What experiences have shaped you?

3. What is Jill most angry about?

4. Jill offers her blueprint for what makes a man. How does your personal checklist compare with hers?

5. What do you think of Jill's relationships with her parents, siblings and daughter?

JILL NELSON, A FREE WOMAN

Published Works: *Volunteer Slavery*, 1993; *Straight, No Chaser: How I Became a Grown-Up Black Woman*, 1997

Home Base: New York City

Literary Hero: James Baldwin

Claim to Fame: *Volunteer Slavery* received an American Book Award and appeared on the bestseller list of *The Washington Post*

Many who have read your work would say the book title *Straight, No Chaser* personally describes you to a T. Have you always been so brutally honest and courageously candid?

I never was good at keeping secrets. I was always the one in the family saying, "What's going on! How come we're not talking about this or that." It's just the way I'm wired. I believe we've got to deal with stuff. As Black folks, we're really secretive, and we spend a lot of time fronting for each other and for the White man. I will say this, though, people don't say, "I don't believe that happened" when they read my books. They say, "Something like that happened to me." Both my books are head-nodding books. I write from a sense of community.

Did you worry about how the personal truths in your books would affect your daughter and your relationship with her?

My daughter has grown up with me, and she's kind of used to my style. When she started to talk to me about her sex life, I didn't really want to hear the details. But she reminded me that everyone in America had read about my sex life in chapter four of *Volunteer Slavery*, and I needed to listen to her. We ended up having a very long, interesting conversation that made us closer.

What was the hardest secret for you to reveal in your books?

That I'm angry. As Black women, we're always told it's unladylike to be angry, and we fear we'll get the reputation that Black women have this big, collective chip on our shoulder. I'm angry, and it's not because I didn't get laid or I didn't get paid, but because just being a Black woman in this culture is so damn hard. We suffer a really unique oppression based on our race coupled with our gender. I'm angry that I can't go out and wear something that's comfortable for me because I might get sexually attacked. I'm angry that so many of us are alone and heartbroken, because too many Black men don't want us. I'm angry that many of us don't have health insurance and that welfare reform is going to devastate our community. To paraphrase Malcolm X, any Black woman who isn't angry is crazy! We have to acknowledge that we are angry and have a right to be so. Readers E-mail me or come up to me when I'm on tour and say, "Thank you for legitimizing my anger . . . thank you for letting me know I'm not alone."

Will your third book also help Black women learn more about ourselves through your life?

My first two books have been very revealing and very wrenching; I needed a break. I'm writing a novel now. It's a satire, and it's political. This time people can speculate if it's me or not.

Some readers have criticized you for airing too much dirty laundry for the White world to see in your books. How do you respond?

That's interesting. It kills me that some of us are so concerned about what the White man is thinking, when the truth is the White man ain't thinking about us. It's impossible to air too much dirty laundry. All of it must be hung out. It's like a wound; if you keep it all packed in gauze, it doesn't heal, it just sits and festers. We've got to let it air. We must be self-critical.

You have criticized the Million Woman March. What problems did you have with it?

Sometimes we confuse symbolism with activism. All those women came together in Philadelphia, and we don't even have a mailing list so we can tap that power. We also don't have an agenda for the work to be done. We need to organize by taking small, local organizations like book clubs, churches, gyms and figuring out a way to create a national network of Black women. I'm working on a project called Triple V— visibility, voice and the vote. I hope to create a mechanism where Black women nationally will be able to vote for the five things that are important for Black women to deal with in the year 2000. On Mother's Day 1999, we would be able to vote through E-mail, an 800 telephone number, by fax or with flyers to determine what our mandate will be. There would be a list of 30 or so goals, and whichever five get the most votes will be where we place our efforts. It will determine the grass roots work we do in our communities, the issues we hold out to our elected officials, the entrepreneurial ventures we take on, the organizations we fund. We're affronted, and we need some power, some visibility, some voice. My commitment to making change is greater than my commitment to making books.

You were turned down by many publishers before *Volunteer Slavery* made it to the bookstore. Why do you believe the road was so rocky?

It has to do with what White people decide Black people want to read. Any fiction about hooking up gets the nod, but when you come with something different, they freak. The popular fiction written by Black people isn't very different from that written by White people. It's for entertainment, not transforming. I read those kinds of books, because it's escapist entertainment, but I hope that my sisters read broadly. I'm personally not that big on self-help books. I'm not a puppy who got injured. I think this literature about healing and self-help can be disempowering. No matter how much you get yourself together, you still can walk out the door and down the block and be assaulted by the violence in this culture. And too often these books blame the victim. I believe we need to do internal work, but I also believe we need to do external work. We all need to volunteer for something. These books are often substitutes for Saturday night dates. Don't read them the whole weekend, get up and do something. Pick up garbage on the block, plant in the community garden, do work at a senior citizen's center, do something!

What do you do?

I do some organizing with women's groups and I do some tutoring, but like Black women everywhere, I never feel like I'm doing enough. But I know that having a commitment to some community beyond the community of self makes you happy; I'm not some miserable, self-sacrificing fool. What I get back is so much more.

In the introduction to *Straight, No Chaser,* you raise the question "What would make us seize the time to care for and love ourselves when most of the signals we get from everyone tell us we are undeserving and undesirable?" How do you nurture and tend to self?

We're always on our way to someplace more important than where we are. A Black woman shouldn't put anyone in front of herself. If you put your kids in front, you do a disservice to them. If I'm healthy, rested and happy, I'm a better mother, partner, community person, a better everything. For me, exercising is my thing. I also get my nails done, go to the chiropractor and get my back and neck adjusted, and sometimes I just go to a park bench and space out. Sometimes I go to the drugstore and spend $20 on stuff—face creams and all that. But it was hard to give myself permission to do that; I had so many periods of burnout. In therapy, I learned the tools to keep myself together, and I've gotten good at my sense of entitlements. Know that it's okay to say no, to put down that ball and let somebody else pick it up. We are not indispensable, but in some twisted way it makes us feel powerful that everyone is depending on us even though we may be doggin' ourselves into the ground. That's not power, that's insanity!

Jill Nelson is the 1993 Go On Girl! New Author of the Year

CHAPTER THREE

A Slice of Life
The Anthology and Short Story Genre

Before books by authors of African descent were being published in such great numbers, anthologies provided talented unknowns with well-deserved exposure. Typically organized by genre, gender, generation or theme, anthologies offer readers the joy of discovery. For the original members of the Go On Girl! Book Club, Terry McMillan's *Breaking Ice: An Anthology of Contemporary African-American Fiction* (1990) was a godsend. When it showed up on the reading list that first year, it was the perfect introduction to the many new voices on the horizon. Several of the books excerpted in McMillan's anthology ended up on the club's list the next year.

Instead of offering a taste of this and a taste of that, like an anthology, short story collections let readers indulge in a plateful of their favorites from one author. For example, those hankering for homespun stories from the heart can devour J. California Cooper's *Homemade Love* (1986), *Some Soul to Keep* (1987), *The Matter is Life* (1992) and *Some Love, Some Pain, Sometimes* (1995). Among the critically acclaimed short story collections that have become classics are Paul Laurence Dunbar's *Folks from Dixie* (1898), Jean Toomer's *Cane* (1923), Toni Cade Bambara's *Gorilla My Love* (1972) and Langston Hughes' "Simple" stories, which began appearing in the Black newspaper *The Chicago Defender* in 1943.

THE GO ON GIRL!
Anthology and Short Story Collection
Reading List

Breaking Ice / Terry McMillan

The Matter is Life / J. California Cooper

*Double Stitch: Black Women Write About
Mothers & Daughters* / Mary Helen Washington

*Memory of Kin: Stories About Family
by Black Writers* / Bell Scott et al

Nouvelle Soul / Barbara Summers

Brotherman: Odyssey of Black Men in America /
Herb Boyd and Richard E. Allen

Some Love, Some Pain, Sometimes /
J. California Cooper

*Honey Hush: An Anthology of African-American
Women's Humor* / Daryl Cummer Dance

A Slice of Life

BOOK PRAISE FROM GO ON GIRLS

"I know I'm in for a treat whenever I pick up a book by J. California Cooper. She writes stories that speak to your emotions. Some Love, Some Pain, Sometimes exposes the many sides to the lives of Black folks—the sweet, the humorous, the loving and the disturbing."

Linda Johnson
Philadelphia, Pennsylvania

"On each patch of a quilt, the stitching tells a story. Double Stitch is many stories in various forms—poetry, essays, narratives and fiction—each one telling in its own unique way of relationships between mothers and daughters. Some patches will make you cry and some will bring laughter. This book is like a quilt that keeps you warm over and over again."

Deb Oliver
Danbury, Connecticut

"Brotherman was a good bedside book. You could pick it up and read a different piece each sitting. The good thing about this anthology is that it introduced me to a variety of African-American male writers. I would highly recommend this book to a brother or a sister."

Yvonne Saab
Plainfield, New Jersey

Nouvelle Soul
by Barbara Summers

Barbara's own words best describe this sophisticated collection of short stories: "Nouvelle Soul begins where labels of race, gender and status end, where lives undress in intimate moments of unexpected challenge." Whether read in one sitting or sampled one at a time, the 24 stories in Nouvelle Soul *will touch your heart and challenge your preconceptions through diverse depictions of African-American life.*

FAMILY

Churchman's had done the last three funerals in the family so it was natural for them to do cousin John's. His casket was closed for the wake. The cancer was swift in taking him, carving away the meat from his hefty brown frame until nothing but skeleton was left. And still he breathed—I wouldn't say lived—until he couldn't. Almost made it to football season, his favorite time of the year. Almost.

I sat with my two boys. Although their father had left three years before, this was their first death.

"Ma, where's Uncle John?" Matthew asked. He was eight, growing on eighty.

"He's in the coffin."

"How do you know?"

"He's in there."

"I want to see him."

"No, you don't."

"I want to see him, too." That was Peter, six, who'd just told me he was going to change his name because the kids made fun of it and him, especially in gym. He was going to change it to Mandela. "I want to see him, too," he insisted.

"No, you don't."

"I do, too."

"He's dead."

"Ma, we know that."

"He was very sick before he died. He didn't look good. And your Aunt Dolores thought it was better to have the coffin closed."

"But I want to see him."

"Me, too."

"It would scare you."

"Not me. He gave me piano lessons. That scared me."

"He gave me candy, a whole roll of Life Savers. Just for me. He was nice."

"Sure he was, and that's how we want to remember him."

"Well, I still say you don't know if he's in there or not."

"He's in there, believe me."

"Seeing is believing."

"Who told you that?"

"You said it when we got my sneakers last week."

"That's something else."

"Is something going to happen here, Ma?"

"No, Petey." Shoot, I'd gone and done it, too. "No, sweetheart, we just sit and think, think about Uncle John and wait."

"See, that's why they call it a wait, dummy."

"A wake."

"He's awake?"

"That's enough."

"Ma, he's inside the box awake?"

"No, Peter. And that's enough, both of you. Let's be quiet now."

"Might be empty or a total stranger."

"Or somebody fell asleep and now he's trying to get out."

"Shhh."

Cousin Dolores wore her schoolteacher plaids and sat in the front row, her short silver hair flippant and uncovered. She smiled and nodded and thanked everyone who stopped by in that high, young voice of hers. It was a relief, she said, and we all understood. He'd been drinking for so long, hurting somewhere inside for so long. Once he took to the bed he never left it. Couldn't eat, couldn't drink—not even water. And yet his body continued to dissolve in streams of soft shit. And the women—relatives and friends who'd never seen him without a tie, let alone this close—took turns spelling Dee by his bedside, turning him over, wiping the mess, cleaning him up and diapering him again. Not one of the men in the family had so much as stopped by the apartment since the hospital had sent him home to die. The death watch was women's work, just like the labor of birth.

Some say men can take it, but I'm not one of them. I don't think they can and I think they know it. They just do their best not to show it. They'd rather fight than feel. Rather buy things than spend time. I'd love to be wrong but you've got to prove it to me. Although I was born and bred right here in Newark, you could say I'm from Missouri. Then, too, I'm divorced and I don't have any stake in supporting men's lies and bad habits. That all falls back on them like dandruff on a dark suit. It's not going anywhere.

Not to say that women are exempt, because after all is said and done, here I am trying to raise my boys to be different kind of men and falling into the same trap—protecting them, always protecting them from what I think they can't handle.

Dolores and John had never had children and now when she returned to the apartment it was to a big and bright but empty space. Family crowded around her wherever she went, trying to shield her from the absolute they all knew was there. She liked the attention, ate little of the food. She was thin as a bird herself. Cousin Bessie declared it took her half an hour to eat one little chicken wing—she'd timed it, she said.

So when at last it was time to leave Churchman's and go back home, Dee didn't lack for company or conversation. Cousin DuBose and Lucille took her in their big maroon Town Car. Took a few proud-faced older folks, too. I lived in the next building over, so after I parked my little Honda and made sure Cece would grill the hot dogs for the kids without causing the smoke alarm to go off this time, I went on over to Dee's as well.

Plenty of people still in the lobby. And why today of all days?

Out of the four elevators only one was running, and for a twenty-five-story building you know what speed that was. Folks try to live in a decent place, try to rise up in the world, and what happens? The elevators get an attitude. Might as well be the projects. That's life in the vertical village.

Dee and some of the others had gone up, but Doobie and Lucille were still there, Lu fussing at him so he would fuss over her. She had put on some serious weight over the years while he stayed thin as our side of the family usually did.

73

"Do I look all right?" she asked, straightening his tie.

"If you'd stop trying to choke me to death, maybe I could say something."

"I was just trying to help. Some men would love that kind of attention."

"And some women would get it if they weren't so busy giving it. Now, isn't that right, Yvette?"

"What would Yvette know? She can't keep a man from breakfast to lunch."

My mouth couldn't find words fast enough before Bessie jumped in.

"And speaking of lunch, Lucille, I see you didn't stay on that last diet too long. Matter of fact, looks like Father Time just keeps adding on to what Mother Nature already gave you plenty of."

That's family for you. Bessie's not that much younger than Lucille and on her third husband, so she's had to take a lot. She's not stingy about giving it back, though. More than forty years Doobie and Lucille've been married. They should have entered Ripley's longevity sweepstakes. Two funny funny people, together so long, believe it or not. We could always count on them for some kind of fireworks at any family gathering.

I was determined to give Lu plenty of room. After all, DuBose was my blood cousin somewhere along the line. We couldn't help being related to each other. But he and Lucille had chosen each other in marriage way before I was even on the planet, back in the days when if you made a mistake you kept on sleeping with it.

The elevator finally came. I pulled mourner's rank and crowded in with eight or nine others. One or two elderly people got off on the lower floors. We were headed for the four-teenth. I used to tease Dee about living there. Just because they didn't call the thirteenth floor what it was didn't mean that it wasn't there. Our whole family were teachers, princi-pals, and professors. It was our job to teach kids—grown folks, too—to count, to think, to fill in the blanks. Dee would tease me right back, saying all my fancy schools and three-let-ter degrees didn't mean a thing if I was still superstitious. I said I wasn't superstitious. I was African. She said fools came in all kinds and colors.

But those were yesterday's good old days. She told me she'd be moving to a smaller apartment as soon as things got set-tled. A smaller place, did that mean a smaller life? All I hoped for was another floor.

We all stood silent, staring at the lights over the elevator door. When the car stopped at 12 it opened onto a flat ugly metal wall. A few inches of open space above our heads showed where the next floor was. We were obviously far off the mark. Somebody's "O shit" came out louder than she wanted and the person nearest the buttons pushed one for a higher floor. The doors closed, we stayed where we were and they opened again. Numbers up and down produced no movement. The doors kept opening on the wide metal wall that felt somehow like the flat blank end of the world. The lit-tle space was like a tease of salvation, too little, too far.

Cruz, one of the building's janitors, happened to be riding with us. He said not to worry in his warm island accent as he pushed the red alarm bell. It had a hearty ring, the sound of instant rescue. Nothing happened. He pushed again . . . and again . . . and again. The bell rang in long loud pleas for help. How could this be happening? Not only were we going nowhere, but we were getting no attention. We all held our breath as if to inhale or exhale would shift the precious balance that held us suspended but steady.

I was scared and furious at being trapped. The bell continued to sound. Nobody said a word. Finally Cruz gave up on the bell. Suddenly it was quiet as a . . . No, no. But quiet, yes.

Then we heard a vague kind of shuffling. Footsteps coming. Yes. Feet stopping here. We saw two pairs of old ladies' shoes topped with round ankles in thick stockings.

"Who's there?" Cruz called.

"Y'all stuck in there?" a thin female voice answered.

"Yeah, we're stuck, we need help. Who are you?"

"I'm Mrs. Palmer and I got Mrs. Marandino here with me."

"Mrs. Palmer, listen, this is Cruz."

"Cruz? Our Cruz?"

"Yeah, Cruz."

"Well, Cruz, I can't bend down to see you 'cause I'd never get up again."

"That's all right, Mrs. Palmer, it's me in here with seven, eight other people. We got a baby in here, too. Could you call down to the desk and get us some help?"

"Cruz, you know that desk phone don't never work in. It just works out."

"Well, get somebody to go down there, one of the kids on your floor."

"Now, that's a good idea but you know kids ain't doing nothing today without no money."

"I'll pay them, Mrs. Palmer, we'll pay them."

"Lady, we'll pay anything. Please, we're dying in here." Lucille sounded frantic.

"Mrs. Palmer," Cruz said soothingly, "listen close. We need help right away."

"I'll do the best I can. I'ma leave Mrs. Marandino here with y'all so you have a little comp'ny, all right? I'ma go on now."

After a few muffled words we heard her feet move slowly across the hallway linoleum. I could feel the tension ease in the elevator. People started talking to themselves or their neighbor in hushed tones of relief. Next to me an Asian couple who had been carrying heavy brown paper shopping bags in each hand finally set them down.

"*Scusi, Signora Marandino, ma parla italiano?*" A stocky young man with slick black hair raised his voice from the back of the car.

"No, sir, I'm from Corsica. You no speak a little French perhaps?"

"No, sorry," he answered.

"*Si, moi je parle francais,*" Chantal, a teenager who babysat for me sometimes and was now holding her own two-year-old, spoke up.

"*Bien, tres bien. On va vous aider, d'accord?*"

"*Merci, madame, on a tres peur.*"

"No, no fear. We get help for you. You come from where, mademoiselle?"

"From Haiti."

"*Bien, tres bien.* We was playing cards and we heard the bell. But Gladys no like to move when she's losing, you know. Well, not me neither. What if she's changing something now back there? Maybe I go."

"No, no," we all protested, maddened by her chit-chat but not wanting the awful silence. Her feet turned around but she stayed put.

"Thanks, man," Doobie said to Cruz, "for keeping such a cool head."

"It's nothing, just part of my job."

"Are you implying that I do not have a cool head?" I knew it was Lucille.

"No such thing, darlin'. The man just helped us out of a tight spot."

"Well, we wouldn't be in this spot if your cousin lived in a better class building."

"Listen, lady," the slick-haired young man said, "I don't know who you are or where you come from but this building is all right, OK? And I got enough to worry about without the insults."

"Doobie, are you going to let some little racist Guido talk to me like that?"

"Who are you calling a racist?"

"Enough of that. Lucille, will you please relax? You, too, young man." I couldn't take it any more either, but Bessie was the one to speak up first. "Why do you always want to start something? We can't go anywhere, we can't do anything, and it's not anybody's fault. Please."

Lucille huffed into a stiff-necked silence. Chantal's baby started to whine. The air was getting warm and close.

"Mrs. Marandino, you see Mrs. Palmer yet?"

"No, Cruz, but two big boys coming."

Two large pairs of white leather athletic shoes stitched with complicated designs filled the space. Mrs. Marandino's shoes moved out of the picture.

"Yo, whassup down there?" Two sets of eyes, one in a strip of tan face, the other in dark brown, squinted through to us. "Cruz, man, whassup? Miz Palmer had us to call the fire department. They said they'd be right over, but you know what that can mean."

"Jeff, listen, call the police department, too. And, listen, have Mrs. Marandino do it."

"Ain't that some shit? A Black man calling for help don't mean nothin'."

"The shit is funked up, man," his partner said.

"Word," said Jeff.

"Peepee, mama." The baby was out and out crying now.

"Dog, y'all got a baby in there, too?"

"Yeah, listen, get going, OK?" urged Cruz.

"Doobie, give the boys some money," Lucille directed. He started to reach inside his jacket.

"Naw, mister brother, we don't want your money. We goin' with the lady. What else you want?"

"Tell who's ever on security to get something happening up here."

"Cruz, you know ol' fat-assed Roger can't climb no twelve flights of stairs."

"Well, just get going, OK?"

"We outta here."

"Wait," I said. One of them peeked down again. "Could you please go up to 14C and tell them they got family stuck in the elevator here?"

"14C?"

"14C."

"You the family?"

"That's right."

"Will do."

"Thank you very much." What else could I say?

The space was empty but we could hear their voices trailing

off. Funked up, paid off, gin, and three levels of laughter. And then nothing. Nothing outside and all the noises silence could contain inside. Even the baby settled down to a whimper.

But I was still scared. I wondered about Matthew and Peter— why I hadn't made a will, if they'd remember me if I died, how long it would take them to forget me, if their father would love them full-time and not just the two weeks a summer. Who would get my books and my clothes? Is that where the second-hand clothes stores got their stuff? From dead people nobody wants to wear anything of? Is dying contagious? Would anybody want the mink coat I was still paying for? What about my old recipe books? *The New Hostess of Today* from 1922? And the pearl-handled .22 in the bottom of the chifferobe? And right next to it the long-ago love letters from Darryl?

And what about my partner, my soulmate, the one I'd been looking for for so long, the one they said everybody was destined to have? If I went, would he go, too,'cause I'd be on the other side and that's where he'd have to meet me now?

"It's all right, Yvette." Bessie put her arm around me and gave me a Kleenex. I didn't know I even needed one.

"So much to think about," I said.

"Truly. Cousin John and now this. I sure am glad Dolores got home OK."

"Don't worry about it, sugar." Doobie's voice sounded masculine and sincere.

"I'm your wife. Don't I get a little comfort?"

"Lucille," he said, taking a deep breath, "you know how I know we're going to make it out of here?"

"How?'

" 'Cause you're enough to try the patience of the Father, the Son and the Holy Ghost combined. They're just not ready to

80

take you yet. And truth to tell I hope they don't decide to jump up and get ready. At least, not any time soon. But you're pushing it, Lucille, you're pushing it and you ought to know that."

"Well, it's the squeaky wheel that gets the grease around here."

"Come on, everybody," Cruz said. "We got to stick together now. We got to be like a family."

"No family of mine. I am not related to poor White trash, bag-carrying boat people, and Haitians who probably got AIDS. Baby probably got AIDS, too. Not me."

The slap sounded like an explosion. Lucille howled.

"I'm sorry, baby, but I just couldn't take it anymore." Doobie tried to put his arms around her. She twisted away in fury.

"What is your problem, Lucille?" Bessie was fuming. "You made him do that. If he didn't, I was gonna have to. Somebody. Why do you do him like that? You got one of the good men. And I know, they're not easy to find. If divorce doesn't get them, dying will. Do you ever stop to think about that? Do you? Think about Yvette here: two little kids and no husband. Think about Dolores: being alone, no one to love, let alone fuss at. Do you ever stop to think what you'd be without him?"

"I'll go before he does."

"What is this, some race to the casket? How do you know that?"

"I just know it."

"What makes you say that, baby? You *want* to leave me?"

Lucille dissolved in Doobie's arms and silence settled in as the answer. Somebody passed around a box of Tic-Tacs. I shook one into my hand and concentrated on the tiny spot of sweet green flavor spreading through my mouth. It felt like a friend.

"O, my God," we heard somebody say in the hallway. Several pairs of feet clustered around our door. Dolores' eyes peeped down.

"Who's in there?"

"We're all here," Doobie said. "Lucille and Bessie and Yvette and some of your neighbors and Cruz. But what are you doing here?"

"They said my family was stuck."

"You got other things to think about, girl," Bessie said.

"Not more important than this. Fire department's on its way. We heard them coming up the stairwell. Just hang in there, now."

That was never one of my favorite expressions—hang in there. Too much strange fruit attached to it, too many sad songs. But I was glad she was there. And Buddy, too, Bessie's husband, who'd been holding down the fort with his broken leg while we were at the wake. We heard his cast thump against the floor and then his silver-rimmed glasses and salt-and-pepper mustache sparkled at us.

"You all right, Bessie?"

"I'm OK, but you shouldn't have come out on your crutches."

"What am I supposed to do? Just sit up there and wait and not know what's going on? Unh unh, not me."

"Thank you," she said softly and then it was Bessie's turn to blow her nose.

Where once there had been stillness, silence, and emptiness, now there was the busy, heavy-footed clanking of a rescue at hand. Noise never sounded so good. The firemen and Cruz pried open the ceiling hatch of the elevator. We could see huge cables stretching away into the gloom of the shaft. The bright little elevator felt almost safer than the tall, deep darkness outside. Two men with ropes and flashlights climbed into the car with us and lifted us up one by one. They took the baby and Chantal first. I didn't look around or down, anywhere but straight ahead where the firemen were saying, "Careful," "Over here," and "Watch your step." But once I was out I didn't feel it was over until everyone else was out. I heard Lucille whining that she'd never squeeze through that little space. I did hear something tear but somehow she managed. I also heard her asking for her husband to be brought out next because he was an old man.

"Who's an old man?" Indignation shook his voice, but they raised him up next and then everybody else and Cruz.

We stood around in the hallway shaking our heads and shaking each other's hands. Strange, it was hard to let go, give up something special we'd probably soon be bragging about. Mrs. Palmer and Mrs. Marandino were there. They looked like twins in their rhinestone glasses and beige cardigan sweaters. We saw that Jeff and his friend in the high-top sneakers had high-top hairdos, too.

Doobie and Lucille were huddled in a corner. I could see tears streaming down his face. He held her close and rubbed her back as sobs shook her body. "Promise?" "I promise" were all the words I heard.

I thanked one of the firemen standing next to me. He said he was sorry we'd had so long a wait, but they'd had a fire in the next building over. Turned out some kids had just burned up some hot dogs.

The Literary Work

DISCUSSION GUIDE

1. Discuss your favorite nugget among this collection of jewels. Why did it catch your eye, touch your heart?

2. In "Panach," "A Good Man" and "Tony the Tiger," Barbara digs below the surface to offer a portrayal that's far from the obvious. Why do you think she's done this?

3. Did "Sam the Man" make you laugh or cry? Why?

4. What does "Nothing Like Daddy" say to adult children about their parents?

5. Discuss the merits of "Fryday." Why do you think it won Barbara an award?

6. Why do you think Barbara chose the title she did for "Family"?

BARBARA SUMMERS, A KEEPER OF STORIES

Published Works: edited *I Dream A World: Portraits of Black Women Who Changed America*, 1990; *Nouvelle Soul*, 1992; *The Price You Pay*, 1993; *Skin Deep*, 1998

Home Base: Teaneck, New Jersey

Literary Heroes: "I have two—
Langston Hughes and Zora Neale Hurston. I've always said I'm their illegitimate child. I relate to them because they both saw life as a comic tragedy."

Claim to Fame: First Prize for Short Stories ("Fryday") at the first National Black Writers Conference at Medgar Evers College

---

When did you get into writing?

I began my writing career as a mature woman. I didn't publish until I was 42 years old. I started by attending a writer's workshop in Brooklyn, New York, taught by John Oliver Killens between 1985 and 1987. He became my mentor. Winning first prize for my short story at the first National Black Writers Conference in front of him meant so much. He died shortly thereafter. As a middle-aged mother and a retired model, to have my first work recognized was really something for me.

85

Why did you choose short stories as the medium by which you would make your literary debut? Aren't novels the more common choice?

I didn't really choose. I'd say short stories chose me. My mother was a poet, and of course poetry is a short form too, so maybe it came naturally. And then all of the other writing I had done before then had been in short forms—articles, book reviews and such. I also studied French literature, and there is a long tradition of short stories in French lit. I've written in the novel form as well, and they are very different mediums.

How is writing short stories different from working on a novel? Do you have a favorite among the many short stories you've written?

One of the advantages to writing short stories is that when the idea comes to you, you can finish it right then and there and move on to the next thing. Once I've written a story and it's been published, they become separate from me. Sometimes I might go back and read something I wrote some time ago and say, "That was really good." But really, my favorite stories are the ones that haven't been published yet.

Reading *Nouvelle Soul* is sort of like being a fly on the wall in an apartment building inhabited by a cross-section of real people. It's a testament to your ability to portray such a variety of characters and situations. How do you capture such diversity and realness?

Again, I think having started my writing career as a mature person, my life experience gives me a wider perspective. So many writers start their careers at a young age, and while they may be brilliant and sensitive writers, their life experience is limited. I mean, at the time I started writing I had had another profession, I had raised a child, been married, been divorced, been around the world and around the block. I know I was also influenced by my work on *I Dream A World*, which profiled 76 women. It was an absolute delight to see how each woman's story was so different. The diversity of their experiences and their expression was thrilling. I wanted my writing to reflect that as well.

How did you choose the title?

The "Soul" part of the title represents Black people. I wanted "Nouvelle" to mean more than just African-American. It gives it an international twist.

While you were creating this collection of stories, did you have any particular goal in mind about what you wanted your readers to get out of *Nouvelle Soul*?

I want people to get the perspective of a variety of African-American experiences. And I also want people to laugh, to enjoy life, to have fun. I find the humor quotient lacking in a lot of widely read modern literature. Humor has helped us survive as much as, say, spirituality. I wanted to get at what allows us to smile through difficult times. There's that fine line between humor and pain. Actually they coexist. The short story is the perfect medium for this.

You have written a short story collection, a novel (*The Price You Pay*) and your second piece of nonfiction (*Skin Deep*). Do you have a preference?

Nonfiction is such a huge responsibility. In working on *Skin Deep*, which is an inside look at Black fashion models, I had so many people and facts to be concerned about. I can't wait to get back to fiction. I want to be irresponsible!

Barbara Summers is the 1992 Go On Girl! New Author of the Year

CHAPTER FOUR

Piece of Mind
The Social Commentary Genre

As a people, we've never minced words when it comes to the
important issues facing our race. The earliest examples of
protest literature challenged the stereotypes of African-American inferiority, stressed equality between the races and
exposed the brutality, physical and psychological, of White
racism. Phillis Wheatley is the pioneer of African-American
protest literature, the first such African-American writer to
gain a wide audience. Wheatley used poetry to call for freedom from slavery. The late eighteenth and nineteenth centuries saw a great deal of protest material, most notably,
Benjamin Banneker's open letter to Thomas Jefferson in 1791.
Leaders of the growing free Black communities in the North,
such as William Hamilton, Russell Parrott and James Forten,
expressed their rage through speeches and pamphlets
denouncing slavery and inequality, and the slave narratives of
the antebellum period were perhaps that period's most persua-
sive protests.

Moving a little bit ahead, it was during the Harlem Renaissance that African-American artists began to talk about the
role of protest in African-American arts, and to question
whether art could or should be propaganda. This controversy
pitted Alain Locke, who saw protest literature as an acknowl-
edgement of the power of White oppression and therefore

something Black artists should not engage in, against W. E. B. DuBois, who believed any African-American art that did not have a social message was worthless.

During the next two decades, Richard Wright used his fiction—*Uncle Tom's Children* (1938), *Native Son* (1940) and *Black Boy* (1945)—to expose the negative effects of racial oppression. The Civil Rights movement of the '50s and '60s saw another debate emerge over the place of protest literature in our art. James Baldwin's essay "Everybody's Protest Novel" (1949) challenged Wright's work and argued that such literature boxed us into the very categories we wanted to escape.

The protest literature of the late '60s and early '70s called the oppressed, not the oppressors, into action. Two influential examples of this more militant stance are Eldridge Cleaver's *Soul on Ice* (1968) and *The Autobiography of Malcolm X* (1965). Later works began to be a bit more introspective, linking protest to a call for self-definition and self-determination. Late twentieth century writers continue in this manner, as exemplified by works such as Shelby Steele's *The Content of Our Character* (1990), Marita Golden's *Saving Our Sons* (1995) and Tony Brown's *Black Lies, White Lies . . . The Truth According to Tony Brown* (1995).

THE GO ON GIRL!
Social Commentary Reading List

The Content of Our Character / Shelby Steele

The Isis Papers: The Keys to the Colors /
Dr. Frances Cress Welsing

Invisibility Blues / Michelle Wallace

Yearnings / bell hooks

Buppies, B-Boys, Baps & BoHos / Nelson George

The Rage of the Privileged Class / Ellis Cose

In the Company of My Sisters / Julia Boyd

Saving Our Sons / Marita Golden

*Black Lies, White Lies . . . The Truth According to
Tony Brown* / Tony Brown

A Shining Thread of Hope / Darlene Clark Hine
and Kathleen Thompson

BOOK PRAISE FROM GO ON GIRLS

"Through reading social commentary, especially The Isis Papers *by Dr. Frances Cress Welsing, I realized that while I joined the book club to read for relaxation, I still need books to challenge, educate and ignite me."*

Evalyn R. Hamilton-Russell
Chicago, Illinois

"Tony Brown's Black Lies, White Lies *challenged me to think differently about affirmative action."*

Valerie Richards
Springdale, Maryland

"I thought Rage of the Privileged Class *had a great premise—that even success comes at a price when you're Black. The author knew our rage, having felt it himself after hitting the glass ceiling. The only problem, though, is after I read it, I still felt rage."*

Stephanie Byrd Harrell
Philadelphia, Pennsylvania

The Isis Papers:
The Keys to the Colors
by Dr. Frances Cress Welsing

*The Isis Papers is a collection of Dr. Welsing's essays
on the volatile subjects of racism and color confronta-
tion. The third-generation doctor of psychiatry is committed to raising the consciousness of people of color
through her writing.*

BLACK WOMEN MOVING TOWARDS THE
TWENTY-FIRST CENTURY (MAY 1975)

Today, the world is going through a period of great turmoil
and change. Individually, we are aware of this turmoil because
social and environmental chaos brings an attendant increase
in the stress we feel in our daily lives as women workers in all
capacities: wives, mothers and individual members of a total
collective that for 400 years has been oppressed. Yes, this is a
difficult period for all of us "hue-man" beings, and it would
not be an exaggeration to say that we are in a time not only of
turmoil, but of *crisis*.

During periods of crisis and stress, the easiest thing to do as
an expression of our pain, despair and hopelessness is to
moan, groan, cry or attempt to escape through alcohol, other
drugs, fantasy, laughter or just fun and games. However,
another possible behavioral response, which channels the
body energy upward and onward as opposed to downward, is

the use of the crisis as a stimulus for analysis, challenge, responsibility, growth and great creativity.

The word *crisis* evolves from the Greek word, "krisis," which means *decision*. A period of crisis is a time for decision: an unstable or crucial time or state of affairs when the decisions that are made and acted upon become all-important for determining future events. Both men and women throughout the world have key roles to play in the resolution of this crisis, but my singular emphasis here is on the role of Black women.

Before specifically defining our present period of crisis and our response to it, we must contemplate our *identity*, the self-image that we carry in our brain-computers. For all that we can imagine doing and all that we will *do or fail* to do is a result of that picture of "self," derived from our total experiences from birth onward. That picture becomes the basis for all our behavioral patterns. Unfortunately, a major part of these self and group images for all too many of us Blacks consists of a brief and inaccurate history. Accordingly, this history began 400 years ago when we were brought to North America in the holds of slave ships by the "very advanced" Europeans (whites); it continues with the "advancement" that we have made since our emancipation in 1863 in becoming full-fledged "Americans"; and, finally, this history insists that many of us now are just like the whites. There is a proverb that states, "The tree grows strong and tall *only* to the extent that its roots are deep and firmly planted in the soil." If Black people are at all disappointed in our present level of achievement, it may be because our roots are not planted deeply enough in the past—resting upon such a shallow, inadequate and faulty data input of only 400 years of history.

The facts of our true identity are that we, as Black people, are persons whose dominant genetic and historic roots extend to Africa, "the land of the Blacks." Men and women of science today, with few exceptions, are satisfied that Africa was the birthplace of humankind and that for many *hundreds of centuries thereafter* Africans, meaning Black people, were in the forefront of all human progress. As John Henrik Clarke states, "It can be said with a strong degree of certainty that Africa has had three Golden Ages. The *first two* reached their climax and were in decline before *Europe* as a functioning entity in human society was born."

Factually speaking, this means that Black women and Black men are the parents of the entire family of people—black, brown, red, yellow and white varieties. Black people can and have produced all of the colors of mankind, including white. White skin is simply the product of a recessive genetic mutation to skin albinism. Whites cannot be the parents of humankind because whites can only produce white. But Blacks can produce a range of colors from as black as the proverbial ace of spades, to as white as the proverbial driven snow. Not only are Blacks the genetic parents of all people in the world today, but Blacks produced the first scientists, architects, musicians, mathematicians, astronomers, astrologers, philosophers, statesman, priests, prophets and generals. Indeed, Africa produced some of the first fighting women generals.

I am reminded of some ancient and important wisdom of Africa, as seen in the following two proverbs: 1) "When you educate women, you educate a nation," and 2) "The hand that rocks the cradle rules the nation and its destiny." With this wisdom of our Black ancestors in mind, let us examine the current world crisis and the role of Black women in its resolution. What is the nature of this crisis?

Critical in the history of white supremacy was the decision not to control Black and other women of color, but to control the men of color. Men are the initiators of the act of reproduction. Ultimately, women are dependent upon their men for protection because of the greater physical strength of men compared to women. If one simply controls the men of a people, the women are controlled also. Thus, the white collective went about the business of systematically developing a plan and power mechanism worldwide to bring all of the world's men of color under their ultimate control. Once this was established, the men of color were informed overtly as well as subtly that if they ever should seek to alter the power relationship of *white* over *non-white,* they would have to fight and many would die. Thousands upon thousands of Black men in the U.S. were lynched and castrated to drive home the message that white men intended to control the "balls" in this world, both on and off of the court!

White males understood that they needed white women as well as Black women to help them achieve and maintain this power relationship. White women always have known what they stood to gain—their own survival as whites. Black women have been confused and less clear in fully understanding how they have been led to cooperate in this deadly power game of white supremacy. Further, Black women do not understand fully that they have nothing to gain and everything to lose if this deadly game continues.

The first lessons to Black women were harsh and cruel ones of sexual assault and abuse, taking their children away and forcing them to watch their men being lynched and castrated.

But then these harsh lessons were followed by milder treatment of Black women as compared to Black men. Black women were given extra food, money, clothing and other gifts for their special personal favors to the masters. They were rewarded for correctly teaching their children to conform to the masters' wishes, as well as for telling their men to calm down and be patient so that they too could be rewarded. Perhaps we (Black women) really became seduced by the illusion of power, being so close to white males.

We have told ourselves that these behaviors were survival tactics and the only way that we could have "come this far." But as our survival increasingly is becoming threatened, we are forced to wonder if we have been mistaken in our analysis and our strategy. But, again, there is something to be learned from our African past. And we must never forget that those who do not learn from "history," "their whole story," are bound to repeat it.

The specific *story* to which I refer is that of the African (Black) queen, Cleopatra. Born in 69 B.C., Cleopatra came to the throne that she shared with her brother, Ptolemy XIII, when she was 13 years old. Egypt was then a Roman protectorate. It was beset with internal strife and intrigue. Cleopatra aligned herself with the Roman general, Julius Caesar, whom she *thought* would reinforce her power and help her people. She saw her political and sexual relationship with Caesar as a maneuver to save Egypt from the worst aspects of Roman domination. This maneuver failed in spite of her second Roman lover Mark Anthony, who came after Caesar's death. Her suicide is a profound statement about the series of decisions that she made. Egypt fell and became a Roman colony. And all of the harsher aspects of Roman rule, which Cleopatra had sought to prevent, settled over Egypt and the Middle East.

There were other Black queens in Africa who fought the white invaders to their death; they did not submit or cooperate with their oppressors. Instead, they moved to resist and destroy that oppressive process. They urged their men to do likewise, thus leaving their marks as heroines and warriors for their people who died in honor. These Black women have not been known simply as "beautiful" queens who committed suicide in their own disgrace.

This brings us to the pertinent question: Should we continue our alliance with the present "Romans," or having learned from the past, should we choose an alternate course? In the context of all that we may want to call progress and material prosperity, we must face the reality that today, Black men die younger than white men, white women and Black women. Black men are the most frequent victims of homicide and they are being killed by one another in increasing numbers. The suicide rate for young Black men is the only Black suicide rate greater than the rates of whites. Black women and Black children are the most frequent victims of rape and other physical assault and violence. Black infant mortality remains two to three times the figure for whites. Black women are more often left alone to care for their children than any other female group in the country. Nearly one-third of our so-called "Black family units," which I refer to as "survival-units," are single-parent families. In the Washington, D.C., metropolitan area, there are over 60,000 Black male children growing up in homes without fathers or other surrogate father figures. We continue to have the highest rates of separation and divorce and, thus, family dissolution. We continue to have some of the highest rates of teenage parenthood, and, thus, immature and inadequate parenting of the next generation. We continue to have high levels of juvenile delinquency, gang wars and drug addiction. Young Black people continue to leave school in record numbers prior to high school graduation. There is a virtual epidemic of low reading and math scores amongst our young people, and as a result, these youngsters are leaving school with totally inadequate preparation for this highly technological, computerized and industrialized social system.

Black people are in a very serious economic depression, while whites are still at the stage of recession. Blacks remain the last hired and first fired, in spite of the supposed achievements of "affirmative action." The relative levels of Black unemployment and white unemployment have not changed since 1945. The housing situation for urban Blacks is not improving. Black men continue to be sent to prison in record numbers, out of proportion to our population percentage. Black men presently constitute 90% of the state prison population. And we now witness the nationwide return of the death penalty.

What must we as Black women do? It is my conviction that the African proverb "The hand that rocks the cradle rules the nation and its destiny" is true. Black women are the mothers and, thus, the first teachers of Black females and Black males alike. With increased consciousness of their importance as the *first teachers*, Black women can determine whether future generations of Black children will be warriors or if we will continue to be slaves living in a highly refined state of psychological oppression, which is no less a death than direct physical destruction. Black women as mothers and teachers can teach the first powerful lessons in pride and respect for cultural, historical and genetic Blackness, while steadfastly refusing to impart any part of the white oppressors' lesson in Black self-hate that we learn as children: "If you're Black, stay back; if you're brown, stick around; if you're yellow, you're mellow; and if you're white, you are all right." Black mothers must cease making their first concern whether or not their babies will have light skin and straight hair.

The newborn infant can tell from the mother's first touch whether she is pleased or disappointed with its color, appearance and gender. Certainly later the child can tell the mother's respect for Blackness by the comments she makes about who is a pretty girl, who is a handsome boy and who has the proverbial "good" and "bad" hair. All of these lessons that we have been taught by our white oppressors to teach our young we must refuse to teach ever again!

But Black women as mothers and first teachers can take their consciousness to an even higher level. They can give the first lesson in what constitutes Black manhood. They can teach all of their sons that they are not their "babies" or their substitute lovers. Black women can be the first to inform their sons, with loving kindness, that they did not bring them into the world to be oppressed. Rather, they brought them into the world to be free men, warriors who have to war to be free, and to die if they so happen to die in the fight for their right to be full men under the stars. Black women must cease saying to child psychiatrists, "I'll never tell my 'baby' anything like that!"

Black women can teach their sons and their daughters that the definition of a Black man is not simply someone who can buy things (a nice home, a car, a yacht and clothes), but rather someone who will respect, support, protect and defend himself, his woman and his children. And finally, Black men are those who will do whatever is necessary to ensure their families' respect, support, protection and defense.

Black women as mothers and teachers consciously can teach their daughters that Black women, as the mothers of all mankind, are the alpha and the omega of women on this planet. They were here in the beginning, and if humankind remains, they will be present in the end. Black mothers can teach their daughters that they should never seek to look like or be like anything other than themselves. They can set the standards of what women will be like on this planet. For this is their responsibility, coming from the tradition of the first mothers and queens. Black women can teach their daughters that respect is not *given* to women by men, but that Black women carry in themselves the highest possible level of self-respect that commands respect from men and women of all races. Black women can teach their daughters how they possibly assist in the destruction of Black men and Black people by allowing Black men to hide out in the vagina. To allow this hiding out (attempts to climb in the womb to be babies or fetuses again) when they know the men should turn and face their oppressors, is an extreme level of self-destruction.

DISCUSSION GUIDE

1. What are some of the key concerns and social issues addressed in this book?

2. How do you feel about Dr. Welsing's strategies for countering racism?

3. How does Dr. Welsing's background as a psychiatrist help her put racism into perspective for people of color?

4. After reading some of her controversial theories, do you agree or disagree with her assessment of why people of color are in the state they are now in?

5. Do you think people of color can truly share in what is defined as the American dream?

6. Most of Dr. Welsing's essays were written to give psychiatrists a better understanding of the impact of racism on people of color. How well do they translate as a book?

DR. FRANCES CRESS WELSING, A PROGRESSIVE THINKER

Published Works: *The Isis Papers: The Keys to Color*, 1991

Home Base: Washington, D.C.

Literary Heroes: "None. I don't focus in that way. If you were to come to my home, you'd see thousands of books. I believe in reading as broadly as your time allows."

Claim to Fame: "I am a Black person on planet Earth who is attempting to participate in solving a problem that is causing the destruction of Black people all over this planet."

What compelled you to write *The Isis Papers*?

The Isis Papers includes the "Cress Theory of Color-Confrontation and Racism," which was the first paper that I wrote. It was written to present to fellow Black psychiatrists, who in the late 1960s were discussing the issue of racism. The paper was presented at the National Medical Association section on neurology and psychiatry in 1970. When I was training as a resident, I realized that the mental health problems Black people faced were intimately tied to racism. I felt if I was going to be an effective psychiatrist, I needed to understand racism in depth. That's how I got started focusing on that topic in a concentrated manner. Also, at that time, I met Neely Fuller, Jr., who had been writing about racism [in] the 1950s during the Korean War. He was the first person to talk about racism as White supremacy, as a global system, not as some abstract, isolated entity that occasionally Black people or other people of color would run into. He was the first to focus on it as a global system of power of White over non-White people. So that was a very critical point in understanding and looking at this global behavioral phenomenon.

What was the initial reaction to some of your theories in the book?

The verbal and written responses to the book have been "this book has changed my life." I receive that type of comment from people at universities, as well as from people who are incarcerated. They say this kind of understanding of racism helps them comprehend the experiences they have had in their life. I didn't originally write the papers for public consumption, so I never thought about a global or national audience. The publisher, Third World Press, encouraged me to put them into a book. So the fact that large numbers of people have had a positive response is always surprising to me, but at the same time, I'm pleased that I have been able to help people. I maintain that Black people greet each other with "What's happening?" because we don't understand what's going on around us. On a surface level, one could say that's a greeting, but on a deeper level, I maintain that we are constantly bewildered trying to move forward in a social system structure and power structure that is poised against us. We haven't had an adequate understanding as to exactly why people who classify themselves as White would have this constant and continuous stance blocking the forward motion of people of color. As a psychiatrist, I believe that you have to understand what is deep within the psyche to cause consistent patterns of behavior.

What would you suggest people of color do to counter racism?

The most important thing at this point in time is for Black people to stop thinking about racism as related to economic exploitation. I maintain that that is not an adequate understanding of racism. The first order of business is for Black people to understand that racism is White supremacy. There's no such thing as Black racism. They have to understand in depth that racism is a local, national and global system of behavioral power and what exactly it is in the psyche of people, who classify themselves as White, that causes them to behave as they do towards people of color. That is as essential as teaching someone what fire is and how it can be destructive if you don't know exactly how to relate to it. Before we enter the twenty-first century, it's my goal that every person who says, "I am a Black person," will understand what racism/White supremacy is and that we would not be referring to ourselves as Black people were it not for the existence of racism/White supremacy on planet Earth. In other words, we would just be people. Simply to say, "I'm not going to refer to myself as a person of color, I'm going to refer to myself as a human being," is not adequate when you have in existence a power construct that is based upon what level of skin pigmentation one has or absence of any skin pigmentation. That's the only classification basically that you have on your birth certificate. You have whether you are male or female, and then you have a classification based on whether you are essentially White or non-White.

There's nothing to indicate what level of income, education or contribution to the planet your parents may have made—just White or non-White. This is the essential element to the maintenance of a system of racism/White supremacy.

What specifically could Black women do to help?

All Black women should realize they are the mothers of humanity. As we enter the twenty-first century, Black women should put the role of procreation second to understanding racism/White supremacy. Understand when it is appropriate to procreate and under what conditions, because that determines what the next generation is going to be about. I believe Black people need to be in their thirties before they procreate, and they should have no more than two children, no closer in age than three years, so that children can have maturity passed on to them in the next generation. This type of procreating will help to produce and advance the maximum development of Black genetic constitutional potential. When people play with sex as we are being conditioned to do by listening to the music and looking at the music videos, we are being influenced to treat the act of self-reproduction as cheap, trashy and frivolous. When people play with sex, the joke is on the offspring. Teachers in the school system don't teach our children; teaching begins with the act of procreation, and the first teachers are the mothers and fathers. We need to bring that level of African wisdom into our efforts.

How did you come up with the name *The Isis Papers* for your book?

Isis was a major Egyptian goddess who believed that truth was more important than silver or gold, so I thought it would be an appropriate title.

CHAPTER FIVE

The Storytellers
The Novel Genre

For nearly 200 years, novels have been written and published by African-Americans. Long fiction narratives centered around a plot or theme with a focus on character development and action; novels represent the area in which Black authors have been most prolific. Perhaps that's because the novel form allows for great diversity in terms of the writer's creative process, and therefore allows us to better see the diversity among us.

In England in 1853, William Wells Brown, our earliest known novelist, published *Clotel*, also known as *The President's Daughter: A Narrative of Slave Life in the United States*. But a woman, Harriet E. Adams, hails as the first Black person in the United States to publish a novel. Her *Our Nig*, otherwise known as *Sketches from the Life of a Free Black, In a Two-Story White House, North, Showing that Slavery's Shadows Fall Even There* was published in 1859. Long titles notwithstanding, these two works are perhaps the best-known novels published during slavery. The authors built their stories around their own personal histories, employing classic features of the popular fiction of the day and setting the context for the African-American novel as we know it today. First, they were autobiographical in nature, which is a still a common characteristic of works by African-Americans, whether it reflects the individual's story or the group's story. Second, these early novels put an emphasis on history.

While the first African-American writers used the novel to influence opinion against the practice of slavery, later writers used the novel to generate a discourse on race. Themes of racial conflict, color and caste discrimination and triumph over adversity distinguishes the works written during Emancipation and Reconstruction. After this period, the focus shifted to uplifting the race and other concerns of the emerging Black middle class. Among the authors offering this perspective were Frances Ellen Watkins Harper, Sutton E. Griggs, Paul Laurence Dunbar, Charles Waddell Chestnut and Pauline E. Hopkins.

As we entered the 1920s, we began to offer literature that reflected an urban perspective. By this time, more Blacks had migrated to Northern cities from the rural South and the Caribbean. We held service occupations and factory jobs. And our cultural expression, especially blues and jazz music, vaudeville and minstrelry, was finding an audience. Feeling freer from outward racial hostility, writers during this period created and contributed to numerous publications and produced at least 50 novels, many of which were experimental in form and technique. This flood of literature became known as the Harlem Renaissance, a period like none before it, when African-American writing was embraced and encouraged. Titles of note include stories of color conflict and passing, such as Jessie Redmon Fauset's *There is Confusion* (1924) and Nella Larsen's *Quicksand* (1928); social satires, such as George S. Schuyler's *Black No More* (1931) and Wallace Thurman's *The Blacker the Berry* (1929); and folk novels such as Claude McKay's *Home to Harlem* (1928) and Rudolph Fisher's *The Walls of Jericho* (1928).

Social realism was the focus of Richard Wright's work, which followed the "New Negro" Renaissance. He was interested in moving the reader to anger, not sympathy. His 1940 best-seller, *Native Son*, demonstrated how the victim of the crime of racism can become the perpetrator of crime. He argued through his work that violence and crime were logical responses to a racist and neglectful society.

In the '50s, Ralph Ellison emerged, offering a decidedly different African-American perspective than Wright. In fact, in his essays, Ellison openly attacked the protest tradition epitomized by Wright's work. Ellison's writings examine the history of the Black American experience through one man's personal journey that ends in alienation. Exploring themes of sin and redemption, James Baldwin, meanwhile, looked at how personal meaning can be discovered through suffering. The visions of Wright, Ellison and Baldwin coexisted during the civil rights movement of the '60s and together formed a blueprint for the contemporary African-American novel. Also notable in these early years of contemporary fiction are Ann Petry, Lorraine Hansberry and Chester Himes, all writers who looked at how changing demographics and politics affected the lives of Blacks.

The late '60s through the early '70s witnessed the rise of the Black Arts Movement, which was Nationalist in nature. Leading literary figures at this time included Gwendolyn Brooks, Sonia Sanchez, Nikki Giovanni, LeRoi Jones (Amiri Baraka) and Ishmael Reed. While this period is noted for promoting Black unity, this school of thought was also responsible for setting a relatively narrow standard for what was authentic enough, Black enough.

As we moved further into the '70s, the African-American

novel began to overstep the boundaries of Black and White and male and female. Most writers in this period created work that confronted historical change and identity and exposed the social impact of racism. There also was a desire among women writers to confront sexual oppression. In fact, this was the beginning of a period of new recognition for African-American women's writing. Critics finally noted that strong female protagonists were indeed present in novels as early as the last decade of the nineteenth century. Recognition of foremothers such as Zora Neale Hurston, Gwendolyn Brooks, Paule Marshall and Margaret Walker proved to be inspirational to women in the mid- to late '70s, who had been drawn to these writers naturally, even before their brilliance was affirmed by the literary world at large.

Since that point, the tables have been turned. Female writers now dominate the market for fiction. For example, the '70s produced writing that was more feminist in tone and substance, and because these new writers were filling a void, they had the chance to write women's stories where there had been none before, or to amend inaccuracies and begin to reflect the complexities in women's lives. These new voices, such as Toni Morrison, Alice Walker, Rita Dove, Toni Cade Bambara, Gayl Jones, Gloria Naylor and Ntozake Shange, were enthusiastically embraced, and went on to achieve prominence during this period. Yet since these writers tackled subject matter previously avoided, such as sexism, domestic abuse and classism, they were not without their detractors. In some corners, this airing of cultural "dirty laundry" was not well received. And while women writers took on a more important role, male authors didn't stop creating during the mid-'70s. One form popularized by them was the "ghetto novel." Penned by authors such as Donald Goins, Iceberg Slim, Joe Nazel, Odie Hawkins, Barry Beckman and Charlie Harris, these novels depict urban street life and the gritty world of hustlers and pimps.

The '80s and the '90s are significant for the sheer number of novels being produced by writers of African descent. The fact that the African-American novel is no longer restricted to the "Black Studies" shelf of most major bookstores is a testament to that. And with so much being produced, there's more variety in subject matter. Generalizing about the African-American novel came pretty easy in past decades. Not so today. Look for themes ranging from cultural affirmation to exploring one's sexuality to the impact of color and class prejudices on human relationships. The one theme that's been getting the lion's share of attention during this recent literary explosion is the everyday life experience of the hard-working, intelligent Black woman. Our relationships, friendships, family ties and careers are being explored in novels rooted in what many critics are calling the "girlfriend culture." The popularity of such works is reflected in the wide audience authors such as Terry McMillan and Connie Briscoe enjoy.

African-American novelists have clearly proven their staying power. The only question that remains is: What themes will be with us in the new millennium?

THE GO ON GIRL!
Novel Reading List

Lucy / Jamaica Kincaid

Baby of the Family / Tina McElroy Ansa

Middle Passage / Charles Johnson

Jazz / Toni Morrison

High Cotton / Darryl Pinckney

1959 / Thulani Davis

Waiting to Exhale / Terry McMillan

Your Blues Ain't Like Mine / Bebe Moore Campbell

And Do Remember Me / Marita Golden

One Dark Body / Charlotte Watson Sherman

Bailey's Cafe / Gloria Naylor

Joy /Marsha Hunt

The Storytellers

A Lesson Before Dying / Ernest Gaines

Ugly Ways / Tina McElroy Ansa

Urban Romance / Nelson George

Coffee Will Make You Black / April Sinclair

Sally Hemings / Barbara Chase-Riboud

The Serpent's Gift / Helen E. Lee

Sisters & Lovers / Connie Briscoe

Chesapeake Song / Brenda Lane Richardson

Brothers and Sisters / Bebe Moore Campbell

The Good Negress / A. J. Verdell

And This Too Shall Pass / E. Lynn Harris

How Stella Got Her Groove Back / Terry McMillan

Knowing / Rosalyn McMillan

Good Hair / Benilde Little

Big Girls Don't Cry / Connie Briscoe

The Literary Work

Ain't Gonna Be the Same Fool Twice / April Sinclair

The Wedding / Dorothy West

Tumbling / Diane McKinney-Whetstone

He Say, She Say / Yolonda Joe

Only Twice I've Wished for Heaven /
Dawn Turner Trice

Tryin' to Sleep in the Bed You've Made /
Virginia DeBerry and Donna Grant

The Seasons of Beento Blackbird / Akosua Busia

Caucasia / Danzy Senna

BOOK PRAISE FROM GO ON GIRLS

"Bebe Moore Campbell's Singing in the Comeback Choir hits a crescendo by taking a look at the hard issues—infidelity, drug and alcohol abuse, AIDS and the deterioration of our neighborhoods. You meet wonderful characters that only Bebe can bring to life with rich dialogue and realistic situations. I was able to identify with many of the conflicts the characters face."

Sandra D. Garrett
Syracuse, New York

"Refreshingly unpredictable, The Seasons of Beento Blackbird by Akosua Busia can't be put to rest. The character Solomon Wilberforce has come up in many of our subsequent book discussions. This touching story dealing with polygyny was culturally different than what we're accustomed to. The intrigue was so great, you had to finish this book."

Kathy Suber
Clinton, Maryland

"Diane McKinney-Whetstone has done it again. Like in Tumbling, the characters in Tempest Rising tug at your heart. Through her portrayal of young sisters Shern, Victoria and Bliss, I got more than an inkling of what it must be like to have that strong sister bond. As an only child, I always imagined it must be special. This touching tale simply confirmed my suspicions."

Barbara Mitchell
Seattle, Washington

Tryin' to Sleep in the Bed You've Made

by Virginia DeBerry and Donna Grant

In their debut novel Tryin' to Sleep in the Bed You've Made, *authors DeBerry and Grant trace the friendship of Patrica Reid and Gayle Saunders, who meet as children, grow up and grow apart while learning about life, love, lies, and finally, the importance of sustaining friendships.*

"... an invisible crack in the world."

1969 QUEENS, NEW YORK

"I gotta pee . . . bad," Gayle whispered to Pat. Fat snowflakes had settled on Gayle's rabbit fur hat and on her bangs, framing her small almond face like a halo.

"You went before we left school!" Pat knew Gayle was stalling to keep from facing her parents with dismal grades. Pat pulled at her green knit cap, trying to keep her hair dry. Her straight-A report card was tucked inside the folded newspaper cover of her math book, but she'd have hell to pay if Aunt Verna had to get out the pressing comb before Saturday.

First thrown together in kindergarten by the random selection of alphabetical order, Patricia Reid and Gayle Saunders were as different and as inseparable as day and night.

Pat had been raised by MaRay, a cake-baking, opinionated woman with immense bosoms and fat, hugging arms, in Swan

City, a hiccup near Raleigh Bay on the North Carolina coast. Lil' Daddy had passed, soon after Pat's hello holler to the world, "But MaRay's here for you, Sugar." Then, when Pat was six, MaRay passed, too. Pat went north to live with her aunt Verna, a hard knot of a woman with no space in her heart or her life for a little girl.

Her first week in the small dark second-floor flat, Pat learned not to mention MaRay and to be very quiet, especially after her aunt's late nights on her job at the Easy Street Bar & Grill. Luckily fall came soon. Since Pat was from the South, which to teachers up North meant she was at least borderline backwards, she was put back a grade, but starting school meant that for at least half a day she didn't have to be quiet, and she wasn't alone.

Pat was chubby and chocolate brown with a wise, wide-eyed face she would grow into and hair that resisted the taming of heat and grease. Her classmates called her "Aunt Jemima on the pancake box" and made fun of her accent, which was thick and slow as the molasses MaRay had laced in her infant bottles. The madder they made her, the more determined she became not to show it. Gifted with keen intelligence nurtured by the strong mother wit of MaRay, Pat quickly proved she was smarter than she looked. In class she always had the answer, which impressed the teacher, but not the students, except for Gayle.

Dainty and honey-colored, with long, wavy "good" hair, Gayle was the answered prayer of Joseph and Loretta Saunders. They married late, past the point when anyone at the venerable Mt. Moriah Baptist Church thought they'd bother. To make up for lost time, they worked hard, saved money for a house, and soon moved from Harlem to St. Albans, Queens, the home of Count Basie, James Brown, and other important people, Loretta was happy to tell you. It was a two-bedroom frame house, with a brick front, pale green siding, a bay window, and, best of all, it was detached, a fine thing to all their apartment-living friends. The lot was even big enough for a carport and a brick barbecue pit in the backyard.

Joseph and Loretta were all set for a family, yet after twelve years and three cruel miscarriages folks said they were too old and ought to stop. Goodness, most of their friends' children were nearly grown. But ever since she was little, Loretta, the ninth of ten in a family where nothing seemed new or enough, had dreamed of being grown and having a daughter. Only one, so she could dress her in pretty clothes bought just for her. She'd have a pink room with dainty white furniture, a room like Shirley Temple must have had, a room of her own.

Just when Loretta and Joseph were beginning to think their friends were right, praise the Lord, their prayers were answered and Gayle Denise Saunders arrived, crying and hollering and demanding to be noticed. Although Loretta was thrilled, she worried that Joseph might be disappointed since she knew men wanted sons, but Gayle landed like an arrow, smack in the bull's-eye of her daddy's heart. He worked for two days with no sleep, laying carpet, hanging Peter Rabbit wallpaper in the nursery, and putting the finishing touches on the new dresser and canopied cradle.

Gayle was their pretty, pampered prize, loved and spoiled by her parents every day, so kindergarten was a rude awakening. She was unhappy to find herself surrounded by dozens of children clamoring for the teacher's attention. Gayle's long hair—worn loose, not braided—her clothes—Sunday-best for other children—and her standoffishness marked her as someone who thought she was too cute, and she was isolated accordingly.

Gayle was so miserable that her good Baptist parents considered enrolling her in Catholic school. But on a day the class had to choose partners for an outing to the park, Gayle decided not to be left alone again. She chose Patty, the other girl nobody ever picked, and a friendship began. To Gayle, Pat seemed like she knew things, and she never seemed lonely or worried, even when she was by herself. And Gayle let Pat into her fantasy world, where anything was possible and it was okay to be a child. They shared finger paints and animal crackers and the hand clap-slap of "Miss Mary Mack, Mack, Mack, All Dressed In Black, Black, Black." They played dolls and blocks, but they always played together, and by first grade, each declared the other her best friend.

Loretta, however, did not approve of Pat, or "her people," meaning she didn't like Verna Reid's job as a barmaid. She kept trying to convince Gayle she could find a nicer girl to be her best friend. Gayle didn't care what Loretta thought on the subject and persisted in inviting Pat over. Lips pursed and nose out of joint, Loretta would complain to Joseph that Verna and her ilk were exactly what they left Harlem to avoid. "Patty's only a child, 'Etta," Joseph had said over the sports page. "Smart one at that. Gayle can learn a thing or two from her." Loretta was so put out with Joseph, she put him out of her bed for a week.

Verna thought Gayle's family was uppity, for no good reason. "Her daddy's a damn janitor and her momma does day work!" Pat sat in silence, playing with a bowl of Trix and pretending to watch *Soul Train* while Verna ranted. "They treat that silly-ass girl like she somethin' special, always tossin' her hair like she White." Verna couldn't figure out why the hell

Pat, with her flat face and eyes like a walleyed pike, wanted to be around somebody who made her look even more homely, but if Pat wanted to be a fool, that was on her.

Now in fifth grade, the unlikely twosome was inseparable. The very children who had disliked Gayle because she was so pretty were eventually drawn to her for the same reason. Pat had all but lost her Carolina drawl, but brains didn't make you popular. She was quiet and a little too bookish, but she could be funny sometimes, she always had the right answers to math homework, and her inexplicable closeness to Gayle sealed her acceptance.

And the girls' walk home was ritual. By three-forty they would reach Pat's street. She had orders from her aunt not to let "any little bastards in my house." Verna called most days at four o'clock to make sure Pat was home alone, so rain or shine, the girls talked outside until three-fifty-five. They discussed schoolwork, sang songs from the radio, and sometimes said things they didn't want anyone else to hear, like how Pat wanted to be a doctor or lawyer, somebody important so she didn't have to work at night like Aunt Verna or wear those clothes that made men click their tongues and talk to her out the side of their mouths. Gayle couldn't wait to be old enough to wear makeup, date, and get married, probably to a prince, because her daddy always had dirt under his nails and her momma's hands were so rough they snagged her stockings. Besides, they worked all the time and didn't seem like they had any fun. Pat inevitably asked the last time she saw a Black prince. "That doesn't mean there isn't one, and I plan to marry him! I'll find a prince for you, too, and we'll have a double wedding!" Gayle would announce, then stroll home daydreaming about gowns and weddings, which she would draw until her mother made her get her homework.

The snow was falling double-time, and car tires whined, spinning for traction. Gayle stomped the caked snow off her boots. "Just went doesn't help when I gotta go now, Patty!" To show the urgency of the situation, Gayle passed up their daily stop at J&T Candy Corner, where she would check for new hairstyle magazines and Archie comics because she loved that Veronica Lodge. Pat would buy a chocolate chip cookie the size of a 45 record to knock the edge off until she warmed the dinner plate Aunt Verna always left her.

"You are the peeingest girl in the world. If there was a pee-ing contest, you'd win." Pat giggled, and Gayle held her stomach and tried not to laugh, but she did anyway.

"Shh!" Gayle chided Pat, as she glanced back and saw Marcus Carter climbing to the top of an icy gray mound, piled high by a snowplow. "Going to the bathroom is girl stuff. Don't let him hear."

Last year, Marcus had moved around the corner from Gayle and appeared in their class and on their walk home. At first they ignored him. He was, after all, a boy, but when Gayle developed a crush on Marcus's eighth-grade brother, Freddy, Marcus became the first male member of this very exclusive club.

Marcus leapt off the bank with a whoop and grinned like a fool as he landed on his butt in the fresh snow. "Everybody pees!" He got up, galloped past them, and snatched Gayle's hat. Trotting backwards he added, "I can pee and write my name in the snow at the same time!" Freddy had just taught him this miraculous feat.

"That's nasty, and gimme back my hat!" Gayle squealed and ran after him.

They arrived in front of Pat's house, and, hat in hand,

Gayle shifted her weight from foot to foot, looking pitiful. She knew Pat wasn't allowed company, but three C's, two D's, and an F in geography meant she'd have to listen to a lecture on how important education was so she could take care of herself and not have to scrub other people's floors and toilets.

"Come on, Patty, I can't hold it. I gotta go . . . now! I can't walk another step." Gayle crossed her heart and her legs.

"You mean if I tickle you, you'll pee all over yourself," Marcus said, his fingers wiggling in anticipation.

"Marcus Garvey Carter, I'll scream if you touch me," Gayle threatened.

Pat hemmed and hawed, yanking at a drooping kneesock. A resounding "whap" interrupted her debate as the frozen sparks of a well-aimed snowball exploded off Marcus's head. His books fell and skittered across the snow as he spun to face his attacker.

"Steeerrrriiike! Right in yo' bean head," shouted Freddy, bounding up to the trio. At thirteen, Freddy, a cocoa-brown length of budding muscle and energy, viewed tormenting Marcus as his brotherly right, secure that he was big enough to call the shots. "Freddy 'Fastball' Carter wins the World Series! Roberto Clemente, eat that! Tell me I ain't bad."

"Baseball is lame!" Marcus yelled, then barreled into Freddy, knocking him to the powdery pavement.

Ignoring the melee, Pat continued, "You only live four more blocks, Gayle. You could make it if you stop talkin' and start walkin'."

"Pleazzzz! It's too cold, and I can't wait!" Gayle looked near tears.

"All right! . . . But you gotta hurry up." Pat swung open the chain-link gate and felt under her scarf for her keys, which dangled from the braided orange lanyard Gayle had made for her last summer in vacation Bible school.

Gayle followed, but a howl stopped them before Pat unlocked the door.

"Aw, Freddy man, you busted my lip. Look, I'm bleedin'." Marcus triumphantly pulled his lower lip down to display the blood collecting around his teeth. "Wait 'til I show Daddy. He's gon' whip yo butt. He tol' you to quit messin' wit me."

"Eeeyew!" Gayle groaned, as Marcus spit out a mouthful of blood that dotted the snow like Redhots.

"Don't be no sissy, man. You ain't even hurt." Freddy lifted his drawstring gym bag and gingerly dusted off the snow. "Besides, I got somethin' in here I was gonna show you, but I can't be showin' no sissy," Freddy said, baiting his hook.

"You ain't got nothing in that stupid bag but s'more a them stupid motorcycle magazines," Marcus said, trying to resist the enticing lure.

"That's what you say. Not what I know." Freddy dangled the bait in front of Marcus.

"What's he got in there?" Gayle whispered to Pat.

Marcus, unable to ignore temptation, bit. "Okay, okay, I won't tell." He prepared to spit again.

"Don't you spit no more blood out in front of my house," Pat yelled, knowing that somehow she'd be blamed for it.

"What I'm s'pposed to do?" Marcus tried not to swallow.

"You could come up to wash your mouth out, and Freddy could come, too . . . so you act right," Gayle offered.

"Gaa-yle." Pat shot her friend a scalding glance, which was answered by Gayle's "Oh come on, just this once" smile. Pat sighed and reluctantly opened the door. "But y'all have to be outta here by four. No kidding." Everybody could do their business by then.

They rumbled up the steps and into the apartment. Pat hurried Gayle into the bathroom and tried to confine the others to the narrow hall, except that meant they were right outside the bathroom and Gayle wouldn't pee until they moved. The boys were remanded to the living room.

"Dag, you sleep on the couch?" Marcus poked the pile of clumsily folded sheets and blankets.

"None a your business and keep your ole nasty hands offa my stuff." Pat emerged from the kitchen and handed Marcus a napkin for his mouth. She missed her bed in Swan City. It was near a window, and she would lie at night counting the stars beyond a clutch of scruffy pine trees except when there was thunder and lightning. Then she would take her covers and hide with MaRay in the pantry, where there were no windows and nothing electric. Ma would tell stories about when she was little while they waited out the storm. The sofa was comfortable, though, and she could watch TV in her pajamas with all the lights out when she was by herself at night.

"What'cha gon' show me?" Marcus zeroed in on Freddy, forgetting his injured mouth.

Freddy knelt on the parquet linoleum and carefully loosened the drawstring of his bag. The hood of his jacket fell forward, obscuring most of his face. "You gotta swear not to tell. You hear me . . . never . . . nobody." Freddy hunched over like a wizard fiercely protecting the secret magic hidden in his pouch. Pat's curiosity drew her closer. "You too. You have to swear." Caution, fear, and excitement tinged his solemn voice. Good sense told Pat that Freddy should take his bag, its contents, and his brother and get out because Aunt Verna was going to call any minute, but her eleven-year-old need to know made her slowly nod yes as she crossed her heart and swore not to tell.

Freddy milked the anticipation. "I shouldn't be showing you this. Y'all just kids, but . . ." He reached inside and slowly, reverently, withdrew his secret by its black, plastic handle.

Patricia's mouth dropped open as she backed away. "You gotta get outta here. Now . . . you gotta leave . . ."

Marcus swelled with an excited intake of air. "Where'd you get it? That's a toy, man. That ain't no real gun." Marcus looked skeptically at the Saturday night special.

"This ain't no toy, chump. I found it. On the way to school . . . next to a garbage can in Baisley Park."

"You like . . . Lemme hold it." Marcus sprang toward Freddy.

Time oozed in thick oily seconds. Pat wanted to be outside again, waving good-bye to Gayle, but she couldn't alter the past or grab hold of the present enough to change it.

"Naw man . . . it's dangerous." Freddy moved to tuck the gun away.

Dense and slippery, the time slick spread.

"I bet you never saw lips like these." Gayle sashayed from the bathroom, her mouth painted with Verna's lipstick in a plum so deep it looked crude. She stopped cold when she saw the melee.

"Come on . . . lemme hold it." Marcus reached around Freddy, grabbing at the pistol.

"Stop, Marcus!"

But he couldn't and the boys locked, struggling over the weapon.

"Marcus, cut it . . ." A crackle, no louder than a finger snap, stopped them all.

DISCUSSION GUIDE

1. What were the life choices that Gayle, Marcus and Pat made? Do you think they made the right choices for themselves? Why?

2. Secrets play an important role in *Trying* . . . Almost everyone has one. What effect does keeping them have on the characters' relationships with each other? How are the relationships altered by the revelation of their secrets?

3. What twists surprised you the most? How essential were they to the story?

4. Compare and contrast the relationships between Gayle and Pat and their parents/guardian. What is Gayle's view of Pat and Pat's view of Gayle? How do they both see Marcus?

5. What are the differences and similarities of the worlds each character has constructed for himself or herself?

VIRGINIA DEBERRY AND DONNA GRANT, SISTER FRIENDS

Published Works: *Tryin' to Sleep in the Bed You've Made*, 1997

Home Base: Donna Grant, Brooklyn, New York; Virginia DeBerry, North Brunswick, New Jersey

Literary Heroes: *Grant:* Jean Toomer is a personal favorite of mine and Ntozake Shange was real important to me. I also like Faulkner, Toni Morrison and Amy Tan. A lot of it has to do with the way they make me feel the story. The character talks to you and the author disappears.

DeBerry: I love Gloria Naylor, J. California Cooper, Zora Neale Hurston, Ralph Ellison, Anne Tyler and Alice Hoffman. I like stories that are not necessarily huge, but zero in on significant moments in peoples' lives, because everyone has those moments.

Claim to Fame: Black Caucus Honor Award from the Congressional Library Association

---

How did the two of you meet and come together to write a book?

Grant: We met as large-size models, both getting into that career by very peculiar methods. I had been working in advertising for the *Daily News*, and someone dared me to model, so I did. Virginia was up in Buffalo and someone encouraged her to try large-size modeling when she left teaching after ten years. She came down to New York and ended up at the same agency with me. It's been after writing this book that we began to trace the history of our friendship. It's been hard, because it feels like we've known each other all our lives.

DeBerry: We should have been enemies. We were always up for the same job and the client was only ever going to hire one Black large-size model. They might hire two blondes [and] four brunettes, but only one Black girl on the job. We figured out really early on just from general conversation at these auditions that we really liked each other. The client was going to decide who to book; it had nothing to do with us, and it never became an issue in our friendship. We ended up producing a fashion and lifestyle newsletter for Hanes queen-size hosiery that was distributed to stores. From that, we had the opportunity to edit a plus-size fashion and beauty magazine called *Maxima*.

Grant: It was a quarterly magazine, but we only did three issues before the backers wanted to do other things with their money. We were left high and dry, and angry. After we were through being angry and upset, we realized that we had to find some way to keep working together. Because that was the rightist thing that either of us had ever done. We both had done a lot of things for a living. We wanted something that nobody could take away from us until we were done with it. And we wanted something that didn't cost any start-up capital because we didn't have any. Throughout the years, books have always remained an important part of our friendship. We've been teased about writing a book together. And we said, "Yeah, we can do that."

So what was the process the two of you used to write the same novel? How did you blend it all together so that it told one cohesive story?

Grant: We plot for a long time, we plot very carefully, and we do it together. The process "what if" becomes what we say to each other. We talk about topics, things that have been important in our lives, situations that could happen, and it kind of works that way.

DeBerry: We probably plotted six months for *Tryin'* before we even started to write the outline. We just kept talking about it and talking about it, turning the characters around and changing situations and adding things and deleting things until we started to get a shape for the story that we saw evolving for these characters.

Grant: And we write pretty much the same way. We mostly sit at the computer together and work. We are both very free with each other's words. No one says, "I wrote that sentence, you can't change that." It's not like that at all. We dance all over each other's work and change it. We both know that we're doing it to make it better. There's not any ego involved.

DeBerry: It's always what's best for the story. It has nothing to do with who wrote it. Does this absolutely work here? Is this something the character would do or say? Does this move the plot along? Those were the questions.

How did you go from putting the book together to convincing a publisher that it should be published?

Grant: It wasn't necessarily easy. We had a literary agent who worked with us for many years before we sold anything. We had another project we worked on that she was not able to sell. The comment she heard from editors was, "We like their writing, but the story isn't working for us. Show us the next thing that they do." That wasn't necessarily the answer we wanted, but we were encouraged. Okay, well they think we can write, so again we dusted ourselves off and started working on the story that became *Tryin'*.

How difficult was it to keep the plot suspenseful?

Grant: Part of what we do is try and think about the drama in people's lives. If you talk to people for more than ten minutes, you'll find there are events in their lives that make you step back and say, "Wow, that happened to you?" If you read the newspaper, you see things that happen in people's lives that are enormous and summons all of their courage and strength to get through. What we wanted to do with this story was look at those events in people's lives that looked kind of regular. They weren't stars. Marcus is an athlete. He had to fight through the situations that caused him pain. It wasn't about the bright lights, it was about his own personal struggle. How many times have you gotten to a point in your life where you say, "I've got this all figured out. I know how this is going to work," and something else jumps up and changes all your very neat plans. That was the part of life we wanted to capture.

DeBerry: While it is fiction, we wanted it to be like life. There are stories that you read, and there are people in these stories that you just don't understand. What happens so often is that the characters seem to have come into the story fully grown in whatever situation there is, and they're dealing with it and you don't know how they got to be who they are. And none of us get grown that way. There are things that affect us that have everything to do with what we are doing today. It was important to give the characters in the story those same kinds of things.

Grant: It was time to explain their interior life. We all have that exterior life where we go out and do what we do, but our interior life tells us why. We wanted to make sure the reader was privy to it.

What message did you want your readers to walk away with?

DeBerry: We wanted them to understand that mistakes are a part of life and that we all make them. When we're young, we can't wait to be grown to do what we want. And what we find out, if we're fortunate, is that being grown is dealing with the consequences of having done what you want. If you can do that and come up on the other side, not bitter or angry over this mistake you made, but wiser, you will have learned something about yourself and the world around you. That's what growing up really is.

Grant: And that's where the title comes from. Titles are very hard. In six words or less, you're supposed to sum up what your 400 pages tell. We went through a lot of them, but we kept coming back to the bed we've all made. It's a saying everybody knows.

Are there any similarities between your friendship and that of Gayle and Pat's?

Grant: The best answer that we can come up with is that we're both neither and both. Neither character translates directly to either [of] us, and the life situations don't translate into things we have gone through specifically.

Virginia DeBerry and Donna Grant are the 1997 Go On Girl! New Authors of the Year

Tempest Rising

by Diane McKinney-Whetstone

The second novel from Diane is as poignant as her powerful debut title, Tumbling. *In Tempest Rising, we are presented with a gentle portrait of an upper-class family eventually torn apart by tragedy.*

The grand stone Victorian tried not to show off, even though it survived that sudden March storm, stood tough while the roof caved in on the house next door, and the front palladian blew out in the one across the street; a half-dead pin oak died for real and crashed through the attic of the house on the corner. But this house blushed inside, still intact with an endless center hall and windows that stretched from the floors to heaven, waiting patiently for Clarise and the girls to get back home. Finally, after all they'd been through leading up to the mammoth March storm, they so deserved this house with its pervasive elegance. Understated, though. Because Clarise knew better than to have an ostentatious house.

Clarise had been raised by her two aunts and two uncles, brothers and sisters to one another, who earned their living making exquisite bar soaps, coconut and honey, by hand. The four had never married and shared a tidy Queen Street row house on the other side of town from where the sturdy, blushing house stood. They dunked their lives into bringing up Clarise, their dead fifth sibling's only child, and had exceptional taste: the uncles; and thick-knuckled attitudes: the aunts.

The sisters were tough, hardworking, ample-chested, husky-voiced women who didn't believe in indulging the child. They both had Georgia-clay red complexions; both were tall for the generation of women born around 1900. And even while they were raising Clarise, through the 1930s and 1940s, and packaged meats had caught on in cities like Philadelphia, the sisters were the type who always bought their pork whole and fresh-killed from the waterfront, drained it, skinned it, hacked it into ham and rump and chops while the brothers and Clarise covered their eyes.

The brothers were soft, immaculate, and artistic; they kept spotless bureaus and chifforobes, played the melody harp, cooked like the French. Both were the color of ginger: one tall and thin, back straight as a paper birch; the other, short and round, no neck, built like a mushroom. They adored Clarise, and from the time she was a baby they would conjure up desserts and make like magicians, pretend as if the tapioca, her favorite, had just gathered itself together from the mist in the air and settled on the table in front of her. They had to sneak, though, when the aunts weren't around, who insisted that too many sweets would turn Clarise into a weak, crybaby type of child.

Clarise was tough in her own right, at least when it came to crying. She could will herself not to cry and shut down her tear ducts so that no fluid fell. She wasn't so tough when it came to men, though. She would go weak for men from the time she blossomed into adolescence. Had to squeeze her thighs together so she wouldn't let herself go wide open every time she got a whiff of Aqua DiSilva, or Old Spice original, or

Noxzema aftershave. She'd been well trained, though, by the aunts, who, tough and celibate as they were, understood a woman's nature, had watched Clarise's strong-natured mother die a hard death from female problems: a growth, a ruptured vessel, a massive bleed, according to the doctors; too many lying men with their tainted naked things getting too close to their trusting baby sister, according to the aunts. They told Clarise what to look for when her own nature came down. Told her to run like hell from any man who said, "Baby, I'm for real." Told her she'd do well to marry young.

So when Clarise was sixteen going on seventeen, and graduated early from high school because she was smart and had been skipped a grade, and Finch was walking through the streets of Philadelphia, taking leave and his final pay from the merchant marine ship where he'd duly served as assistant cook, he saw Clarise in the cream-colored graduation dress that had been hand-sewn by the uncles with beads at the top and layers and layers of voile. Clarise took note of Finch's eyes, how they went liquid for her like brown gravy seeping down the curve of a rump roast; she knew then he was the one she would marry even before he tried to woo her with his financial worth. He'd flash a wad of bills, lick his index finger before he peeled off the dollars to pay for their drinks at the Showboat.

But Clarise knew it was all for effect. The sailors whose ships always docked at the navy yard made similar spectacles of their earnings. Even when she was a child walking through the streets of downtown, she'd watched them, pausing before they went into the penny arcade, or Horn & Hardart, or McCrory's dime store. They'd hoist their pants up higher on their waists before digging deep in their pockets to bring up a mound of paper money. And if Clarise appeared even minutely impressed, she'd feel her aunt Til tug her arm. "Man with real money doesn't flash it in public for all to see," her aunt would say.

So even though Finch tried to show off his money, which Clarise knew meant that he was broke as a grasshopper in the snow, she sensed that he was the type to turn a dollar into twenty time and again. It wasn't just the way he puffed his cigars and mashed his feet flat into the earth when he walked or the way he'd slap the backs of the men in the clubs, with a gregarious authority; it was the way the air smelled around him. Clarise had a heightened olfactory sense that revealed more about a person or thing to her than her eyes could see. And whenever she stood within two feet of Finch, no matter how much his Old Spice tried to get in the way, she detected the unmistakably crisp scent of heavily inked, fresh-cut, new paper money.

Plus Finch was dark, meant the children they'd have together would have some color. She herself didn't have much color. Her father was rumored to have been an Italian from the other block of Queen Street, so Clarise had an odd look: skin color like the shell of an egg when it wasn't quite a brown egg, but not a white egg either; eyes the tint of a dusty gray dawn; long silky hair that went bushy when it was humid out; well-defined nose; nicely padded lips. She was often teased about her look. Would run home after school and stand straight as a board in front of the aunts, hold her tears like she was trying to keep from wetting herself. "They called me a half-white African," she'd say.

"You tell them you as white and as African as their mommas," her aunt Til would say.

"They called me shit-colored," she'd say.

"You tell them shit comes in all colors, even black like their mommas," her other aunt, Ness, would say.

The aunts helped Clarise to be tough and unflinchable in the face of hurtful childhood insults. They knew firsthand the starchy taste of persistent teasing. Spinsters, they'd been called; old maids, hags, he-women, funny honeys. Had to teach their baby sister, Clarise's mother, how to hurl the insults right back when she'd come home crying, telling the aunts the names they'd been called. So they were expert when it came time to help Clarise become a master at quick come-backs to the assaults on her strange looks. Soon the other children were so terrified of Clarise's ability to string words together like beads on a necklace, wrap them around some child's neck, and send that child home crying and choking, they promptly stopped calling her half-breed, mulatto, massa's child, witch's nose. And even though her odd look as a child metamorphosed itself into an exotic form of beauty when she became a teen, she didn't want her own children to tote the barge of her childhood looks. She knew Finch would dilute her looks in their children and give them thick, pressable hair and earthy-toned complexions. Not only was he dark brown, but he had very nonextreme looks: a normally round face, a typically short nose, eyes and lips that were neither large nor small. Plus he had nice, amply sized legs, an appetite like a country preacher, and his very chest expanded when he looked at Clarise, as if he were saying, "Right here, pretty baby, lay your head right here," meant she wouldn't have to worry about dying young like her mother did from the taint-ed, naked parts of lying men.

When the time came for Clarise to sneak out of the window on the Queen Street row house and spare her dear aunts and uncles the expense of a wedding, she wrote two letters. She'd had to write only two letters because she'd known no other family, no grandparents, no cousins. One letter she left in the shed where the aunts cured their ham; she thanked them for advising her so well. The other letter she propped next to the uncles' lead crystal sugar bowl in the center of the breakfast-room table; she wrote how much she'd miss their tapioca and begged them not to cry. Then she climbed out of the dining-room window into the alley that smelled of honeysuckle and bleach mixing well with Finch's Colgate aftershave.

Finch stood there wide-backed, flat-footed, trying not to sneeze. He lit up the alley he was beaming so, and patting his breast pocket that held their bus tickets to Elkton, Maryland, where the justice of the peace was, and then to Atlantic City to the Cliveden Hotel on Kentucky Avenue for their honeymoon.

The aunts knew the very second Clarise snuck away from their home. Ness, the younger, softer sister, sat straight up in her bed when she heard the hushed giggles before they evaporated into the alley like blowing bubbles. She called across the room. "Til," she said. "Til, she's gone."

"We knew it was coming," Til said.

"But he's a poor man, Til."

"What colored man isn't?"

"Daddy wasn't."

"Daddy's dead. Whole breed of colored men like Daddy gone to glory. Probably looking down and shaking their heads at lesser versions of themselves that don't even own a pot to piss in."

"You think this Finch will do right by our girl, Til?"

"We did right by her."

"Lord, yes, we did."

"And she knows not to settle for less than what's she's used to."

"Pray, pray she knows it."

"Strong child."

"Well, well. Thank you, Sister, she is strong."

"And we got her inheritance stitched between the mattress springs should they really fall on hard times."

"I'm so thankful, Jesus."

"And our hacking knives stay sharp if he turns out to be the mistreating kind."

"You a mess, Til, a natural mess."

They laughed easy laughs, and then the air got stilted, as they both realized at the same instant it seemed the startling truth to Til's words: how Til had almost made two separate spheres out of Line 'Em Up Larry's face who'd lurked around after Clarise's mother died, insisting that the toddler Clarise was his child and he'd come to claim her, to take her to live with his sister, Vie, and him on Bainbridge Street.

Til told him he was either crazy or drunk. Anybody could look at Clarise and see she was no seed of his, black as he was, blacker than pitch tar, plus everybody knew his pecker had been crushed long before that short spell when he took up with Clarise's mother, when he jumped bad with the Irish during the union riots and they crashed him in his middle with a fifty-pound bag of sand, so he just better keep his black ass away from their house. He didn't heed Til, though. Came back again, talking about "my child, I'm here for my child, me and my sister, Vie, gonna raise my child." And Til told him to just wait right there, she was gonna split him in half. He waited. That became a family joke between the brothers and sisters. If they were talking in superlatives about how stupid somebody was, they'd sum it up with "He's stupid enough to wait in the living room while Til goes to get her sharpest hacking knife to split his head in two; in fact, if there's anybody else around, he organizes a line and claims his spot at the head." Line 'Em Up Larry survived, but that didn't stop two burly detectives from arresting Til and charging her with attempted murder, spurred on by Larry's sister, Vie, who boasted connections at City Hall, said she'd see Til under the jail. Til was found guilty but only slapped on the wrist with a suspended sentence since Larry's sister was only a low-level clerk down at Family Court.

"Ness," Til said, after they had both breathed and sighed and stirred up the bedroom air with remembrances of Til's fight to protect their baby niece, "you getting ready to cry, aren't you, Ness? I can hear it in your breathing."

"I am. Won't deny it. I'm just gonna miss our girl so."

"And you thinking about her mother, right, Ness?"

"How can I not think about Baby Sis at a time like this and the painful ending to her too-short life?"

"Clarise will have a better ending, Ness. But you go ahead then. Go ahead and cry. Just don't let Brother and Brother hear you. As it is, we gonna be wiping up their spilt tears for the next week once they realize our girl went and eloped."

"All right, Til. Stop talking then. Just let me cry, and while I'm crying, I'm gonna pray for the peace and love of their union, and for their prosperity; I'm praying real hard for their prosperity."

Clarise's aunt Ness wasn't the only one praying for their prosperity. Finch had moneymaking on his mind from the start of their holy matrimony. Clarise's type of beauty begged for mink and silk. But before he thought about such large-scale purchases, he knew he'd want to keep her in sheer, lacy nightgowns. He'd noticed right away after he'd carried her over the threshold of their honeymoon hotel on Kentucky Avenue in Atlantic City and she'd unpacked the quality tweed suitcase that belonged to the uncles, there was only one fancy nightgown. Lord have mercy, he thought, she'll leave me for some other cat if I can't keep her in good lingerie. He could hardly concentrate on satisfying her appetites that night thinking about that nightgown. She'd teased him so, played peeka-boo and hide-and-seek with her one nightgown before she'd let him poke his fingers through the holes the lace made.

Finch just lay there staring at the ceiling that entire night while Clarise snored softly against his chest and lightly ground her teeth. Instead of counting sheep, Finch ticked off the mammoth hidden costs of having such a beautiful bride. In addition to nightgowns, there would be fine nylons, imported scents, luxurious skin creams, manicures, and pedi-cures, and even though he loved her hair when it went soft and bushy and looked like cotton candy, felt like it too when it bounced all up and down his chest to the rhythm of her body working his manhood like it had never been worked before, he knew she'd want to get that cotton candy hair pressed out on a regular basis, and not at someone's kitchen table either, she warranted the finest, full-service salons.

The list of expenses kept accumulating in Finch's head even until the morning, when Clarise woke glowing and chattering about that delicious ocean breeze sifting through the screen in the Kentucky Avenue hotel.

"Come on, Finch"—she giggled—"let's hurry and swim in the ocean early before the beach gets crowded and people let their untrained children stir up the sand in our faces and pee in the ocean and scatter wax paper from their bologna and cheese sandwiches all over the shoreline."

Mercy, Lord, he thought. He hadn't even gotten to children. Children would be a whole separate list. As it was already, he'd have to work night and day as a short-order cook at the Seventeenth Street Deweys. But he couldn't work night and day. Surely Clarise would get bored waiting for him to come home to play peekaboo games with her nightgown.

He was so plagued with thoughts of some prosperous cat showering his exotic beauty of a bride with see-through lacy lingerie that his steps lumbered heavier than usual as they walked to the beach. Clarise tickled him and tried to entice him into a game of tag; she slapped his butt, blew into his ear, called him honeybunch, and jumped up and down like a squirrel as they walked. Finch hardly grunted. "Got things on my mind, pretty baby," he said.

"But the sun is overhead, the ocean's in our sight, the day is young, and so are we, Finch. What could possibly be so pressing on your mind?"

Before he could tell her that it was money, the type of money he'd need to treat her, to keep her, to do right by her as her man, a seagull released its creamy droppings right on Finch's hatless head. "What the fuck," he said as he patted his head and looked up, only to have the loose-boweled gull go again and again and again, substantial plops, until Finch had to cover his head and run around in circles.

Clarise was laughing and really hopping now. "Oh, Finch, it's glorious, it's the most wonderful thing. I knew it! I knew it! I was right. Thank you, Lord, I was so damned right."

"What the hell is so freaking wonderful about a nasty gull

shitting on my head?" Finch asked, wiping his forehead furiously, trying to keep the shit from his eyes.

"It's luck, silly fool." Clarise continued to laugh. "Bird shit, just a dripping, on your head means prosperity. And look at you. You're covered in the shit. We're going to be rich, rich, I tell you, Finch. Filthy rich. So rich we'll move to a huge, brick, single heaven of a house. And that's what we'll call it, Finch. Heaven. We're on our way to Heaven, my wide-backed, flat-footed man." She wrapped her arms around his shoulders and kissed at his face, even where the milky omen of their prosperity dripped and ran.

Finch bought into the bird shit legend. After that it made sense for him to parlay what little he had left of his merchant marine final pay into his own enterprise. Cooking. He became a caterer.

The Storytellers

DISCUSSION GUIDE

1. The beginning of *Tempest Rising* reads almost like a fairy tale. Why do you think Diane chooses to portray the family in this magical way?

2. Is it merely coincidence that Clarise and Finch's home is so rich in the abundance and variety of food and Mae's is not?

3. Wealth and material comfort seem to offer the characters a sort of redemption. How does Clarise and Finch's pursuit of success, or even Ramona's, differ from the greed exhibited by Mae?

4. Redemption is a powerful message in *Tempest Rising*. Which characters are seeking it and why? What do you make of their hidden stories?

5. Does there seem to be an ambivalent slant to the religious feelings expressed by the characters in *Tempest Rising*? Do they really have faith? Does it help them?

6. The title *Tempest Rising* comes from a church hymn. Discuss its significance.

DIANE MCKINNEY-WHETSTONE, EXPLORER OF THE HUMAN CONDITION

Published Works: *Tumbling,* 1996; *Tempest Rising,* 1998

Home Base: Chadds Ford, Pennsylvania

Literary Heroes: "Toni Morrison, for what she does with the language, and Gloria Naylor, for the wonderful tales she's spun."

Claim to Fame: 1997 Zora Neale Hurston Society Award for Creative Contribution to Literature; Pennsylvania Council on the Arts Writer's Grant

---

How did you begin writing?

I was working as a public affairs officer for the USDA Forest Service, but I had always thought at some point I'd write fiction. I was in my late 30s and realized if I didn't at least make an attempt before I turned 40, I may never do it. Besides, I was no longer able to ignore the gnawing.

You're married, and at the time you started writing, your now-teenage twins were younger. How did you juggle family, writing and a full-time job before you were awarded the writer's grant?

I started writing *Tumbling* between five and seven in the morning, before I had to get the children fed and off to school

144

and myself ready for work. Initially, everyone was encouraging. In fact, my husband often reminded me that I had always said I wanted to write and kept asking me when I was going to get to it. But when I became so immersed in the process, they were surprised at the way it took me over. It began to spill outside the five-to-seven period. I'd look up and realize the kids were going to be late for school or that I had forgotten to pick my son up from Little League. I would just get so absorbed by the characters.

That's easy to imagine, since your characters are so fully drawn. Where do you get your inspiration?

My characters come to me as I'm writing. I certainly draw on a sprinkling of people I know. But quite early on they become like real people. They feed on my imagination and I feed off of them. It's a very symbiotic relationship between the characters and me.

Did your own mother figure into your portrayal of Clarise?

She does remind me of Clarise—the way Clarise is described as a little offbeat, but a good, strong woman. She is nurturing in the way that Clarise is and a bit eccentric in her look.

Did the relationship between the sisters in *Tempest Rising* mirror that of you and your four sisters?

I was able to draw on how my sisters and I have had to come together at points of crisis. I also picked up on us as children in the way the girls argued and bickered.

Both *Tempest Rising* and *Tumbling* are set in Philadelphia, your hometown. What was it like growing up there?

It was a Philadelphia of corner stores, where the owners knew everybody and everybody's payday. Aunts and grandmothers lived around the corner or sometimes in the same house. You knew not just who lived next door, but who lived down the street. The scene in *Tempest Rising* where the girls are jumping double Dutch exemplifies some of the Philly I knew—where girls would play and help each other unknowingly.

Music plays a tremendous part in setting the tone and texture of west Philadelphia in the 1960s, the setting of *Tempest Rising*. Why did you choose to use music in such a significant way? What kind of music do you like?

A song will sort of set a scene for me, and then it becomes a backdrop. I could hear the music as I wrote about Clarise walking up 60th street. I heard the Impressions singing. I could hear Clarise in her living room singing "You Send Me." Personally, I like jazz vocalist Sarah Vaughan, the Motown sound and some of the R&B my teenagers listen to now.

There are very few thoroughly "bad guys" in your novels. Ramona in *Tempest Rising* and Ethel in *Tumbling*, for example, are quite complex. Is it a conscious decision to portray an antagonist's good *and* bad aspects?

The characters that interest me most are those that have shades to their personality. Ramona started out as just a sentence, but almost tried to take over the book. She was going to have a lesser role and Mae was going to take the bigger role. But I found myself looking beneath the surface to see what was going on with Ramona, and as a result, she became more prominent than originally planned.

Why have you included in each of your novels a character blessed with some heightened sense?

Culturally we have often relied on things that we don't see with our physical eye. It seems that at least one of the characters should do this in a discernible way. It seems to be a clairvoyance, but it is just a greater attention to things. It seems to give them a greater power, but it has to do with them just putting their attention where it needs to be.

The infidelity story line in *Tumbling* proved to be a hot topic of discussion for the Go On Girls. Tell us what you think.

It is never right, never acceptable. But as I was writing, there was an attraction between Herbie and Ethel that I couldn't ignore. It challenged me to come up with a way to give him an out, so it at least would be okay. The incident from Noon's girlhood happened late in the writing of the book just to accommodate Herbie and Ethel being together. I liked Herbie too much. I didn't want to not like him because he was running around. I listened to what the characters were saying and it gave the book another dimension.

In *Tempest Rising,* the father's disappearance is a bit dubious. Do you think we might see the return of Finch in another novel?

So far, book number three is not about Finch, Clarise and the girls. I may have made Finch's disappearance murky because it was hard for me, since I lost my father not long ago. I think it may have been personal experience mixing with the art. I haven't decided if Finch needs to come back because the story needs him or because I need my own father back. But for right now, he's gone. My next novel moves from the '50s into the '90s. It's about a young woman who moves to Philadelphia from the South.

Diane McKinney-Whetstone is the 1997 Go On Girl! Author of the Year

The Itch
by Benilde Little

Like the critically acclaimed Good Hair, *Benilde's (Be-neel-dee) new book,* The Itch, *is a humor-laced expose of life and romance among the talented tenth.*

Confirmation of what she knew all along. As much as she had wanted proof, she also knew she didn't want to know that her husband was fucking around. Abra sat on the flow-ered-chintz chaise and stared out of her bedroom window. The phone rang, and she wouldn't answer. She didn't have the energy to face anybody. She couldn't talk to Cullen. She didn't want to talk to Natasha. She sat at the window for hours, not getting up even to go to the bathroom. She wanted to feel frozen, as if somehow, if she remained still, she could keep her emotions immobile as well.

By the time late afternoon came, she was still in her paja-mas, still hadn't brushed her teeth or returned any of Natasha's calls. At dusk, she'd managed to move to the bed where she drifted in and out of dreams. In one, she was walk-ing through a jungle thick with leaves and branches that attempted to block her path, and she fought through—elbows out, arms getting scratched and cut, her blood creating rivers around her as she moved. In another, she saw her mother and father having sex on the sofa, both drunk with passion, sweat-ing, and watching her as a little girl watch them. They were

149

laughing at her. Abra woke up and tried to remember if that had ever really happened. If she'd ever seen her parents having sex. She closed her eyes and began to sob. It was the first time she'd cried since she found out about the chlamydia. First they were silent, deep sobs, then she began to groan and got louder and louder until she was screaming and thrashing and looking around the bedroom for something to break.

A silver-framed picture of Cullen and her on their honeymoon in France, propped on his nightstand, was the first thing she spotted. She hurled it across the room where it shattered and nicked the television screen. She got up on the bed and grabbed a lamp and threw that against the wall, creating a huge gaping hole in the plaster. She got down off the bed and went into Cullen's office. His degrees and awards were framed and in a box. She took them out, one by one, and jumped on them until they were smashed sparkles in the carpet. She opened the drawers, saw his perfectly filed folders and took them out, handfuls at a time, and emptied them onto the floor. She grabbed a brass desk lamp and banged on his computer terminal and keyboard until it was a pile of plastic and glass.

Looking like a primate in search of food, breathing hard puffs through her nose, she went searching for something that meant something to him. A devious smile crossed her face when she remembered his beloved collection. He'd accumulated two thousand bottles in his wine cellar. She threw open the door, raced downstairs into the basement, entering the perfectly climate-controlled 55 degrees–70 percent humidity of the vault crammed with shelves of burgundies, Bordeaux, chardonnays, champagnes, cabernet sauvignons, Graves, ports. She grabbed a couple of bottles and flung them to the Spanish-tile floor. Heady, fragrant grape immediately filled her nostrils. She stopped for a moment, thinking about which were his most prized bottles. She didn't want to waste energy breaking the unimportant, easily replaceable ones. Which ones, which ones, she thought, commanding her memory to kick in. Yes.

She climbed up the stepladder. She wanted to hurt his ass. She recalled the Australian phase and quickly trashed several $200 bottles of Penfold Grange. Then, like a gift, she remembered the most coveted in his collection, a Domaine de la Romanée-Conti, a $650 burgundy that they'd picked up in Provence. She cradled the precious bottle, remembering their honeymoon, how happy he was to find this vintage, and how thrilled she was just to be with him. As her tears dropped onto the label she softened at the memory of them, as a young couple. So excited to be in love and in Europe for the first time. The sense of freedom and fear all mixed together, creating a new feeling that they wanted to hold on to forever. Sure they would always be this happy. Then she remembered his betrayal. She threw the bottle to the floor with the force of a major-league pitcher. As she watched the glass, liquid, and paper slowly meld together on the cellar floor, Abra began to feel a smile cross her lips, then a laugh. First it was a small chuckle, then a giggle, then a wave of uncontrollable gut tickles so strong that she had to sit down on the stepladder to keep from falling.

Abra's outburst had been a release valve. Laughing in the face of what she had been dealt scared her, made her feel as if she might be losing touch, losing her mind. She threw some T-shirts and a pair of jeans into a nylon overnight bag. Got herself dressed and in the truck.

Odessa still lived in the two-bedroom, two-bath apartment in a complex of high-rises that had been a part of Lyndon Johnson's Great Society. When Abra was a baby, and it had become clear to Odessa that her life would be lived without Rayford, she looked around for the best place for her money and her child. Myrna and Sylvia had become New Jersey suburbanites and were close enough to help out with Abra in an emergency. Back when she and Abra moved in, the apartments were luxury cooperatives in Newark, right on the bus line into Manhattan. The units were built to sell as cooperative housing, creating a class of owners, instead of just tenants, who would take care of what they owned. While it looked like early public housing in terms of brick and size, there were no graffiti or fetid smells that later overran the projects. To many it was a haven, but once Abra was in high school, the place began its descent and now it was surrounded by overgrown weeds and covered in spray-painted names like Shakim and Boo and LaQwanda.

As Abra drove the luxury truck around the neighborhood, she realized that she didn't care if it was stolen or vandalized. She parked near a bus stop, didn't put on the Club and grabbed her bag. Crossing the wide street, the used-to-be maple-lined boulevard, she realized that while her house was less than an hour away, it might as well be in Utah. All the residential property in Brookville was zoned for a minimum of two acres. Odessa's entire complex was crammed onto less. During the day the courtyard was filled with adolescent mothers pushing expensive carriages. Occasionally gunshots would keep Odessa awake. In Brookville the only sounds to prevent sleep were the sometimes unbearable nothingness, punctuated by the sporadic noises of animals foraging for food. Abra's stomach knotted as she waited for the elevator and thought about the many arguments she'd had with Odessa about moving her out. Her mother simply refused. This is my home, she'd say, marking the end of the discussion. Abra had traveled so far between worlds, a different person would have been paralyzed by the whiplash. Right now she was grateful she had someplace to go, and this place, with all its vicissitudes, would always be the place where she felt safe.

The apartment was empty when she entered and for a moment her reflex was to look for a snack and bolt the door. She remembered that it was Friday, and that was the day her mother got her hair done. She went into her old bedroom and sat on the twin-size bed that she'd slept in throughout her youth. Her mom had changed the daisy-print spread for a more contemporary blue horizontal-print bed-in-a-bag number. Her posters—a faded picture of a scorpion and one of the Jackson 5 and their *ABC* album—were still on the pale-blue walls, held by aged, topaz-colored tape. There was a Princeton flag hung over her headboard. A picture with her freshman housemates featuring Abra's lone, sad, brown face sat atop the chest of drawers. The same multicolored rug covered the middle of the floor, and even her component set hadn't been moved. She sat down on the rug and leafed through her albums stacked in a red plastic crate. There was Marvin Gaye in the rain, Chaka Khan in a rabbit-fur bra, and Michael Henderson dressed in a white suit, standing in front of a Rolls Royce. She had kept her ABBA, Carpenters, and Bee Gees in a separate pile so that she could easily hide them whenever a few of her neighborhood friends came over.

The smell of bergamot mixed with pressing comb snaked

into Abra's nose. "Hi, Ma!" she yelled from the back to keep from scaring her mother into a heart attack.

"Arabella? That you, baby?"

"Yeah."

"What you doin' here?" Odessa said, removing her coat and going into Abra's old room. She found her daughter sitting on the floor, legs crossed, with albums spread out around her. "Baby, is everything all right?" Odessa asked, sitting down on the bed.

"I'm okay, I just came to stay for a while . . ."

"Stay? With me? What? Where's Cullen? You scared to stay in that house by yourself?"

"No . . ."

"So, what're you doin' here?"

"Oh, Mom." Abra leaned against her mother's knees and began to cry.

Odessa patted her daughter's hair. "Just get it out, just let it go," she said.

"Cullen's seeing someone . . . he gave me chlamydia . . ."

"What? Chlamydia? What the hell is that?" Odessa asked, now holding her daughter by the shoulders.

"It's a sexual disease . . . he got it from screwing somebody."

"Lawd ha' mercy. What the hell . . . baby, you sure?"

"I'm sure. The doctor had the lab rerun the test."

"My Lawd . . . are you all right?"

"Yes, I'm taking antibiotics."

Odessa, who was usually quick with the tongue, was stunned into silence. Her baby, was all she could think about; how she hurt for her child, knowing intimately the pain Abra was feeling. Nothing was like the hurt that a man whom you truly loved could put on you. She wanted to pick Abra up the way she used to whenever Abra tripped in her street skates; to kiss the pain of the boo-boo away, make it all better. But her girl was a woman now, and there was nothing she could do to ease her pain. Knowing that caused Odessa's heart to ache.

Abra was sobbing loudly now, pleading with her mother to make this thing make sense.

"Oh, baby, I know, I know," Odessa said, tears now streaming down her face, holding Abra's head tight to her chest.

"How could he do this to me, Mommy? Why?"

"Baby, I don't know, but the Lawd does. All things happen for a reason . . ."

Abra let out a noise that sounded so rough and raw, as if she were being tortured. She pushed away from her mother and began rocking herself with her arms wrapped around her knees. "Ma, I don't know what to do. How am I going to go on without Cullen? He was my whole life."

Odessa felt a flash of anger run through her. While she felt her daughter's pain, years of struggling to raise her daughter right had created a steeliness in her. *I'll be damn. How could you think he's your life after all that you have, all I've sacrificed to give you? An education, good skills, manners, you could do anything you want to do. The hell with some man! How have I missed teachin' my girl to be independent and strong? How did she get to be such a mess, so damn crippled? You stay or you leave, but you don't let him crush you like I let Rayford do me.*

"Baby," Odessa said, carefully measuring her tone, "Cullen is just a man. He don't walk on water or turn it into wine."

Abra looked at her mother and tilted her head to one side, like a German shepherd.

"Every man is gonna slip and fall. You just settle yourself down some, I'm gonna get you some tea." Odessa pulled Abra up from the floor and put her on the bed. She arranged the stiff polyester comforter over her.

In the kitchen, she searched her cabinet for some peppermint tea as she tried to find an answer to where she went wrong in raising her child. *Didn't she see me make a way for her? Didn't she listen when I lectured her on the importance of an education? "Nobody can take it from you, once you have it," I would say over and over to her. "Always stand on your own two feet."* What she hadn't figured, though, was what her daughter *didn't* have. It was so simple that it escaped Odessa. Not having had a father every day was a hole in Abra that never healed, and it pushed her to Cullen, made her create an illusion of Cullen instead of realizing who he actually was. In Abra's mind he *could* turn water to wine, if he'd wanted. Sure, she went to good schools, got good grades, got a graduate degree, but that had nothing to do with filling up her hole. Cullen became her entire life, her reason for living. It was something Odessa would never be able to understand. She'd had her daddy and that daddy loved her, something she was incapable of passing on to her fatherless child.

After she drank her tea, Abra took a nap. Odessa sat in her kitchen, staring out of the window that faced a courtyard, and retraced her mothering steps. Maybe the fact that she and Rayford never married had scared Abra. Maybe the way she was absorbed with her own blues had harmed Abra. Who knew what kind of message she was sending to her child, being with a man, sleeping with him without being married to him? In her mind, Odessa figured she'd just raise Abra to be an independent, free-thinking woman, who wouldn't need a man. Odessa picked up the cigarette that had burned almost to the tip and drew a long drag. She blew out curly smoke and rubbed her face, now puffy with age. She looked around her kitchen at the faded orange-and-yellow floral wallpaper and thought about how different Abra's life was from hers. She wanted her daughter to be happy, but how was that achieved? People in Odessa's generation didn't put a lot of stock in happiness—what was that, anyway? Her outlook was different, she knew, from Abra's. Odessa believed that you got up every day, thanked the Lord for waking you up, and put one foot in front of the other. She had let go of her great expectations of life. Maybe that was her mistake.

DISCUSSION GUIDE

1. Compare and contrast the similarities and differences between Natasha and Abra.

2. Abra signs up for a workshop series dealing with women's issues and fatherlessness, but she only goes one time. Why do you think she, like so many Black people, has a phobia about getting professional emotional help?

3. The book deals with issues of infidelity and passion. Do you think it's feasible to expect passion in a longtime relationship?

4. To look at Abra, she is perfect. Why does she (and so many other Black women) invest so much money and time on her exterior?

5. What examples clue us in that Natasha's sister Natalie is very impressed with her well-off self, but not with how her family acquired its wealth? How can parents, who want to provide the best of everything for their kids, keep them grounded and unashamed of their roots and of the less fortunate in the race?

6. Oftentimes our upbringing guides our destiny, but if you want to break your family's blueprint, how do you do it?

BENILDE LITTLE, A "CLASS" ACT

Published Works: *Good Hair*,
1996; *The Itch*, 1998

Home Base: South Orange, New
Jersey

Literary Hero: "James Baldwin. He
lived and wrote his truth."

Claim to Fame: *Good Hair* held the number-one spots in
both hardcover and paperback on the Blackboard best-seller
list; it was optioned twice for Hollywood by Natalie Cole;
and Little was nominated for a 1996 NAACP Image Award
for literature.

**In your debut novel, *Good Hair*, readers wondered if you
were the main character, Alice. Are you now being asked if
Natasha or Arabella from *The Itch* is really you?**

Yes. Alice was much closer to me in temperament and early
experiences. Like her, I was raised middle-class in Newark
and began my writing career as a reporter for the *Star-Ledger*
there, but that's where the similarities end. If I had gone to
the private high school my mother wanted me to go to and
then on to a college like Mount Holyoke, I fear Alice is who I
could have been. I'm sure I would have been much more conflicted about class had I not gone to Howard University. In
The Itch, Natasha goes to Howard, but she and Abra [Ara-

bella] met and became friends as little girls growing up in Newark. I think I'll always have some Newark thing, because there's something very poignant about home. The general theme of *Itch* is that searching for something more. Not more things, but more fulfillment inside, and I've certainly been there. Once you get to a certain age, you realize that that old cliche, "Money can't buy you happiness," is really true. It's somewhat unique to oppressed people to think that once we achieve financial success in life, everything is going to be wonderful. Many of us are the children of the dream, but we give up so much of our cultural stuff so easily—the fish fries and all of that—and in that distancing, we damage our kids. In the book, Natasha is a second-generation graduate of Howard. Her father Norwood is a very successful entrepreneur, generating his wealth by expanding on the rib joint business his Mississippi father started. Natasha doesn't feel at home easily. The Black bourgeois is like "We don't eat ribs," and White people never really accept her, because the money has grease on it.

Do you believe that classism is creating two separate and distinct Black communities, where never the two shall meet?

I'm interested in writing about what happens when the two do meet, but the culture has moved, more and more, to the haves and the have nots. How do we come together? It's a good question, and again I write about it, but I don't know the answers. The 400 years often keep those of us who have tended to do well from looking back. There is a gap geographically too. We live in White communities and we don't see each other at work either. Then there are those who have the

"Black like me" syndrome: They only want to be around Blacks who have all the trappings they do.

Both of your books have very provocative titles. How did you arrive at them, and what's behind each?

The books are about a number of things, so it's always a problem to come up with that one title that captures it. Though I turned the book in twice without the title, I finally arrived at *The Itch* because it really gets at that feeling you have when you know there's more than what you're living, but you just can't get at it, can't scratch it. As for *Good Hair*, my original title was *Good Hair and Other Plantation Baggage*. I don't use the term good hair, and I wanted people to know that to me it represents heavy baggage. But my publisher thought the longer title sounded too much like nonfiction. They just didn't get it.

Like *Good Hair*, *The Itch* is filled with wit, but what lasting messages do you hope readers hold on to?

I'm leery of people preaching, so I hate to answer this one. The nice thing about a book is that people get all kinds of stuff from it, some of which I might not have even intended. But I guess the one crucial thing is you've got to pay attention to your stuff. Life is a process. You just don't get to one point and stay there and it's all groovy. You get there, then you've got to move. When I worked at *Essence*, people would say "Oh, wow," and for a while, I felt that way too. Then I realized there was something else calling me, and I had to move. You have to listen to yourself, and I've learned that when I don't do it, I always get in trouble—like with the cover of *The Itch*. I didn't like the first version, but everyone around me who I respected and trusted loved it. I tried to live with it by suggesting a few minor changes, but when that was done, it still didn't work for me. Then I finally just said, "No." The new version the artist came up with was just perfect, and everyone around me loves it as much as I do. In the book, Abra learns to listen to herself, and she realizes the work is on the inside. At the end, Cullen comments that though her physical appearance hasn't changed, she looks like a different person. That's because there's no false comfort, she's done the work.

With your newfound literary success and all the trappings that come with it, how do you keep yourself grounded so you don't become one of those people you write about who have no shortage of things but a shortage of peace?

That's really easy when you're a mother. My preschool daughter doesn't know anything about it, and doesn't care. I'm so glad it [the success] happened after she was born. I was talking on the phone the other day to another writer about to sign her first deal, and my daughter came into the room and stood right before me and squeezed a whole tube of lotion onto her feet. She was like, I don't care about big deals and writer's contracts, I just want to play with this lotion right now. With her, I'm mommy first. I'm trying to be honest for her. I want to leave a blueprint for her so she doesn't have to reinvent the wheel. She'll have a jumping-off point to do better—not financially, but emotionally. I also try to stay close to old friends; they're more like gold than ever. It's all about people who really know me.

After the success of *Good Hair,* was it easier or harder to write *The Itch*?

It was horrible, much harder. I have so much anxiety about this book because of the expectation. *Good Hair* sold so incredibly well that I felt the pressure of trying to duplicate my success. One of my writing instructors—a very wise woman—told me, "You just have to pretend none of this happened." She's right. I just want the work to be as good as it can be. I feel a responsibility to my reader.

Infidelity is dealt with in the book, but perhaps an even stronger theme is the lasting effects growing up fatherless has on girls. You grew up with both parents in the home, but what are your observations of the challenges women face who have not had that experience?

When I was at *Essence*, I came in touch with many sisters who would have everything on paper but couldn't find or keep a man. When I would start questioning them, I would usually discover that they didn't have interaction with a father or that there had been some kind of sexual abuse. Then one of my best friends who I grew up with revealed to me her pain of never having contact with her father. She said that when we were young, she liked coming to my house because there was a father there, and she liked watching the interaction between a husband and a wife. Another time, a single woman I know was sharing how the young daughter she had recently adopted immediately started asking for a father. That led to her discussing how difficult her own personal relationships with men had been because she too grew up fatherless. She was constantly seeking affirmation of her womanhood, and in most cases, the men were also clueless because they too had grown up in homes where there had been no man to emulate. I know that with my own daughter, there's a deep love and a soul-connection, but there are things she can only get from my husband. Like when I dress her up and fix her hair real pretty, I'm constantly telling her how beautiful she is. But she can't wait to be done to go and get praise from her daddy. And as soon as he says you look pretty, the shoulders relax and the peacocking begins.

You've said that James Baldwin is your literary hero, and you've even named your daughter after him. Why are you so moved by this major twentieth century writer?

I named my daughter Baldwin because I wanted a name that meant something, and I wanted it grounded in America. We are here, and we made a great contribution here. I admire Baldwin because he was trying to be who he was—brilliant, sensitive, gay and Black—at a time when nobody wanted to be bothered with any of that. Like him, I'm trying to live my truth.

Benilde Little is the Go On Girl! *1996 New Author of the Year*

The Men of Brewster Place
by Gloria Naylor

Gloria Naylor has spent much of her literary career writing stories about our neighborhoods and the color-ful characters who inhabit them. In her latest novel, she gives voice to the men in our communities.

If Brewster Place has something like a heartbeat, it can be found at Max's place. Max runs an old-fashioned business; he'll shave you and cut your hair, that's it; none of that unisex stuff where both men and women can go to get their hair done. It's not that women aren't welcome—even though they're not—but a woman would have no reason to come. It's real clear just by the smell of the place and look of the place that this is where men have a chance to hang out and talk. I go there about once a week myself, sometimes I'm taking a rest from the tenants, but most times it's just to chew the fat—or hear it chewed—with other men from the neighborhood.

It's nothing much. Just a small shop with four leather seats and the two barbers—Max and Henry—there to serve the customers. Those seats bear the imprint of the hundreds of men over the years. And the place has the pleasing smell of Old Spice aftershave, hair pomade, and talcum powder. The men who sit in there, reading the papers, playing checkers, or just socializing done solved every problem in the world before the shop closes each day. And they're in there the next day to solve 'em all over again. It seems that no one's listened to them and so the world stayed in the same mess from the day before. It's a thankless job, being an armchair—or barber chair—politician. The issues they solve boil down to three subjects: white men, black men, and women. The white man carries all the guilt for messing up the world; the black man gets all the blame; and women are just a downright confusing issue that a hundred barbershop politicians wouldn't be able to solve. Why are women so difficult to get along with? "They practice," said Henry. "They practice all the time." This brings a good laugh and opinions from a half dozen others who want to top it.

"Naw, they don't practice. They're born that way."

"It's their mothers. They train 'em to be evil."

"Maybe their fathers too. I got me three girls and I tell 'em everyday to watch out. There's some real dogs running around in the streets pretending to be men."

"Yeah, and all they make is babies. I told mine too, don't you bring no babies in here without showing me a husband first."

"But where she gonna find one? These young bucks today don't want no responsibility—that is, them that's left over and not stuck in jail."

"Amen to that. And it's making the white man very happy to see us caged up like animals in jail."

"The white man. The white man. I'm so sick of hearing about the white man. When are we gonna face up to our own lives and the stuff we do? The white man ain't in that bed helping these girls get pregnant just to then run off and leave 'em."

"That's exactly where they been our whole history—laying up with our women in slavery and us too scared to say anything. Look at all these colors here. Since when you see pictures of Africans that look like us. We is brown and beige and tan. Some of us pure yellow. Now where that come from but slavery and the white man's blood running in our veins."

"And our blood is running in them too. Years ago it weren't nothing for a high, high yellow black man or woman to slide on over the color line. Mixing and matching blood don't run one way, but you never hear about that."

"And you never will either. They don't wanna be reminded that there's black someplace in a lot of their families."

"Yeah, tell that to a white man, he'll haul off and die. But there's a little soot in many of them pots."

And the talk would go on like that for hours—round-robin—unless Greasy came into the shop. Whenever Greasy stumbled in, the shop would get silent as a tomb. To look at him the way he is now it's hard to imagine that this man once had a job, a home, and a future. But when crack started eating away at his brains, he lost it all in just that order: first his job as an airline ticket agent, then his brick home complete with a wife and two kids, to finally be left with a future in which his head was an empty shell, allowing only space for the winds of his nightmares to keep howling and howling. But somewhere in the back of his mind is the single thought left from his sane days that every month he must get a haircut. And so he comes in, smelling to high heaven, the seat of his pants slick as mud, and dropping the nickels and dimes that he gets from begging as he tries to count out the cost of his haircut. It's pitiful to watch him chasing the dropped coins that he can't keep in his shaking hands. And it's always the same reaction from Max. "No charge today, Greasy. Just sit on down and relax."

Max is the only barber in the place that will work on

Greasy's head. It's too unpredictable when he'll start pounding on his chest and yelling, "I'm a man . . . I'm a man . . ." Any comment can set him off and so the other men have learned to just stop conversing when Greasy's in the shop. Some will even get up and leave, saying that they can't stand the stench from his unwashed body.

"You need to get off that shit and get yourself together," Max says.

"I'm trying, Max. I'm trying."

"You ain't trying hard enough," someone else will say.

"And when you gonna put some water on your stinky ass?"

Greasy laughs with the rest of the men. "I'm trying, Bullet. I'm trying."

"Now don't get him going," Max says, "or I'll never finish his head."

"Max, you need business that bad you gotta work on him?"

"Every man is entitled to a shave and a haircut. For some of us, what else is left?" Max replies.

"Yeah," Greasy says, "because I'm a man—right, Max?— I'm a man . . ."

"Now look what you done, you got him started. I oughta make you work on his crazy ass. Sit still, Greasy, or I'm kicking you out of here."

But no matter how deep the pain; how tangled the threads of this man's life; Greasy's isn't the only sad story that's sat in Max's chairs. If those chairs could talk, they would be at it day and night with sadder and sadder stories. Brewster Place is a small street but it seems there's an endless supply of I coulda, I shoulda, but I didn't. Can you call it any man's blues? I don't know, but you can definitely call it the black man's blues. There's something about us and pain that keeps spinning out there in the universe to return again and again. And when you're sick and tired of being sick and tired, sometimes you get like Greasy. And if not that low or that bad, then you get like us. Hoping to solve the problems of the world so that we forget—or put the knowledge on hold—that our own lives need attention.

Yeah, if these seats could talk. They could tell you like I couldn't about Mattie's son. I knew it was Basil who spoke to me that one day in the street before he stopped by here to get his hair cut. Whenever I was up in Mattie's apartment working on a bad pipeline or doing some plastering, I saw the little shrine she kept for him. A wall of pictures from the time he was little until a grown man. Did I tell her he had come by? No. Because what could she have done with the knowledge? Say, thank you, Ben and then go up to her apartment to grieve a little more? To me that woulda been messing with the order of things. It's not my job to bring grief to a nice woman who never had nothing but a kind word to say to me.

And then there was Eugene who came here on the day of his baby's funeral. I had spoken to him earlier in the morning and seen pain so thick I coulda cut it with a knife. You going to the funeral? he asked. No, I said, too sad with it being a baby and all. Yeah, he said, I know what you mean. I was going myself, but the way Ceil's friends look at me, damn, like I was filth or something. But I knew Eugene wasn't going to be able to take that funeral, even though he stopped by the barbershop to get a clean shave and a cut. He was grieving too hard to accept that child was dead. And I knew that his was the kind of grief that could swallow the whole world—himself included—if you let it get out of hand. I saw suicide in that

169

boy's eyes and I prayed for him to get a grip on things. Just let the pain and the regrets wash over you; you won't drown although you'll feel like you will. No, the one fact about regrets is that they do ebb in time and you're faced with the hard decision to let your life go on or not.

Those are only two stories but these chairs have seen hundreds more. You can change the name and occupation, go up or down with their ages, and it's like it's the same man sitting there each time. What they got in common is the blues. And like they say, the blues ain't nothing but a good man crying for help. These chairs done seen many a good man as well as the bad, and the ugly. They done seen rejoicing and they done seen grief. Although a man grieves different from a woman, a whole lot more is kept inside to bite him a little here, a little there, until the blood begins to flow. And when the blood begins to flow, it'll have to fill up every space in his body before you finally see it in his eyes. Men cry as much as women—but most just cry inside.

And maybe things woulda worked out different if we had realized that was the case with Greasy—he was bleeding inside. But we were so busy being thankful that we weren't him, so busy judging and feeling superior, pitting our half a minds against his none, that we forgot he was our "brother" and where he goes we go—if we like it or not. Yeah, if we had remembered that things might have turned out real different that muggy day at the end of October.

The shop was more crowded than usual 'cause we had the weather to talk about—an Indian summer that showed no signs of letting up. And this one time I was hiding from the tenants 'cause some were gonna want me to fire up those furnaces regardless of the weather. The shop door was kept open to let in what little breeze there was and some men had stripped down to T-shirts and short pants. "It's all them rockets they sending up to the moon," said Max. "Been messing up the weather since then." Every time we had a different twist on the season—a warm winter or a cool summer—Max lay the blame on rockets being sent into outer space.

"Yeah," Henry agreed. "Things ain't been the same since them white men starting messing with the moon. Can't figure out shit to solve the problems here on earth, they gotta go take their nonsense to the moon."

"You'll never get me up there," one of the customers said.

"And me neither," joined in another.

"I didn't hear nobody asking for your monkey ass to go to the moon," Max said. "They too sick and tired of you black people right here on earth to take you someplace else. You know how that goes, let you black people move in and the neighborhood goes to the dogs."

"You black people? Since when you turned white?"

"The day I figured it might get me a shot to be an astronaut. I don't mind admitting I might like to see what's really up there."

"Turn around and look in your mirror and you'll see exactly what ain't getting up there—your black butt."

"They got black astronauts. I seen 'em in a magazine."

"Yeah, but you see any of them walking on the moon? I told you before, they don't want your monkey ass walking on the earth, so why they gonna send you to walk on the moon?"

"You see, that's what's wrong with the black man—always so negative."

"He's right about that. Before you know it, they're gonna

even have black women astronauts. Wouldn't that be something?"

"Yes, Lord, that'll solve all our problems—send their nagging butts right to the moon."

As the men were laughing Greasy stepped into the shop. He had on a clean shirt and pair of pants, even though both were wrinkled. His clothes meant that he'd been picked up and taken to a shelter that he managed to escape from again and again. But at least he'd stopped smelling so bad.

"You're looking good there, Greasy," Max said. "You ain't getting married on us, are you?"

"I'm trying, Max, I'm trying."

I often wondered how much Greasy understood what folks was saying to him. He had only two phrases anyone's heard him say: "I'm a man." And "I'm trying."

Max was still working on a customer's head so Henry, who had just finished a head, took Greasy into his chair. The house rules were if Greasy walked in he was the next customer no matter what—get him in and out fast. But this day it wasn't fast enough. For no reason—or at least I should say, for no godly reason that anyone could tell, Greasy moved toward Henry's chair, grabbed the straight razor on the counter, then grabbed Henry from behind and held the razor to his neck. Every man in there became still as a stone.

"I'm a man . . . I'm a man . . ." Greasy kept saying over and over.

"Yeah," Max said, trying to edge closer and closer to him. "You're a man . . . You're a man, Greasy, so just put down the razor."

Greasy's eyes were vacant and wild as he tightened his hold

on Henry's neck. All the life had drained from Henry's face as he tried not to move an inch or even breathe too deeply. A few of the other men got up and started edging toward Greasy as well. "You're a man, Greasy," they kept saying as if they were cooing to a baby—quiet and smooth—"You're a man."

"So just put down the razor, okay?" Max said softly. "Put it down and let Henry go. I gotta cut your hair, right? See, it's me, Max, I always cut your hair. So put down the razor, okay?"

"I'm trying, Max, I'm trying." And Greasy began to cry.

"That's okay," Max said, "I know you're trying. So just put it down, okay?"

A circle of men were within three feet of him now. And Greasy was getting confused, trying to look at them all, to make eye contact as those wild winds howled in his head. "I'm a man," Greasy said as he let Henry go, "I'm a man."

And then suddenly he took the straight razor and slit his own throat. Blood from the artery in his neck gushed so forcibly that it sprayed all along the mirrors and on every man in the shop. And the fall that Greasy took, hitting his head against the floor, almost tore his head from his neck.

"Aw, shit," Max kept saying over and over again. "Holy shit."

Max's place was closed for a week, and when he reopened we had plenty to talk about. And believe it or not, it was never about what happened to Greasy. We all remembered what it was like to go home and wash his blood from our clothes, our faces, and above all, our hands. To have to look into our mirrors and lie to ourselves it wasn't our fault. We had not made him the whipping boy for all of our troubles. We had not held that razor to his throat and slashed. If for all the times we had called him brother, if we had really meant it, somehow Greasy should be alive today. But we let him down and let ourselves down as we used him for the garbage can to hold all our fears.

There's talk that Brewster Place is to be torn down. And if it's true, Max's place will be the last holdout. "They better take me out in chains and handcuffs," Max is always saying, " 'cause it's the only way I'm leaving here." But he'll leave, like the others leave, with the bitter taste of defeat in his mouth. Myself, I would hate to see Max's barbershop go. But it's only fitting that he would make a grandstand and fight till the end. This is the only place for us men to get together, to look into each others' eyes and see what we need to see—that we do more than just exist—we thrive and are alive.

The Storytellers

1. Which of the male characters in this collection of life stories touched you the most? Why?

2. Compare and contrast the characters. How do they differ from each other? How do the female characters in the book view the male characters and vice versa?

3. From a broader scope, how different are the lives of these men from the lives of Black men today?

4. Besides the location of Brewster Place, what else connects these men to each other?

5. If you've read *The Women of Brewster Place,* which characters in the male version connect with the females in the previous book? How does the story seem different to you now looking at it from the male perspective?

6. What are some of the social issues facing the characters in the book? How do they deal or not deal with them?

7. What details does Gloria provide in setting up the neighborhood of Brewster Place? How do you feel about the place from her setting?

GLORIA NAYLOR, OUR NEIGHBORHOOD WATCH

Published Works: *The Women of Brewster Place*, 1983; *Linden Hills*, 1985; *Mama Day*, 1987; *Bailey's Café*, 1992; *The Men of Brewster Place*, 1998

Home Base: Brooklyn, New York

Literary Heroes: "I don't have any heroes. There are people I enjoy reading, and they're mostly a lot of women writers. In school, I studied Black women writers, and I think discovering them helped inspire me to write—people like Zora Neale Hurston and Nikki Giovanni."

Claim to Fame: National Book Award and the Guggenheim, and a National Endowment of the Arts Fellowship

---

You are perceived as our neighborhood watch. What is so appealing to you about writing about neighborhoods?

It allows me to address a whole profile of different characters, and it doesn't limit what I can do with it as a writer.

Your books tend to take on many social issues. Do you feel as an African-American writer that you have a responsibility to address the issues that are important to us?

Not as a writer I don't. As a private citizen, yes, it's important to be part of the community. When I'm working on my fiction, I'm trying to tell the best story I know how.

So many female writers are criticized for their portrayals of male characters in their books. What was your experience with *The Women of Brewster Place*?

I never apologized for the stand I took for Black women. Never. I tell my audience, I am telling your mother's story. Now what could be wrong with that? I don't think that Black women have been hard on Black men. And no one ever asks about the invisibility of Black women in the work of Black men. But we're not there. To tell the truth, I did not care about the criticism. It really was just a small number of people asking, "Where are the men in this book?" And I said, "They were not meant to be in this book, it's not their book, read the title page and you'll see." I feel very strongly that artists should be able to write whatever they want to write; there's a lot of self-censorship in our community, which I think is really a shame —people feeling that they have to write role models, as opposed to just writing good characters.

Why did you find it necessary to revisit Brewster Place, this time from a male perspective?

I just wanted to look at the other side of the coin from the women and give those men, who really didn't speak in the first story, a chance to tell their own story. I didn't have an epiphany. My father passed away and then there was the Million Man March. Those things slowly added up to my writing about the men. What crossed my mind was the stories I would tell now; my heroes, if you will, would be all different types of Black men, speaking to make a microcosm of the Black man in America. I decided to use the same strategy that I used in *The Women of Brewster Place* and for almost the same reason—to show multiplicity.

So your father was an influence in writing *The Men of Brewster Place*?

In some ways. He was married to my mother for forty-some years. And he worked damn hard all of his life. And he stayed in the marriage probably when he might have been happier somewhere else, but the fact is that they're from that generation that believed in family first. So he was just a solid kind of person.

Why did you bring Ben back to tell the story?

Because he was the observer to all the events that went on in *The Women of Brewster Place*. He was always perched on top of the garbage can, so he would be the ideal observer again to tell about the men.

Eugene's character was the father of the child who dies in *The Women of Brewster Place*. Why did you decide to make Eugene gay in this book?

I didn't choose that. A lot of things you don't do consciously. But as I began to think about Eugene's story, it unfolded that he wanted to be gay. But I didn't start out saying, "I'm going to make Eugene gay or make Basil this or make Ben that." It's just that once you get into a work, different truths are revealed to you.

All of the characters in your books are well developed. Is there one that's a favorite of yours and why?

No. That would be like choosing one child over the other. Each character has brought me something different.

Gloria Naylor is the 1992 Go On Girl! Author of the Year

Big Girls Don't Cry
by Connie Briscoe

In her second novel, Big Girls Don't Cry, *Connie examines the issues faced by a young Black woman determined to be successful both professionally and romantically. Any woman who has faced the frustrations of glass ceilings, the pain of loss and sacrifice and the perils and pleasures of love will immediately relate.*

As soon as the morning recess bell rang, everyone in Mr. Parker's Algebra 101 class sat up on the edges of their seats, waiting to be dismissed. Naomi thought Mr. Parker got a kick out of torturing them like this, holding them for a few extra seconds while he piled on the homework. Sometimes it seemed like he was purposely adding extra chapters and equations while he stood there stroking his chocolate-colored chin. The minute he said "class dismissed," thirty-two pairs of feet in various hues of brown made a beeline for the doorway.

During recess, all the girls gathered on the playground in their little groups and did different things. There were the fly girls. They were mostly in the eighth and ninth grades, always had the finest boys hanging around them, and wore the latest styles in dresses and shoes. Some of them even wore makeup. Naomi had tried to get Mama to buy her a pair of Nineteens or Sebastians. They cost twenty dollars a pair and looked so fly. But twenty dollars was far more than she could afford with her allowance, and Mama said there was no way she'd buy them. Not because of the money but because she didn't want her daughter looking like one of those "fast girls," as she called them. Besides, that would mean letting Naomi wear stockings and a garter belt, something else Mama didn't want her daughter to do yet.

Another group was the squares or, if you wanted to be a little nicer about it, the bookworms. They were mostly seventh and eighth graders. They got all A's, dressed corny, didn't seem to know boys existed, and never got into any kind of trouble if they could help it.

Then there were the hard girls. They mostly lived on the other side of Rhode Island Avenue, where the houses and apartments were older and smaller. Some of them were even projects. At school, these girls stood around on the edge of the playground wearing black leather jackets, sneaking cigarettes, and joning on each other. It was harmless teasing when they did it among themselves, kind of a game to see who could throw out the worst insults. But sometimes one of the hard girls would crack on somebody in another group—say nasty things about them or their mother.

In Naomi's opinion, if that person was smart she'd smile and go along with it or maybe pretend she didn't even hear it, depending on the circumstances and what she thought would work best to keep from getting her butt whipped. Especially if it was Henrietta Jackson joning on you. Henrietta was the baddest fighter in school, had even creamed a couple of boys who were bigger, and most girls didn't even want to look at her the wrong way. A few of the girls in the hard group were really OK, though. They looked and acted tough but they would speak to you in the hallway and not mess with you as long as you minded your own business.

Naomi was in a group that was somewhere in between the fly girls and the squares. Most of them were in the eighth grade. They tried to dress cool, even if their parents didn't allow them to wear the really fly clothes. They were all pretty smart and studied hard but tried not to seem like bookworms. And they cared about boys enough to sneak and put on make-up at school, even if the boys didn't care much about them.

If one of the hard girls was in the mood to pick a fight, it was usually with one of them. The squares seemed so odd to everybody, Naomi thought the hard girls didn't know what to make of them. And the fly girls always had boyfriends to protect them. That left her group.

Today everything seemed pretty calm. The girls in Naomi's group had changed into their gym shoes and tossed their fall jackets aside and were racing each other. Two girls would run from one marker—a tree, a pole, a crack in the sidewalk—to another. The winner would race the next girl and so on. Naomi had come to love this game, since a week ago she won for the first time ever. Last year, she would have been more likely to curl up under a tree with a good book than participate in the races. But since taking up ballet that summer, her legs were becoming stronger and she felt surer on her feet.

The races finally came down to Naomi and Vicky, a tall skinny girl who was pretty fast, but Naomi beat her last week and was pretty sure she could do it again today. Debbie, her best friend since third grade, had lost way back.

"Shoot. I don't even know why I bother," Debbie had said, putting her eyeglasses back on over her big almond-shaped eyes. "I'm pitiful at this stuff."

They both laughed, because it was so true. Debbie was funny and one of the smartest girls at Monroe Junior High, but athletic she was not. So she picked a spot on the sidelines to root for Naomi as the other girls gathered around her and Vicky. This part got loud as some of the girls who favored Naomi tried to get Vicky's friends to bet on the race. Just as the two of them got into place at the start line, a girl from the hard group named Barbara came over to watch. Barbara was one of the OK ones. She always spoke in the hallways and they'd even talked a few times, so Naomi wasn't bothered. She kind of liked it that Barbara was there watching; if she won, Barbara would go tell the other girls in her group, and that would make her look cool.

She puffed her chest out, knowing the race was hers and the word would get around. Then she crouched a little as one of the girls said, "Ready . . . set . . . go!" Naomi flew down the track and beat Vicky easily, barely breathing hard at the finish line. Naomi and Vicky hugged between deep breaths of air and walked back to join the crowd.

Debbie ran up to Naomi and they gave each other five. Debbie's mahogany face was all smiles. "How do you do it, Nay? How'd you get to be so fast all of a sudden?"

Naomi shrugged. "I don't know, you know? If I feel someone closing in on me I just make my legs go faster and—" She stopped as Debbie's big eyes got bigger and moved to something behind her. Naomi turned to see Barbara approaching them. She flicked her cigarette on the pavement and smiled.

"You really fast, girl," Barbara said, shoving her hands in the pockets of her leather jacket. "I seen you race last week, too. You're good."

"Thanks," Naomi said, trying to act as if it was no big deal.

"She's the best. Can't nobody beat her," Debbie said, slipping into her tough-girl dialect.

"Oh, yeah?" Barbara said, smiling. "Think you pretty slick, don't you?"

Naomi shrugged, trying to maintain her nonchalance. Truth was, she felt ten feet tall.

"I'm always telling her we gotta find somebody who can beat her," Debbie said.

"Yeah," Barbara said. "Hey, I know somebody you can race."

For some reason, hearing that made Naomi feel like she'd shrunk down to two feet. She was fast, but she knew one thing. She had never raced any girls outside their cozy little group.

"You know Henrietta?" Barbara asked.

Now she was down to two inches. She was too nervous to say anything, so she just nodded her head.

"She my number-one ace," Barbara continued. "Sometimes we try, but none of us can beat that girl. Maybe you two should race."

Naomi still couldn't speak. If she said no, Barbara would run back and tell her friends Naomi was chicken. Barbara was standing there waiting for an answer, so Naomi kind of nodded her head to let Barbara know she heard the question while she tried to think how to get out of this mess.

"All . . . right!" Barbara shouted, leaping into the air.

At first Naomi didn't understand what she'd said or done to get the girl all excited, then she realized she'd goofed big time. Barbara thought her little nod was an agreement to race Henrietta. Naomi thought she would pee in her panties.

Barbara backtracked toward her friends, and Naomi finally found her voice. "Wait. I didn't mean—"

"I'll go tell 'em. Be back in a second." Barbara turned and ran off.

Debbie grabbed Naomi's arm. Now Debbie's eyes looked like they were about to pop out over her glasses. "You're not really going to race Henrietta Jackson, are you?"

"How am I supposed to get out of it?"

"You'll find a way. You're always good at working around things."

Naomi shook her head. "Not this time."

"Then just come out and tell her you can't do it."

"So she can tell everybody I'm chicken?"

"Well, shoot, Nay. Better that than if you beat her and she kicks your butt till it's black and blue."

"I don't think I'll beat her."

"How do you figure that? You're way too fast." Debbie's eyes lit up. "Hey, I have an idea. Let her beat you."

"You mean throw the race?"

"Yes!"

"I guess I could do that."

"You have to do that."

There was no more time to discuss it. A herd of leather coats marched their way, with Barbara and Henrietta leading the pack. Not only was Henrietta tough, she was also pretty and light-skinned, with reddish hair down to her shoulders. Henrietta approached Naomi, and the seven or eight girls with her stood behind. By now, some of the others on the playground had sensed something big was happening and were starting to come over too. This included Steve, a boy Naomi had liked since seventh grade but could never get to notice her.

"I hear you want to race me," Henrietta said.

Uh, not exactly. But how could she say that with Steve and half the school looking on?

"Well, do you or don't you?" Henrietta asked, sounding like she was ready to beat Naomi's butt either way. Naomi stole a glance at Steve. He was looking straight at her with that cute baby face of his.

"I'll race you."

The way Debbie looked, you would have thought she was standing over Naomi's casket.

Everybody got into position on the sidelines. Then someone from Henrietta's group got the idea to make the race longer, and they moved the finish line to a tree farther away.

All this was a blur to Naomi. Her mind was whirling, trying to decide what to do. If Henrietta was able to beat her, fine. But what if it looked like she could take Henrietta? Should she deliberately slow herself down? She didn't have a lot of time to think about it, because Barbara was telling them to get ready. As Naomi stood at the start line and looked out at all the excited faces, she made up her mind. She would do her best to beat this girl. She might end up with a black eye or worse, but she could never throw a race in front of all these people, especially Steve. If she won, he'd probably think she was bad. Everybody would think she was bad. In a way, she felt relieved now. Instead of worrying which way to go, she could concentrate on winning.

Barbara picked up a stick and held it in the air. She waited for everybody to quiet down some. "Ready . . . set . . . go!" She lowered the stick and they were off.

Henrietta shot out ahead of her. Naomi's first instinct was to let it stay that way. But she couldn't. She willed her legs to go faster, pushing them as hard as she could. She thought of ballet, where she willed her body into all sorts of odd shapes and had become the best dancer in the class. She thought of the pride she felt whenever Mrs. Johnson singled her out to demonstrate a movement to the other girls. She thought of Mama, so tickled with her progress she often came early to pick up Naomi and watch from the sidelines. This was no different, Naomi told herself, as she caught up to Henrietta. All she had to do was push a little harder. The finish line was just ahead, so she didn't have much more time. She forced every ounce of energy in her body down to her legs and sprinted ahead of Henrietta and over the finish line.

She bent over trying to catch her breath. They were both breathing so hard neither could speak. Henrietta had surprised her. She was better than anyone Naomi had ever raced. But Naomi was more surprised with herself. She'd had to dig deeper than ever before to win this one, and it felt good to pull it off. She just hoped—

"Bitch. Think you bad, don't you?"

Naomi heard it, but she didn't want to believe she heard it. She straightened up and tried to keep her knees from trembling. "No. It was just a race."

"You cheated. You started before Barbara said go."

By now the others had gathered around.

"She did not," Debbie said, coming to stand beside Naomi. "You were out ahead of her at the start."

Henrietta glared at Debbie. "Who the hell asked you? This between me and her."

"Yeah, stay out of it," somebody from the crowd said.

Debbie backed down wisely, and Henrietta turned to Barbara.

"Didn't she start before you said go?"

"Yeah," Barbara said. "I wouldn't take that shit if I was you."

Some of the other girls chimed in. "Yeah, don't take that shit."

"Bitch don't play fair."

"Whip her mothafuckin' ass."

So much for Barbara being OK. "Wait a minute," Naomi said. "No need to get all worked up. If you want, we can do it over. That would settle it." She was trying to be civil here.

"I don't want to race no cheating hussy," Henrietta said. " 'Sides, I never could stand your stuck-up ass. Think you cute 'cause you got all them fancy rags." She shoved Naomi in the shoulder. "I'ma whip your sorry ass."

"You gonna take that?" somebody asked.

Naomi wouldn't have had any problems taking it if she and Henrietta had been alone somewhere, since she'd never been in a fight and Henrietta was the last person she wanted to learn from. But she couldn't just stand there and let somebody shove her around and call her a snob in front of all these people. Just as she was about to hit Henrietta back, the school bell rang, and a couple of teachers came out and told them all to get moving. Talk about being saved by the bell. She had never been so happy to hear it.

Henrietta wasn't through with her yet, though. She stood inches away and pointed her finger in Naomi's face. "Meet me back here at three-thirty. I'm gonna whip your butt good." Naomi didn't say anything, but she'd just as soon eat a bag full of worms as show up at 3:30. As if reading her thoughts, Henrietta added, "And if you don't come, I'll find you tomorrow or the next day. Either way, your ass is mine."

"What are you going to do?" Debbie asked as everyone headed back.

"Good question," Naomi said, as they walked slowly toward the building. "Guess I'll have to come back. It's now or later."

"Are you crazy? You can't come back here. Even if you could beat her, she'll have some of her friends with her and they'll probably all jump in."

"Don't scare me like that. Maybe she'll come alone."

"Henrietta Jackson? She never goes anywhere without her crowd following her. There'll be at least five of them."

"You got a better idea?" One of the things Naomi liked about Debbie was she always got smack to the point, but that trait was getting on her nerves now.

Debbie sighed. "Guess not."

"That's what I mean. Might as well get it over with."

"You want me to come back with you?"

"I don't see what good it will do if it's just the two of us. It's not like we've got a bunch of friends to invite to stand up to Henrietta and her crowd."

"Two of us is better than one."

"You can come if you want. But maybe if it's just me, I can talk Henrietta into leaving the others out of it. If she sees you, she'll probably just get madder. So just stay home." Naomi couldn't help but notice the look of relief on Debbie's face.

"Why didn't you just let her win?" Debbie asked.

"I don't know. Once we got started, I couldn't hold back. I just don't have good sense, I guess."

"Sure it didn't have anything to do with Steve standing there?"

"No, I'm not sure it didn't have anything to do with Steve standing there."

Debbie got this weird smile on her face. "What?"

"I bet he knows who you are now," Debbie said.

The Literary Work

Discussion Guide

1. What details does Connie provide that so wonderfully evoke the setting and people of a Washington, D.C., neighborhood in the '60s? How does D.C. in the '60s differ from her depiction 20 years later?

2. How do Connie's female characters differ from her male characters, and how do they view each other?

3. What do we learn about Naomi's personality as a child and how did it help shape her as an adult? What type of relationship does she have with her parents and her brother Joshua?

4. The color line is drawn in the story from the very beginning. Why is it important in the telling of this story? What effect does it have on the people in the novel? How does Naomi deal with it?

5. Naomi and Dean's relationship has major ups and downs. Why do you think they can't get it together initially and become a couple? What finally brings them together?

6. When does Naomi begin to take chances and enjoy life? What are the things she finally realizes are important to her?

CONNIE BRISCOE, A SISTER WHO CAN RELATE

Published Works: *Sisters and Lovers*, 1994; *Big Girls Don't Cry*, 1996

Home Base: Falls Church, Virginia

Literary Hero: Zora Neale Hurston. I love the vibrant language and the cultural traditions depicted in her work.

Claim to Fame: *Sisters and Lovers* debuted to rave reviews and appeared on the best-seller lists of several leading daily newspapers; it is also being made into a television miniseries. *Big Girls Don't Cry* has enjoyed best-seller status as well.

Both you and Big Girl Naomi Jefferson grew up during the 1960s. Were your childhoods similar?

In some ways. In addition to being baby boomers, we both grew up in Washington, D.C., in Black middle-class neighborhoods. Naomi's personality is different from mine, though. I was quiet and shy until I reached my late teens, and I had no idea what I wanted to be when I grew up, unlike Naomi.

Were you born with a hearing loss? How has your deafness affected your personal life and your writing, if at all?

I was born with a mild hearing loss that got progressively worse when I was in my late twenties. I've always lived in the hearing

191

world—hearing family and friends—although I know deaf people from my years working at Gallaudet University. Deafness doesn't show up in my writing, but I definitely believe that losing my hearing was one of many things that motivated me to write and to keep at it until I was successful. I thought of it as a way to get ahead in life where my deafness wouldn't hold me back.

One of the most interesting issues you examine in *Big Girls Don't Cry* is the prejudice within the African-American community based on differing skin tones. Do you believe this prejudice still exists and does it still play a role in our relationships?

It definitely still exists, although maybe it's more subtle now, at least among adults, because we went through the "Black is beautiful" thing during the sixties and seventies. I'm told that teenagers can still be downright blunt about the light-skin, straight-hair thing even today. Some of it may be maturity: As you get older you come to realize how superficial a thing like complexion is and that character is what matters.

Both of your books explore the lives of contemporary, middle-class Black women. What specific issues does this group face that you try to illuminate in your writings?

The same things that working class and poor Black women face, in a sense. Race and sex discrimination are alive and well in all segments of society, whether you're a cleaning woman or a CEO. The point for all of us, though, is not to let those things cripple us, or not to allow ourselves to feel victimized to the point of despair.

In *Big Girls*, Naomi experiments with politics as a method for change, and ends up deciding that maybe politics is not

the best course of action. What do you think are the most effective ways to combat racism?

I think politics can be *one* way. The problem is that we've generally focused on politics and ignored everything else. African-Americans have held every political office except the presidency and vice presidency, and we're probably less than a generation away from achieving that. We need more people in the top echelons of business, technology, the arts, media, entertainment and all the rest of it.

At one point in the book, Naomi laments that many African-Americans have forgotten that making sure their children have a better life than they did is the best way to progress. Do you agree with her? If so, why do you think so many have forgotten this and how do you think they can be reminded?

Yes, that shared goal of making a better life for the next generation, even if you had to make sacrifices yourself, seems to have been lost. I guess part of the reason is that progress has come so slowly and people are getting tired of waiting. And sometimes it seems that no matter how many get ahead, there are still so many left behind. All I know is that progress is being made, even if it's inch by inch. The boom in African-American authors is one example.

Your novels reveal the difficulties sisters have finding available and desirable men, and some would accuse you and other African-American female novelists of "male-bashing." How would you respond to such criticism?

If we can't look at ourselves and our experiences and be able to criticize each other, then we'll never get anywhere. We're far from perfect, and that goes for brothers *and* sisters. Self-improvement comes from self-criticism. How are we going to improve if we can't be honest about what needs improving? Or if we can't air our opinions, even when they differ? Some of it is understandable. We get beaten up so much by the society at-large that it's hard to take criticism from within too. But isn't it better to get it from each other than from those whose motives may be suspect?

Big Girls Don't Cry is a refrain many young girls grew up hearing. Is it true, and what do you believe to be the best ways for releasing disappointment and grief?

Of course we cry. But the point is, after you have a good cry, dry your tears and get on with your life. Don't sit around feeling sorry for yourself or thinking your situation is hopeless.

We eagerly await your third novel. When will it be published, and what is its focus?

It will probably be published early in 1999. This one is different from the first two in that it's a fictionalized account of the female ancestors on my mother's side of the family. I'm able to trace back four greats to a woman named Clara, who was a slave on President James Madison's plantation. This novel looks at issues that Black women face, like the first two did, but it will look at those issues in times past.

Connie Briscoe is the 1995 Go On Girl! New Author of the Year

Singing in the Comeback Choir
by Bebe Moore Campbell

In Singing in the Comeback Choir, *we learn about forgiveness, hope and redemption through the lives of Maxine McCoy and her grandmother Lindy, who are fighting against declining communities, alcoholism, emotional despair and workplace stress.*

Maxine heard her name as in a dream, traveling to her through a mist. But the voice was too relentless to be a nighttime fantasy. She turned on the light and picked up her watch. Four A.M. She went to her door and opened it. She heard her name again, a cry for help. Not a dream. Nowhere near a dream.

Lindy's bed was empty. She wasn't in the bathroom. Maxine switched on the hall light and started downstairs. She smelled the smoke before she hit the second step.

Then she was running, taking the steps two at a time, her heart sprinting.

The sofa pillow was ablaze. Lindy's frightened swats were ineffectual. "Move," Maxine shouted, and stomped on it. She ran to fill a pot with water and doused the remaining fire.

Lindy wouldn't answer any questions and seemed afraid to look her in the eye. Maxine saw the half-full glass of scotch on the coffee table and next to it an ashtray filled with ashes but few cigarette butts. Lindy's gloomy silence fueled the flames inside Maxine.

"Suppose I hadn't been here? Suppose you'd been in this house alone or, God forbid, with Toby or the twins. You want to be responsible for killing children?"

Not a word.

"You want people to say you burned up in a fire because you were drunk? Huh? Is that what you want the world to say about you? 'Once brilliant singer dies in fire.' Is that what you want my baby to know about you? Don't I have enough bad memories?"

A whimper then, with shaking shoulders. Maxine stared. How could Lindy be so foolish? What was she becoming? Maxine looked at her grandmother until Lindy turned away.

"Please don't look at me like that. I didn't know I'd gotten this bad." Her voice was tinged with incredulity and grief. Then it grew lower, as though she were talking to herself. "I don't want to be like this," she said. "I *can't* be like this."

Maxine went into the kitchen and made two cups of peppermint tea. They sipped in silence as they sat on the sofa. From time to time, Maxine glanced at Lindy, whose face was so devoid of expression that she seemed to be in a trance. She had the same vacant look when they climbed the stairs to go to bed, as though she were confronting something she couldn't quite make out.

Maxine stood at Lindy's door; she watched her get into bed, then turned out the light. In her room, Maxine picked up the phone and called Satchel. It was well past one in Los Angeles, and she knew that she was waking him, but she needed to talk. "I just put out a fire in the living room," she said. As she told him what had happened, she was too tired to get emotional.

"Are you both safe? You sure you put it out completely?" Satchel sounded alert and willing to be in charge.

"Yes. It's out."

"You're sure? It was just the pillow? The rest of the sofa didn't burn?"

"Yes, yes. Satchel, what am I going to do? First she fell and hit her head. Now she set the house on fire. She won't move. She doesn't want anybody living with her. What am I supposed to do?"

"Right now there's nothing we can do. Calm down. Go to sleep. When you talk with her in the morning, see where her head is. Maybe this was scary enough for her to be more open to moving or getting a companion. If not, we'll have to figure out something else. But for now I want you to go to sleep."

Satchel's words were reasonable and orderly. This goes here; that goes there. But if there was comfort in them, Maxine couldn't find it.

The next time Maxine was awakened from a deep sleep was almost as bad as the first. "Maxine," Patrick Owens said, "I found you."

She looked at the clock on the table beside her bed. It was barely eight in Los Angeles. She put her pillow behind her. "Is there a problem?" she asked. But she knew. Patrick Owens wouldn't call her unless something was wrong.

"Have you gotten everything squared away with your grandmother?"

"It's taking longer than I anticipated, Patrick."

"I see."

Maxine waited, heard faint tap-dance steps collecting in her head.

"Ted's not the same with you away, Maxine. I went to the tapings Friday. He was off. Way off. You won't be able to use those shows for sweeps. I don't have to tell you that we have a lot riding on the May book." He paused. Maxine could hear his fingers drumming on some hard surface. "When were you planning to come back?"

"I talked with the supervising producer about that show. The warm-up was ill."

Patrick acted as if he hadn't heard her. "When are you coming back?"

"Next Monday."

He seemed to mull this over.

"That's not going to work," he said. "Ted's no good without you. I want you back in charge as soon as possible. Be here Thursday morning. Today I want you to call Ted. Work some magic."

Her mind leaped away from the phone. To get back by Thursday morning, she would have to take a late plane tomorrow night or a very early flight on Thursday morning. Either way, she had only today and tomorrow in Philadelphia. "Patrick, getting back on Thursday is going to be very difficult."

Patrick cleared his throat. "Please don't think I'm being insensitive to your situation, Maxine, but my professional responsibility is to the show. I'm afraid you'll have to come up with some other arrangements to take care of your personal life. Ted needs you at the studio, and so does Vitacorp. Thursday."

Maxine was able to hold in her anger until after she hung up, then it spilled out of her. She slumped down in the bed, trying to piece her thoughts together as her jangled nerves settled.

Dammit! A few more days, that's all she wanted. Maybe by then she'd talk Lindy into moving. Lisa wasn't incompetent. She'd made a mistake sending Ted out to a cold audience, but in general she knew what she was doing. Why had Patrick let her come to Philadelphia so readily—first class, no less, courtesy of Vitacorp—only to demand her return before she could finish what she'd set out to accomplish? Why was he trying to make her think that things were falling apart just because she'd been gone for a couple of days? How could she leave her grandmother now? What was going to happen when she left? "Something's not right," Maxine said out loud.

She was a hired hand, she reminded herself. A hired hand with sliding ratings. She had to toe the line, do what she was told. It was too early for Ted to be at the studio yet. She dialed his home number, and just as he answered, it occurred to her that maybe Ted had told Patrick to call her.

His hello was a bit groggy, but he sounded less like someone who'd just awakened than someone who hadn't slept all night.

"Ted, I'm sorry I lost my temper yesterday. Sweeps are coming, and we're all a little edgy."

"You're not the one who goes out there. You don't have to face that crowd."

"I know that, Ted. I had a talk with Lisa. Things are back on track. You had a right to be angry. But you didn't have a right to talk to me the way you did. I've been with the show for eight years. Been the EP for three. I think you know I'm loyal."

"There's a lot going on with me, and I don't trust anybody but you. I didn't mean to yell at you. I'm sorry."

"I accept your apology. What's really bothering you, Ted? I mean, besides the ratings. What's wrong?"

"Ahh," he began, but he didn't finish his thought. "When are you coming back?" She heard anxiety in the question.

"I'll be in this Thursday for the taping."

"Great." Maxine could hear the relief in his voice. "Is everything all right, then—with your grandmother?"

"No, everything isn't all right. Last night she started a fire. I can't get her to quit drinking and smoking. She refuses to move. Doesn't want anybody else moving in. So no, things aren't all right."

"I had no idea. I just thought she was, you know, old and sick in a regular kind of way. Do you think you could get her committed?"

"Ted, she's not crazy. I couldn't do that to her."

"How bad was the fire?"

"I was able to put it out before it did any real damage."

"What did she say?"

"Something like, 'I didn't think I was this bad.' She was embarrassed. I fussed at her."

"What do you guys talk about?"

"What do you mean? We talk about everything."

"Like when you were a kid and stuff like that?"

She was taken aback by the wistful nature of his question. "Some of that and some of what's going on now."

"You know each other really well, don't you?"

"Sure. She raised me."

"Right. That's really good." He grew quiet and in that silence she heard his cry.

"Ted, have you spoken to Patrick recently?"

"Not in a couple days. Why?"

"No reason."

After hanging up, Maxine put on jeans and a sweatshirt. She tried not to think about who was lying to her. Why would Patrick force her to come back, for no good reason? She went to the door and listened for any sounds of activity from Lindy's room. She heard nothing: Lindy was asleep, or pretending to be. Either way, she wasn't ready to face her granddaughter. It was just as well. Maxine was too angry to talk.

She went downstairs and stood in front of the broom closet. She felt like slamming her fist against the door. Instead she opened it, grabbed a broom, a dustpan, several paper bags, and went outside.

The wind was blowing, but Maxine ignored it and began sweeping the patio, the front steps, the sidewalk around them, with all the fury that was in her. She scooped up the trash at the curb and dumped it into the bag, then she started cleaning Mercedes' front. She had nearly finished, when the door opened.

"Whatcha doing there, girl?" Fauntleroy asked. He was in his bathrobe; the worn fabric puffed out around his sunken chest.

"Trying to sweep away the evil I feel," she said.

"I heard that," he said.

Her broom moved steadily down the block, picking up speed like machinery gone wild. She went inside for more bags, then moved farther along the block. At Nora Kelly's house, she detected a slight movement at the blinds, a presence behind them. No way I'm sweeping her front, Maxine thought. She left the litter in front of the white woman's house untouched and was about to go to the other side, when the wind lifted pieces of paper and blew them toward Lindy's home. Maxine crossed the street.

She could see eyes peeping at her from behind the boards at the crack house as she beat the pavement with her broom. Maxine filled all the bags she had with debris and had to get more from the house. She hauled them back to her grandmother's in two trips, stopping to sweep up the bits of paper that had blown down the street. Graffiti was scrawled across Lindy's window box, a scramble of letters that spelled nothing. Misused symbols. Maxine stared at the lines and squiggles.

The letters fought back. Maxine scrubbed in vigorous circular motions with a scouring pad. She pressed harder and harder, envisioning Patrick's face. Both the Magic Marker and the ancient paint on the window boxes began slowly to disintegrate. She stood back, unable to determine if her work was an improvement. The box, with both its defacement and its aged adornment scrubbed away, seemed oddly forlorn. It needed paint and flowers.

The telephone was ringing when she went inside.

"How are you doing, Maxie Mae?" Bootsy's voice was raspy.

"Mr. Bootsy." She felt moist and gritty; her muscles were throbbing.

"How's it going, Miss California?"

"I'm fine. How about you?"

"Doing okay for a young man. I was wondering if you had a chance to talk to Red about that music festival."

"She doesn't want to do it."

"Because of Milt?"

"Exactly."

Bootsy's breathing sounded like fall leaves being crunched underfoot. "It's like that, huh?" He cleared his throat. "What you gone do, put her in the old folks' home? Red ain't even seventy yet."

"Hmm," Maxine said, stifling her retort. "It's not an old

folks' home. And she doesn't want to leave this house. Did you ever talk with her about that?"

"Aww, that won't do no good. Just make her mad. You want something outta Red that she don't want to do, you have to be careful. You approach her head-on, she's just gonna fight you. Ain't no reasoning with that woman." He was quiet for a moment. "Only time I ever seen Red really behave herself was when she was taking care of you and when she had to go on that stage. If she was singing that night, she didn't speak to nobody all day long. Didn't smoke. Saved her partying for after the show."

He left her another space for cogitation as he coughed and sputtered. Maxine pictured her grandmother in the old days, sipping her hot water and honey before the show, pointing and whispering, doing her sit-ups, all so she could shine that night. "Sometimes Red doesn't know what's good for her. That's how come we never got married."

"You asked Grandma to marry you?"

"More than once. And I think a couple of times she was close to saying yes. Then she stopped singing and I pretty much stopped playing and . . . it's funny what makes a change in your life. After that our love got real quiet."

"Mr. Bootsy," Maxine said.

"Yeah?"

"I'll ask her again."

"Do it in a roundabout way. Your grandmother's that horse folks talk about, the one they can lead to water. You gotta make her know—"

"—that she's thirsty."

"Make her know it's the water that will save her life," he said.

Lindy ate the oatmeal and the slices of toast that Maxine put in front of her, but she didn't taste it. If she concentrated on opening her mouth and chewing, maybe she wouldn't think about how she almost set the house on fire. She tried to remember how many drinks she'd had the previous night. No more than two. Maybe three. Lord, was she becoming a drunk? She couldn't bear thinking of herself that way. When she finished, Maxine cleared her place. Lindy remained at the table; her head was crowded with images that she didn't want to see. What is wrong with me? she asked herself. She heard Maxine say, "Why don't you get dressed and we'll go for a walk." She sounded as if she were talking to a child. I deserve that, Lindy thought. She went upstairs and put on some clothes.

The Storytellers

DISCUSSION GUIDE

1. What key social and human issues does *Singing in the Comeback Choir* address?

2. Why do you think it's so hard for Maxine to forgive her husband for his indiscretion?

3. How does Bebe weave the theme of music throughout the story?

4. Compare and contrast Lindy in her heyday as a singer to the Lindy Maxine now has to deal with. Why did she become so bitter? Do you think she's justified in not wanting to perform again, even if it means work for her old musician friends?

5. How does the Philadelphia neighborhood Maxine remembers as a child differ from the one she visits today? How have the familiar faces that are still there changed?

6. How has Maxine's relationships with her mother and grandmother affected other relationships in her life?

7. What similarities do you see between Maxine's workplace issues and those many of us face?

BEBE MOORE CAMPBELL, OUR SOCIAL CONSCIENCE

Published Works: *Successful Women, Angry Men: Backlash in the Two-Career Marriage*, 1987; *Sweet Summer: Growing Up With and Without My Dad*, 1989; *Your Blues Ain't Like Mine*, 1992; *Brothers and Sisters*, 1994; *Singing in the Comeback Choir*, 1998

Home Base: Los Angeles, California

Literary Hero: "Toni Morrison because she writes so powerfully well. I like the fact that Toni keeps evolving; she's not resting on her laurels. She's got guts and the proper amount of arrogance."

Claim to Fame: Being Maia Campbell's mother

Most of your books deal with social issues that affect the Black community. How do you know or even decide which issues to choose to write about?

Well, it's all emotional. With *Singing in the Comeback Choir*, I really am a music appreciator. I really do love our women singers, especially the older ones. At the same time, it gives me the horrors to look at the disintegration of our communities. I was thinking about them in the same way as some of our old jazz singers, fallen down on their luck. I was trying to connect those two strands. With *Brothers and Sisters*, I lived through the civil unrest here, so that was very pressing on my mind. I kept thinking about Rodney's question, "Can we all just get along?" I really wanted to explore that. In dealing with *Your Blues Ain't Like Mine*, Emmett Till had been running through my mind for years. I write about whatever is on my heart at the time.

Speaking of *Your Blues Ain't Like Mine*, you had to be very young when Emmett Till was killed. How did what you heard about this tragedy impact you and compel you to write a story loosely based on this incident?

I was five, and I can only imagine that I heard bits and pieces of it then. But people were still talking about it when I was ten, and then when I was 15. This incident helped usher in the Civil Rights era that continued with the March on Washington. So this boy's name was raised like a banner all throughout that decade at the end of the '50s into the early '60s. This was something that was talked about, and I was a child who listened to adult conversations a lot. In a sense, Emmett Till really hasn't left us.

You say you especially love old jazz female singers. Any in particular?

I was profoundly impacted by seeing Alberta Hunter. She was an old blues singer who was hot in the '20s and '30s and had been on Broadway. She went into obscurity and took a job as a practical nurse. Somewhere in the late '70s, someone rediscovered her and she made a comeback. The voice was still there, and they ensconced her in the nightclub The Cookery in the Village in New York. I went to see her perform. She had one of those voices that filled a room without a mike. It was that powerful! Because of all that power, I expected that when she was done singing, she would stride off the stage, knocking people out of her way. But instead, she hunched up and shuffled off like a little old lady. I thought, *She's old, but she came back.* That really left an impression on me. I like people who make a new beginning, like Lindy in *Singing*, WT and Tyrell in *Your Blues*, and like Esther, Tyrone, Mallory and Humphrey in *Brothers*. They realize they made mistakes but turned their lives around. When I can find somebody that is a real-life example of that, I sort of warm to that person.

So was Alberta Hunter your inspiration for Lindy?

Not just Alberta Hunter, but Baby Washington, Maxine Brown and the people who made me dance, like Gloria Gaynor. What happens with a lot of these sisters in the later years, when their glory is gone, is that they become people who are on welfare or are in pink-collar jobs, or they succumb to alcohol and drugs, because we didn't support them their whole lives. Many of them didn't survive the onslaught of the Beatles, when American radio really stopped playing Black folks, except for James Brown, because they couldn't duplicate him.

How do you feel about your new role as a spokesperson on social issues within the Black community?

It's a very interesting role. *Brothers and Sisters* is now being used on campuses across the country for race relations to help people understand each other. Prince Georges Community College started with it as its communitywide book club book.

They had an Oprah-style book club discussion talking about issues Black and White. So it has been very helpful in that respect. But at the same time, I'm uncomfortable with being a spokesperson, especially when I'm on those TV shows where they set you up with other people who have a contrasting view. It's much easier for me to write about the issues.

As a writer not in the nine-to-five corporate world, how do you capture that scene so well?

I used to work in corporate America for AT&T, but not very long. My husband worked in corporate America for many years. He was a banker, and that's where I got all the information for Esther in *Brothers and Sisters*. And with Maxine, my girlfriend was an executive producer of a talk show, and I would talk with her about her job. I do the research through people I know who are doing what my characters are doing. For *Your Blues Ain't Like Mine* I had to go to Mississippi. I had never been there. I'd like to write a book where no research is necessary, but in all three of my books, I've had to do it. For *Singing*, I read Ruth Brown's autobiography so I would understand her struggle in suing Atlantic Records to get back royalties. I also read books on Motown and Etta James' life story.

How do you develop the relationships between your characters in *Singing in the Comeback Choir*?

I use memory. One of my grandmothers was very feisty, and when she was ready to die, she gave me all this stuff, like Lindy was giving Maxine. It was like she had a feeling she was about to go. With Lindy, it's premature, and this is tripping Maxine out. So, I can relate. Also, the ten years I spent in the magazine world interviewing many people influences some of the relationships I develop for my books. And I watch people and my own reaction to things.

Bebe Moore Campbell is the 1993 Go On Girl! Author of the Year

Ain't Gonna Be the Same Fool Twice
by April Sinclair

With crackling dialogue and pure authenticity, April introduced us to Stevie in the coming-of-age tale Coffee Will Make You Black. *In the sequel,* Ain't Gonna Be the Same Fool Twice, *Stevie fully explores her sexuality and takes us into the lesbian community, which is rarely visited in our contemporary literature.*

"You meet the same peoples over and over again in life," Grandma warned from the doorway. I didn't give her my full attention. I was too busy cramming wool sweaters into a suitcase full of jeans. Despite my sweaty, well-toasted skin, I knew I'd need warm clothes in a month or so.

"They names and they faces might be different. But they will be the same peoples," Grandma insisted. Her words hung in the humid Chicago air like the smell of chitterlings cooking on a stove. She pulled a paper towel from her apron pocket and wiped the sweat off her fudge-colored forehead. Grandma wore one of those serious aprons that you had to stick your arms through. There was nothing prim and proper about her.

I was the first person in my whole family to go away to college, and I was excited. But I knew that "book learning" wasn't everything. Grandma says experience is the best teacher. And she is no one to take lightly.

Mama joined Grandma in the doorway. The two of them could barely fit. They were both big women. Neither of them were fat, just big in the way grown women are supposed to be, according to Grandma. She'd often say, "Chile, don't nobody want a bone but a dog." But I was content with my slim figure. Thin was in, especially in white America, where I was headed. After all, Twiggy was the model of the hour. And besides, I certainly wasn't skinny. I did have titties and booty to speak of.

There sure were a lot of memories in this bedroom. The walls had been yellow, pink, and finally blue, my favorite color.

I shook my head at the now worn-out-looking white bedroom furniture that had looked so magnificent the Saturday afternoon they carried it home in my uncle's truck. Mama and Daddy bought it used from a house sale in Lake Forest, a rich northern suburb. I'd thought I'd died and gone to heaven. Aunt Sheila took one look at the gleaming white furniture and declared that we'd arrived.

I gazed at my bed. The quilt that Grandma made me years ago was almost in tatters now. I'd bought a brand-new, lime-green corduroy bedspread with some of the money I'd made this summer helping Grandma at her chicken stand.

Mama looked sad, like she hated seeing her only daughter go. You'd never know by her puppy dog expression that Mama had swung a mean switch in her day. She'd also done a lot of preaching over the years. And I'd been the mainstay of her congregation. My two younger brothers could never be held hostage long enough to listen to her sermons. Boys were "outside children," they "liked to go," as Mama would say. I wondered if David and Kevin would finally have to help her out in the house. She might make them wash a few dishes, but that would probably be about it.

"Well, Mama, you won't have me to kick around anymore," I teased.

"Just don't let some man make a fool out of you and you'll be all right." She sighed. Her smooth pecan complexion only showed wrinkles when she frowned.

I didn't have a boyfriend right now. I'd gone to the senior prom with a dude from the school band who'd asked me at the last minute. I'd barely known the shy, husky trumpet player drew breath until he'd mumbled, "Stevie, will you go with me to the prom?" They call me Stevie at school. My family calls me Jean. My name is actually Jean Stevenson. I'd swallowed and answered, "Yeah, I'll go with you." Paul was shy and quiet, but kind of cute. At least he wouldn't expect me to put out, I figured.

Our date had been pleasant enough. I even had fond memories of resting my head on Paul's shoulder as we slow-danced to the prom's theme song, "We've Only Just Begun." It was a white tune by the Carpenters; and our class of 1971 was all-black, except for a couple of Puerto Ricans and a Chinese girl. Some people had complained about the honky theme, but the prom committee prevailed. Only three other white songs were played during the prom, Carole King's "It's Too Late" (which everybody agreed was hot, white girl or no white girl); Bread's "I'd Like to Make it With You" and Bob Dylan's "Lay, Lady, Lay." Of course no dudes could complain about the last two.

Paul and I had gone to the Indiana Dunes for the senior class picnic the day after the prom. And Paul had been a perfect gentleman, lightly brushing my lips only when he'd said good-bye. It would give me a sweet feeling, just thinking about it. Something might have come of our connection if we'd had more time to get to know each other. But we didn't; Paul's draft number was pulled. He jumped up and joined the navy and shipped out right after graduation. Paul figured if he was in the navy, he'd have a better chance of staying out of Vietnam.

"Jean," Grandma said, interrupting my thoughts. "We're expecting great things outta you."

I chuckled as I stuffed underwear in the inside pocket of the large suitcase. "Grandma, I'm just going away to a state university, so don't y'all expect me to come back a Rhodes scholar."

"I know you'll do us proud," Grandma said, dabbing her eyes.

Suddenly, I felt a lump in my throat. I was sad to be leaving everything familiar, even Mama.

"You just keep your head in your books," Mama admonished. "And don't let men distract you. Men are nothing to get excited about, remember that." It was obvious that Daddy no longer excited Mama. The two of them reminded me more of business partners than lovers. She often passed Daddy like a vegetarian walking by a steak house. I wondered if the earth had ever moved.

"I don't know what you talking about." Grandma winked. "Men are too something to get excited about! Jean, if you can't be good, be careful."

Mama folded her arms. "You oughta be ashamed of yourself, talking like that at your age!"

"You the one who should be shamed," Grandma insisted, stepping into the bedroom and swinging her full hips.

"Chile, there might be snow on the chimney." She laughed,

pointing to her Afro. "But there's sho' nuff fire down below!" She snapped her fingers and did a boogaloo step.

"Get it, Grandma!" I laughed, clapping my hands.

"Poppa must be turning in his grave," Mama sighed.

Grandma rubbed her nose. "My left nostril is itching. Some man is talking about coming to see about me right now. And if he cain't cut the mustard, he kin least lick the jar!" Grandma rushed out of the room.

Mama shook her permed head in horror.

Grandma said her good-byes in Chicago. She shoved a twenty-dollar bill in my hand and then we hugged for the longest time.

As soon as my brothers, my parents, and I were out of Chicago good, we saw corn for days. I don't mean that literally; it was only a four-hour drive. But I don't care if I ever see another cornfield again, no matter how much I like eating it.

I've been assigned to a coed building, modern twin towers with twenty floors. Mama says she would've preferred for me to be in an all-girl's dorm. Daddy agrees with her, like he usually does on matters involving us kids. I don't know why Mama's tripping. We're on two different sides of the building. We even have different elevators.

It got a little emotional in the parking lot for us and plenty of other families. Everybody hugged me, Mama, Daddy, tall, lanky David—who will be a junior on Southside High's basketball team—and cute, chubby Kevin, who I can't believe will be a freshie this fall.

There wasn't a dry eye among us, including my father's narrow dark eyes. He's due for a dye job, I thought, noticing the gray around his temples. But Daddy still looked strong and athletic in his bowling shirt.

Grandma says white people are born actors. So, I'm not sure how my roommate and her family really felt when they discovered that I was black. I'd moved into the room first. My family was long gone by the time Barbara, her parents, big brother, and little sister trooped in with her stuff. Everybody was cordial; none of them tripped out like they'd seen Godzilla or anything. But who knows how they really felt?

Anyway, thank goodness, my roommate seems like the sweet type. Maybe because she's so homely. She probably figures she has to be extra nice. I hate to be cold, but the girl's face is hurting. Barbara is tall and skinny, downright gawky. She's got long, stringy, brown hair and pinched features. I don't have to worry about any latent homosexual tendencies being aroused by the sight of her, that's for damn sure.

I know that I can be attracted to a girl. I got a crush on the school nurse back in high school. Nurse Horn said it was normal for adolescents to develop same-sex crushes. But it still bothered me that good-looking girls turned my head.

Barbara is from a small town—Quincy, Illinois. She goes to bed at nine o'clock and plays a lot of Barry Manilow and even some classical. I'm thankful that she plays it real low. I try to be considerate, too. I don't blast my Motown sounds unless she isn't here. I made up a riddle. Why do white people go to bed so early? The answer is, because they're "tired." If you don't get it, that means you're "tired" too.

Today, I finally found the ivy. I'd always pictured a college having old, stately, brick buildings with ivy hanging from them. But I've only seen one place like that on this campus. The newer buildings outnumber the older ones, about two to one.

I like most of my classes. Only one of my teachers seems racist. Not anything overt, just a feeling I get. But that's nothing new. I can't trip on it. I have to keep my eyes on the prize, like Daddy says.

In class, my answers better be right. I feel like I have to represent my race. If I look dumb, we all look dumb. It's a burden. Sometimes I envy the white students, who can just blend in.

It's a trip suddenly to be surrounded by wall-to-wall white folks. And it's really strange living in the same room with one. It's a mindblower to look over at a pink face sleeping in the bed across from me. I keep waiting for the girl to go home, but then I remember she lives here.

In the cafeteria, when I sit with white girls from my floor, I cut my chicken with a knife. And I surely don't suck on the bones. I pretty much avoid watermelon altogether.

In the second week of September, I made my first trip into town. The place reminded me of that song "I Wanna Holler, but the Town's too Small." There are no signal lights or busy intersections. But there is a statue in front of the courthouse of some dude on a horse. Every small town probably has one, I thought.

I was sitting on the bench waiting for the campus bus. I'd just finished buying a flashlight and some tampons. The weather was perfect, about seventy-five degrees and very little humidity, for a change. Suddenly, I heard somebody shouting "Nigger!" Then I felt wet spit on my arm. I looked up as a truckload of men passed by, leaving a cloud of gravel dust. It all happened so fast, I was stunned.

I felt anger, fear, and humiliation all rolled into one. The white people walking by and the campus bus pulling up to the curb became a blur. Since I couldn't kill the assholes in the truck, I simply wanted to disappear. Somehow, I gathered my composure and boarded the bus. And I was able to stare out of the window at the postage-stamp-size town just like anybody else.

But tears ran freely down my face when I told Mama on the phone what had happened. She said in a calm but concerned voice, "Baby, I'm sorry that happened to you, but you will just have to tough it out. Lord knows, we as a people have come through slavery, survived the KKK, and the dogs being set on us in Birmingham. And you will just have to survive getting a college education in rural Illinois; so long as they're giving you a four-year scholarship. It's too bad, but that's just the way it is." Mama paused. "Sometimes, your soul looks back and wonders how you got over."

I'm thankful for the camaraderie I feel with the other 500 or so black students on this campus of 20,000. Most black folks speak to one another, whether we know each other or not. The few who don't are scorned as "Uncle Toms" by the rest of us.

I met a sistah named Sharlinda in the dorm bathroom. She had Noxzema all over her face. We nodded and introduced ourselves before I brushed my teeth. Then Sharlinda said that it was hard getting used to not seeing roaches running every which way when you turned on a light.

I could've turned my nose up and acted insulted. Just because I'm black doesn't automatically mean I'm acquainted with roaches, does it? But despite Mama's vigilant efforts, we keep us a few roaches in residence. Not to mention occasional mice and a rat every blue moon.

So, instead of copping an attitude, I laughed and said, "Girl, I know what you mean."

Sharlinda confided that she'd never slept between two sheets before in her life. She said it had taken her a whole week to figure out what the second sheet was for. I laughed and told her I could relate.

It seemed like by the time I'd rinsed the toothpaste out of my mouth, Sharlinda and I had become fast friends.

Sharlinda is cute and "healthy," not a size eight like me.

She's light-skinned with sharp features and curly hair that you could barely call a 'fro. You might think she was born to purple until she opened her mouth. Sharlinda talks like a stone sistah. She can butcher the king's English with the best of them. She was probably raised on a boot and a shoe.

Sharlinda grew up on the West Side of Chicago. I came up on the Southside. She says the West Side is the baddest side of town. I don't disagree with her.

I'm a journalism major. Sharlinda's major is undeclared. She's in the "Reach Out" program. Mama would say that they had to reach *way* out to let Sharlinda into somebody's college.

Mama seldom likes my friends, and I know she wouldn't approve of Sharlinda. She prefers seddity people and I don't. I like it that Sharlinda is funny and down-to-earth. I'm often drawn to people like her. Mama would say that's my downfall.

Anyway, it's nice having a friend to hang out with. Especially since I don't have a boyfriend yet. The competition for brothas is a little stiff because more than half of the black students are female. A few of the dudes have been checking me out, especially a handsome, clean-cut type named Myron. But so far nothing has materialized, just a couple of smiles and one long, lingering look in the campus bookstore. Maybe I'll give Myron some play soon. Blood seems nice, I just hope he isn't too square for me.

Yesterday, Sharlinda and I went shopping in town. I was nervous, but at least I wasn't alone. Besides, I knew I had to conquer my fear. There were almost no other black people in sight. We felt like aliens until we found this cool store run by hippies. Sharlinda bought a black light and a reefer pipe. That's how I know she smokes dope. I've still never even tried it. But I'm ready to.

I bought two posters for my room, one of a woman with a big rainbow Afro and another of a peace sign.

Speaking of peace, I marched in my first demonstration against the war last night. A few dudes even burned their draft cards. That's when the campus police ordered us to disperse. When we didn't disband fast enough, they sprayed us with tear gas. I hated that shit. My eyes and throat were burning all the way back to my dorm.

There was a long-haired photographer taking pictures at the demonstration. I told Sharlinda that I might end up in *Life* magazine. She said I'd be more likely to wind up in a CIA file. That worried me a little. But Sharlinda said, "Don't trip. You're small potatoes, ain't like you're Bobby Seale or somebody."

Tonight, my roommate and I were interrupted from our studying by a big commotion outside. We stuck our heads out the window into the warm Indian-summer night to find out what the deal was. I thought it might be another antiwar demonstration.

But to my surprise, what I saw was as traditional as the Fourth of July. I'd heard about panty raids but I never thought I would actually witness one in 1971.

Girls were sliding the window screens open and panties

were raining down on white boys' heads. They sniffed them like they were fresh-baked rolls.

They talk about us being wild, I thought. I swear, white folks are something else.

"I have half a mind to throw my funky drawers down there," I said aloud. I forgot I was talking to square-ass Barbara.

"Let's do it!" She smiled wickedly.

I was as surprised as if a nun had invited me to an orgy.

"Who knows? This may be the last panty raid. It's the end of an era." Barbara sighed. "This will at least give us something to tell our grandchildren."

"Yeah, we won't be able to say we were at Woodstock, but we can say we were in a panty raid."

"Well, it beats swallowing goldfish or stuffing yourself inside a phone booth."

"OK, let's go for it then." Barbara and I reached under our long nightshirts and pulled off our drawers.

We giggled as our panties, still warm from our body heat, were quickly snatched up.

DISCUSSION GUIDE

1. In college, Stevie forged friendships with Sharlinda, Today and Celeste. Contrast and compare how they each relate to one other. Why do you think Stevie, who feels close to them, can't tell them her fears about her sexuality?

2. April paints a vivid picture of college life for Stevie. What are some of the written and unwritten rules of college life that Stevie learns to live by?

3. After college, Stevie winds up living and working in San Francisco. What did she learn about herself in this city? Did she really thrive in San Francisco?

4. Contrast Stevie's life in college with that of her life in San Francisco. What were the major changes for her? What was similar?

5. In San Francisco, Stevie meets two women, Traci and Cynthia. How did they each change her life? What were the differences between Stevie's relationships with both of them?

6. What was Stevie's relationship with her family like? Were you surprised by the reactions of her mother and grandmother when she told them about her sexual orientation?

APRIL SINCLAIR, A MARCHER TO HER OWN DRUM

Published Works: *Coffee Will Make You Black*, 1994; *Ain't Gonna Be the Same Fool Twice*, 1997

Home Base: Berkeley, California

Literary Heroes: Maya Angelou, Toni Morrison, Alice Walker and Langston Hughes

Claim to Fame: The American Library Association's 1994 Young Adult Fiction Book of the Year Award for *Coffee*

Considering that society, in general, and the Black community, in particular, is still very much homophobic, was there any fear in bringing bisexuality out of the closet in literature, and why was it important to you to do so?

I had some concern about what people's reactions would be to a female character with bisexual experiences, but it was a story that needed to be told because it's been so neglected in today's mainstream writing. I got some flack from a few readers who met me on tour, and I had one live interview that was terrible. The reporter was clearly uncomfortable with the subject, and it made for a very tense interview. When it was over, she revealed that it [lesbianism and bisexuality] went against her church and her beliefs. For the most part, though, people were open-minded, even more so than I expected. Stevie as a character is very warm, and a lot of people feel a kinship with her. There's a lot of humor in the books, too, and that helps to relax people and make them comfortable.

After reading your books, did people want to know if you're gay?

Did they! They hounded family and friends, anybody, to find out. Let's just say inquiring minds definitely wanted to know.

So, what did you tell them?

I'm unusual, because I'm not big on labels. Sexuality, for some people, is not so cut-and-dry. You can be open to a relationship based more on the individual. A person's gender is not the deciding factor in my choice of who I have a relationship with. Most people say that's bisexual, but that label doesn't work for me either, because that means you cut it right down in the middle—men and women. Again, for me, it's the person.

You humorously revealed how painful it can be for children whose parents don't talk to them about their sexuality. What words of advice would you offer parents on this subject?

Read *Coffee*. I don't mean to be self-serving, but a book can be a springboard for discussion. If both parent and teen read it separately, then getting into a conversation about sexuality can be easier. Parents often are uncomfortable with their own lives in many ways, and they're afraid of revealing too much to their kids. Many are even uncomfortable with discussing their sexuality with their own spouse.

How did your mother handle "the talk"?

My mom was basically old-school and reserved. There wasn't a lot of leeway in her thinking. It was basically "don't do it." That's good advice for teenagers if you back it up with a lot of conversation on the issue. I do believe, though, there's something in between abstinence and intercourse, and it might be a good place to be for older teenagers today. Basically when I meet young girls—and they turned out in large numbers when I was on tour for *Coffee*—I tell them you've got to love yourself; never put a relationship ahead of you. I also tell them to get a spiritual relationship with God, because everything else falls into place from there. They don't have to swallow the Bible whole, and parents and other adults should help them develop a relationship with God that's self-affirming—not punitive. Focusing so much on sin is a turn-off for young people, because it's a negative. If you come at it from a positive, then it's empowering. They won't be so torn by peer pressure. I also encourage girls to ask themselves one question before they do anything: "Does this make me feel good about myself as a person? Do I feel strong, safe and free?"

Same Fool is set in the go-with-the-flow '70s. How did you put yourself back into this place and time when writing the novel?

I was only a few years younger than Stevie in the '70s, so I basically went down memory lane. I also listened to some of the music of the day.

You have been a fellow at Djerrasi, Yaddo, McDowell and Ragdale artists' colonies. What is that experience like?

Going to an artists' colony is a great opportunity to work (there's not as much sex as they say!). You can share your work with other artists of different disciplines, and the cross-pollination can be very enlightening. People stay about a month, and there is some socializing and many intellectually stimulating conversations. The surroundings are usually beautiful and natural, and you get your own cabin and good food.

In the bio notes on the jacket of your last book, it says you're taking belly dancing lessons. Well, can you stir it up?

I'm still a beginner; I took lessons for about a year. It's been helpful in the writing of my next book, because one of the characters is a belly dancer and the main character is taking lessons. I needed to try it for myself to really know and feel the spiritual side of belly dancing.

Spiritual side?

It's really hard to understand unless you've done it, but belly dancing is very opening. It's a lot about trusting yourself.

Your third book is due out in spring 1999. Do tell.

Well, there's no Stevie. It's about a woman in mid-life looking for love in the "I feel your pain" '90s. She's a radio deejay in Chicago, who, in searching for her other half, discovers her own wholeness. She struggles with her weight and issues of self-esteem revolving around a childhood drama. She has close ties with younger people, so the book spans the generations as it explores what we've gained and lost as a community.

I'm sure it will have your trademark humor. Have you always been funny?

Yeah, I've always been funny, but there's a thin line between joy and pain. Growing up, my humor was a kind of defense. Sometimes you laugh to keep from crying. My childhood wasn't tragic or anything, but there's just always stuff. I'm the oldest of four, and the next one is only eleven months younger than I am, so I never got to be the baby. To a certain extent, I also felt I didn't fit in with other kids. I was more intellectual than a lot of kids, and yet I was spunky. They couldn't put me in the good or bad category. I therefore had what I call "the-halfway-cool experience."

April Sinclair is the 1994 Go On Girl! New Author of the Year

Chesapeake Song
by Brenda Lane Richardson

Brenda made her fiction debut with Chesapeake
Song, *the eloquent story of a wealthy and educated
African-American farm-owning couple. Charles and
Tamra have everything except what they really want—a
happy marriage. When we are given details of their
parents' marriages, their own childhoods and their
shared tragedy, we begin to understand why love truly
is not enough to keep a couple together.*

TAMRA AND CHARLES
JULY 11, 1977

She would always remember the fluid movements of the
heads, nearly three hundred of them, turning, mouths fishlike
in *oohs*, as she and Harlen began their journey. The gospel
choir, a cappella, sang a wordless, soul-deep rendition of the
wedding march. Each row of pews was festooned with gar-
lands of wild grape blossoms, which grew white and lavender
in raucous abandon along the roads and creeks of Nanticoke.

Even with her steps paced to the slow rhythm of the chants,
she'd expected the faces along the way to be an unrecognizable
blur. She was mistaken. They all greeted her, old men with new
haircuts, elegant ladies in small hats and brightly colored silks,
their half-smiles apologetic in their unfamiliarity; Virginia's
sorors, she assumed. Here and there, youths, often as wide-eyed
as the young women with sloping hats who sat beside them.

228

She brushed off the momentary sadness that threatened to seize her. It was Charles's father, and not her own, with whom she walked. Harlen took measured steps, his eyes downward, as if embarrassed by the elegance of his tuxedo. She wanted to thank him for stepping in, knowing he hated the spotlight, but finding speech impossible, she looked away from the gazes. An unhappy thought flitted through her mind, like a bird soaring over a silent stretch of water. Daddy would never see this, the same man who twenty-five years before had spun tales when she was new to the earth, offering his voice as balm, cheerful, happy endings.

She tried to picture him through an infant's eyes, his mustache like a strip of velvet. She'd known his voice since utero. When she could walk, they'd danced. Standing on his shoes she'd learned the tango. What had happened to that joy? What of that man, that father? Breathing deeply, she swallowed the sadness.

In a shaft of light a swarm of fruit flies twirled. As girls, she and Wadine had called this a wedding of flies. She blinked hello to Aunt Florida, who wore a shiny navy suit, her hair in rolled-up clumps, as if, after removing the curlers, she'd forgotten to comb it out. A row ahead and only knee-high, she saw the small, laughing face of a squirming boy, an unknown second cousin perhaps.

Her daddy was alone and maybe her mother had been right about him being ill. She pictured him in a tuxedo, stretched out, and grew aware of a sudden pressure on her arm. Harlen had squeezed it to his chest. She smiled at him, saw the sprinkling of freckles across his cheeks.

Shifting the bouquet of white roses, she glanced frontward, her head tilted toward the high ceilings of carved mahogany and the double rows of balconies. The church had been designed in the early nineteenth century, for whites to sit in the nave, free Blacks, including, eventually, the Lanes, in the first balcony, and slaves in the uppermost reaches. Today this largely Black group was scattered with the faces of Charles's white business associates, and up front, seated with his family, Eve and Art Reardon.

She looked toward the draped, flowering altar, where Charles waited. The photographer's light, hidden somewhere behind, casting a hazy glow. He held his hands behind his back and was dressed as an African groom, in white brocade with threads of gold. He wore a skullcap with a pattern along the brow, a hip-length shirt with short, wide sleeves, pants that narrowed at the calf, and a long draping shawl hung from a shoulder.

Her attention was pulled away by the voices of older twin cousins, smiles of approval illuminating their round faces. They raised their heavy bodies on tiptoes. "Go on, girl," one called as she passed.

"You lookin' good, honey," another said.

"*Allll right,*" they said together, their voices tingling her skin, as if tiny lights had been strung across her. She would not have cried. But the nearest twin reached out and touched her elbow, saying softly, as if they were alone, "You gonna be fine, you wait and see, ya hear?" Words of condolence, of seeing through, which tipped her tears beyond the veil, onto her chin and breasts.

Virginia and Big Mama seemed to be holding their breath, prepared to breathe for her. Her mother wore glasses, the lenses catching the light and masking her eyes as she held her chin up.

As Wadine laid her flowers in a wide basket, Charles

reached under her veil, wiping a tear from her face, a public act of love, as if comforting a child. He smiled, whispering something. She tried sniffing, but it came out as a sob.

"Think you can do this without making me look like a fool?"

"Piece of cake, my brother." She sniffed. "If you don't watch it I'm going to embarrass you for a change and kiss you before the ceremony starts."

He lifted her veil. "Go for it," he said, and moving quickly, she grabbed his shoulders, kissing him roughly on the mouth. There was a burst of startled laughter and applause. She held onto him, riding the cheers, her arms about his waist, holding on, so thankful for him. He'd pulled her to dry land.

Reverend Noel's voice interrupted the whistles and cheers, each of his words in deep timbre, like a separate song. "Dearly beloved: We have come together in the presence of God."

She looked closely at the cleric, who had been educated at Princeton, and who, like her, had returned. Was he happy here? His bright blue and scarlet doctoral hood, which hung from around his neck and over his shoulders, added a festive splash to his black robe. ". . . If any of you can show just cause why they may not lawfully be married, speak now; or else forever hold your peace."

She heard tittering and turned to see Charles staring threateningly into the crowd, as if daring anyone to speak out.

When Harlen had finally given her away, they sat, the two of them, as Reverend Noel moved to his pulpit and took a long drink of water. "Some folks wonder why you'd even need a preacher at a wedding. Tamra and Charles already have our goodwill and prayers on this occasion; and from what I just saw, they certainly know what they want to do."

The congregation laughed heartily at this.

"I suppose they could simply exchange vows and we could get on with the party." There was a scattering of applause. "But I am here to remind you, for this one brief moment, about the importance of marriage." A man in back called, "Amen."

Reverend Noel continued. "A lot of you are just meeting Tamra for the first time. She's a town girl, and in her young life has traveled extensively." He said that while he hadn't traveled as much, he'd just returned from Kenya, where he'd visited Machakos, Nairobi, and Lokitaung.

Charles whispered: "I think he picked up the wrong sermon. This sounds like his travelog."

"On one of my favorite tours we visited a protected area filled with giraffes. With the mists swirling about their long necks and legs and spotted bodies, it was like watching a slow-motion ballet. But I learned something important that day. When these animals drink from a river it is not an easy task, for they are so tall, and it is unsafe. Low to the ground they can easily be attacked by enemies. So when they drink, they go in pairs, like partners . . ."

"*Umm hmm*, now that's all right, Reverend," a voice called.

Charles whispered, "That's your uncle back there." Tamra pretended to ignore him and covered her smile with the white Bible Dalhia had given her. It had served at family weddings for over a century.

The minister's voice rose. "While one drinks, the other stands guard."

The voice from the rear again. "Um hm, now put some salt and pepper on it."

Charles poked his elbow into her side. "You didn't warn me about all these countrified Negroes in your family." Now she fought laughter and discovered Charles was a master at keeping a straight face.

The pastor continued, saying that Tamra and Charles represented a marriage of science and nature, and that one should not be separated from the other. "Like most scientists who have an exacting approach to viewing the world," he said, "Tamra has discovered something about the relationship people must have to nature. We can't be detached because we are immersed in God's world. We are learning we can't get free from it, stand over it, or manipulate it for our ends without extraordinary costs to ourselves and the whole of creation. We are part of the very material and structure of the universe itself."

Tamra found herself leaning toward Charles as she continued listening to the preacher.

"In a very real way, they are influencing the course of creation. And what we can expect from them is that they will do nothing less than change the world."

The voice from the rear again: "Preach on in heaven."

"Tamra and Charles, you are saying to the world, 'We are better as two than as one.' It is a testament to enduring love . . . whether one is up or down . . . that God intends for human relationships."

The sermon ended, they stood to return to the altar, when a frail, elderly woman in a straw bonnet walked on stage with sheet music and a metal stand. Tamra wondered if there was something in the schedule she'd overlooked. Charles sat and urged Tamra to do the same.

The woman unfolded the legs of the stand and arranged

sheet music. Backstage, someone could be heard fiddling with the audio system, placing a needle to a record.

The congregation rose. It was the national anthem. Tamra turned, narrow-eyed, toward Virginia, who stared defiantly back. It confirmed a nagging fear: This was the same soror Virginia had mentioned months before, who'd retired from half a century of teaching, and who'd taken up singing. When Virginia had first suggested this woman be allowed to perform at the wedding, Tamra had vetoed the idea. She saw now that she'd been overruled, and with "The Star-Spangled Banner," of all choices, for a wedding! The old gang of college militants who she'd invited would be sure she had lost her mind.

"*O say! Can you see . . .*"

Oh, dear, she was off to a shaky start, and off-key, wavering, fake soprano. She turned toward Virginia and smiled with tiger teeth. Charles whispered loudly to the back of her head. "Loosen up, baby." She let her shoulders drop.

"*Whose broad stripes and bright stars . . .*"

As her voice rose Charles began to howl like a coon dog.

"*O'er the ramparts we watch'd . . .*"

"*Owwwwwwwwwwwwwww.*"

"*And the rockets' red glare . . .*"

"Yowwwwww . . ."

Tamra nudged his foot. When he persisted, she stepped on his toe, but he only howled louder. She looked around to see how their guests were reacting to his howling. Except for Virginia, who looked furious, a few others fought grins. Hoping to drown him out, she raised her own voice, singing along with the final chorus.

"*Oh, say does that star-spangled . . .*"

234

The congregation and choir joined in.

"O'er the land of the free . . . and the home of the brave."

Silence followed as the soloist gathered her music and left. Tamra looked smugly at Virginia. Finally she had someone who could handle her mother's manipulations.

Virginia nodded determinedly toward the altar. It was time to resume their position up front. Tamra grabbed Charles's hand and gave him a scolding look. He smiled like a saint. She'd been right about him all along, she'd never be able to stop him from doing anything he wanted.

At last, Reverend Noel asked the questions she'd waited for years to answer. "Will you have this man to be your husband; to live together in the covenant of marriage? Will you love him, comfort him, honor and keep him, in sickness and in health, and, forsaking all others, be faithful to him as long as you both shall live?

"Oh yes, I will," she answered, silently adding the words, *gladly, delightedly, assuredly, passionately,* as the pastor questioned Charles.

The ceremony concluded with: "Those whom God has joined together let no one put asunder," and she and Charles moved up the aisle greeted by a crashing round of applause that sent them spilling into the sunlight. They stood together, thanking their guests and posing for photos. Through the sumptuous buffet, she hardly knew what she ate or said. Cousin after cousin whispered in her ear, speaking of her good fortune, of the joyful life ahead, assuring her she'd found the perfect mate.

She rushed back to the dressing room to prepare for their three-day honeymoon. When she'd changed her clothes and was returning to the hall, she was startled to find Charles waiting behind the church with the surprise Virginia had tried to warn her about. He sat on a black charger that was decorated with pastel ribbons and tiny, pink roses. The scent of the flowers failed to mask the horsey smell, and the beast stamped its hooves threateningly as she approached. He then turned in circles, finally nudging her with his snout. She was awed by the animal's strength.

Charles said: "You're always calling me your prince."

Eyeing the saddle of brown, tooled leather, she wondered if she could actually fit up there with him. He told her to hurry and climb up, but she looked dubiously at the neighing horse. "You don't actually expect me to . . ."

"Did you know there was a war lord named Tamerlane?"

"You're making that up . . ."

"I swear, baby. Fourteenth century. Somewhere in Asia. Genghis Khan's great-nephew or something. Christopher Marlowe wrote a play about him."

"There's a point to this?"

"Well, I asked myself, what mode of transportation would be fit for his namesake, and on her wedding day?"

She backed off, protesting. "That thing's huge. I can't." The horse stamped, a large wet eye watching her.

"Come on, Tamerlane, give me your hand, hurry. Your suitcase, everything's in the car. Hurry."

"Can't wait to be alone with me, eh?" she taunted, while walking cautiously to the front of the horse, trying to work up the nerve to mount it. She decided to just get up and not think about the discomfort. Charles extended a hand as she struggled to figure out which foot to hook into the stirrup. He pointed to her right one. Her palm was clammy and slipped from his grasp as he pulled her up. The acetate travel dress clung to her skin. Before she could settle in, the horse reared up. "I don't think he's too crazy about all this."

"Skyrocket was thirty-one last week. He's tired, that's all."

No matter how much she twisted, comfort was impossible. It felt like she was sitting on the corners of two heavy boxes.

'What took you so long, anyway?" he asked, urging Skyrocket along.

"Had to call Daddy," she said, "but that's not important. I haven't had time to tell you what went on back there in my dressing room. First Wadine, then my mother and Big Mama gave me the strangest . . ."

"I want to hear about it, baby," he said, "but hold on. I've got to find a john."

She reached under his shirt, her fingers moving in circles. His belly was hard, flat, and the hairs on his chest so wiry they peppered her fingertips. She thought about it. They were really married. The wonder of it. Skyrocket picked up speed, and she said through giggles: "So this is the way you introduce me to the realities of farm life?"

"I didn't think we could fit on a hog."

Their laughter broke the silence of the road, and as Skyrocket moved beneath them, she was surprised at how fully she enjoyed the warmth and trembling of the horse's body through her stockings. On one side of the road, they passed a green field of young wheat, on the other, an idle plot gone to chickweed, wild garlic, and flowering dandelion. And she thought, as the horse began to trot, that she liked seeing the world from up high.

The Literary Work

D I S C U S S I O N   G U I D E

1. Based on the details of her parents' marriage, what patterns did Tamra pick up that may have had an adverse affect on her own union? What about the history of Harlen and Dalhia, Charles' parents? How has it influenced their son? Do you accept the premise that patterns are destined to repeat themselves in generations to come?

2. Relationships often require sacrifice. What things do Charles and Tamra give up in the name of marriage and family? How does this affect their relationship with one another and their children? Are there viable solutions?

3. How can a tragedy like the one Charles and Tamra experienced impact a relationship? Why do you think the author included an incident like this?

4. Cousin Johnny really got under Tamra's skin. Discuss that chemistry.

5. Tamra's grandmother gave her some advice on her wedding day that Tamra acknowledges she never mastered. Do you agree with those words of wisdom? Do you think they could have made a difference in Tamra's relationship?

6. What did you make of the therapy sessions Charles and Tamra attended with Wadine? How effective was it to use a therapist that knew both partners and some of their history?

7. When the novel opens, Tamra is thinking about divorcing her husband. When you reach the conclusion, do you think they have a chance at making it work?

BRENDA LANE RICHARDSON, A ROMANTIC AT HEART

Published Works: *Story Power: Talking to Teens in Turbulent Times,* 1991; *Chesapeake Song,* 1993; *Love Lessons: A Guide to Transforming Relationships,* 1993; *The Language of Fertility: The Mind-Body Path to Conception,* 1997; *What Mamma Couldn't Tell Us About Love,* 1999

Home Base: Piedmont, California

Literary Hero: "I love many many authors, but there's been none more supportive than Terry McMillan. She does something a lot of 'big-time' authors don't do. She talks us up to other people. She phones the store where you are going to appear and orders the book in advance. She makes it a point to invite you to the premiere of her movie, to send you a note. I've heard other Black authors say the same thing about her, and I have never heard of other African-American women in this business doing that. She's my hero because she's got three things going for her: She's a good writer, she has this tremendous business acumen and then she's supportive to other sisters. Readers pick up on that. When they buy a Terry McMillan book, they buy her, as well as the words between those covers."

Claim to Fame: 1993 PEN Oakland Literary Award for *Chesapeake Song*, and the Ford Foundation, Alicia Paterson and John Knight Journalism fellowships

---

Few African-American authors have built their novels around a love story. Much of what's out there depicts us on the dating scene, not working at the stability of marriage. How did you come to choose this as your topic?

Well, I suppose because my first marriage was very unstable. I followed my mother's footsteps and walked out the door when I didn't like what I had. And I know that hurts children. When the second one wasn't working out, I decided that whatever it took I was going to figure out how to make it work. The one thing I had learned from working on *Love Lessons* was if one person changes in a relationship, you can also change the relationship you're in. Even if you are not in a relationship, if you make some changes, you will attract different kinds of men. You can't sit around and say, "Well, brothers are no good." It's a matter of you doing your own personal homework. That's what I did. I stopped pointing a finger, which is basically what my novel is about. The fact that I was writing about a marriage grew out of my own life. I wanted to know how to make a marriage work. I had never seen one work, except on television and with White folks.

That explains why the subject of relationships seems so close to your heart. Even your nonfiction work focuses on relationships.

Yes, even the fertility book I wrote. Unless you have a good relationship with yourself and until you figure out what's happening in your body and your mind that's not allowing you to conceive, you don't conceive. My first book, which is not even out in print now, was about getting along with your teenagers. So my writing has always centered around what I don't know and am trying to learn more about.

While *Chesapeake Song* is indeed a love story, it's not all hearts and roses. Right from the start you pose the eternal tough question: If two people love each other, why is marriage so difficult?

People miss the boat. They say, "I left because I wasn't getting along with them [my spouse]." Well, I think that's exactly the way God devised it. We were supposed to be attracted to people with whom these issues were going to come up. Whether it be drinking, overspending, or not being respectful, whatever the issue is, that relationship represents what has not been worked out in our childhood or in our young adult lives that needs to be worked out. By staying and working it out, guess what? *You* become a whole person. It's not just the marriage thriving. It's not just the relationship doing better. It's you being at peace.

In the book, Tamra is conflicted about giving up her career to stay home with the children. You're a mother of three and have a career. While the way you make your living doesn't require you to go into an office every day, how has this difficult balancing act impacted your marriage?

It's very hard. Housework and the division of labor has got to be one of the biggest issues going on between couples today. Everybody's angry. He's thinking, *I've been out working all day, so I shouldn't have to do a thing except put my feet up.* Meanwhile, she's thinking, *What's his problem? He needs to be getting up and helping me. I'm doing this all by myself.* My husband and I had that same issue going on, but until I learned so much about who I am, much of what I was doing to try to get him to do what I wanted was really destructive. I learned to turn that around and say, "What's really going on with me, not with my husband, but with me." I sat down one day and began writing my husband this really furious letter that I never ever planned to send. After I wrote this letter, I asked myself, "Now who am I really writing this letter to? Who wasn't there for me? Who expects me to do all that?" First Mom turned up, because I was the good little girl who was always cleaning the house. We all know this story. We didn't want our mothers coming home to a mess. They worked hard. They went out of their way for us. My sister was the one who sat there with her legs crossed and did nothing. So, I was angry with my mother. Not that it was her fault, it just so happened that she was the mother and I felt compelled to do this for her. I was angry at my sister for not doing more, and I was furious with my dad because he was never there to make things better anyway. So here was all this fury from the past, and my poor husband would walk in the door not even knowing he was dealing with feelings and issues from a generation ago.

We can't just say, "Okay, I know that's what happened" and then it's over with. You really have to work through it. I knew I had worked through it when we were having a conversation one day about all the burdens we were carrying, and I did not feel the need to try to control him by making him feel really guilty—and you know a lot of us are controlling. We learned that if we love somebody, the only way to hold onto them was to be really controlling. That was one of the lessons we learned in slavery because we lost people so easily. My latest book looks at how the intergenerational lessons about men and love we've learned from early ancestors are working against us. There are also some strengths we are not using that could help us have better love lives.

Once you recognized your long-standing issues around house cleaning, what did you do?

This time I simply said, "I know you have a lot to do and I have a lot too, but when you're sitting there working on your next lecture and I'm here scrubbing these floors with the stress of all my other responsibilities, like the deadline for my next book, I feel there is no one in the world who cares about me. That I am just by myself." He responded with, "That sounds pretty miserable and I'm sorry that you feel that way." Then we didn't talk about it anymore. Later I had to go out to meet a friend. When we came back to the house, the first thing that hit me was the scent of Pine-Sol. He had done the floors in the rest of the house. And next thing I knew, he was coming in with a tray of herbal tea. I thought, *Thank you, God! I am the first woman in my family who has finally learned how to talk from the heart.* He finally heard me because it was the right way to say it.

As you tell Charles and Tamra's story, you also relate a family saga. Why did you choose to include this history?

Because it is so important for us to understand from whence we came. None of us start off fresh. If we came from a family where women were abandoned, then that's going to be the theme for the rest of our lives. It will be your children's theme— even if they grow up with a father—until we make some corrections. It is important to see the whole scope of these people. The way to make this interesting was to put it in story form. I had tried the self-help book. Some people buy self-help books, but a lot of people like reading romances. I like reading romances too, so I thought, *Let me go through a different door*. Suppose I showed how you can have all these material things. You can have the education, the looks and the fine man, and it still may not work out. As a matter of fact, I received letters from women saying, "You know, you helped me with my marriage. Thank you." Interestingly enough, I received more letters for *Chesapeake Song* about that than for *Love Lessons*.

It's interesting that you introduce couples therapy in your novel. Traditionally, therapy has not been a popular means for dealing with dysfunction in the African-American community. What motivated you to include this story line?

I wanted to give people an opportunity to see what goes on in this setting and why therapy does work. When working on *Love Lessons*, I got to see my best friend and coauthor on that book [Dr. Brenda Wade] at work. I sat in the back of the room and saw her work with couples, who I just knew she wouldn't be able to help. But soon, I saw this change taking place that was just incredible. I wanted more African-Americans to know how powerful and effective this can be. I highly recommend therapy. But I'd have to say a lot of therapists miss the boat when it comes to African-Americans because they don't include our intergenerational histories of slavery and racism. That's why we haven't taken advantage of therapy in great numbers. We haven't been able to trust the system. We go in and someone may be trying to make a point by pounding their hands on the desk in front of the psychiatrist's White secretary, and he's labeled a psychotic. There have been studies that show we are misdiagnosed often by White therapeutic professionals.

You mention watching your coauthor at work. We Go On Girls kept saying we just knew Wadine in the book was Dr. Wade or at least inspired by her. How much of your life is played out in the story of Charles and Tamra?

That wasn't too far of a leap with that name, was it? I just love my best friend so much, and when I saw how good she was, I thought, *God is in our midst now.* I had never thought of a therapist as being called by God, but she is making a difference in lives. I've got family and friends all through that book. Tamra is named for my sister, who died when she was only 34 years old. She was sort of a mother figure for me while we were growing up. A lot of people thought I was just not so bright, but Tamra knew something was going on. It wasn't until many years later that I found out I had a learning disability. Tamra was the one who would drag me to the library and pay me to read from her babysitting money. As a sixth grader, I started picking up things like Sigmund Freud and *War and Peace.* That built the foundation for my love of these sweeping sagas and my fascination with the realm of the mind. I wanted to pay homage to my sister by giving her a fuller life than the one we had through the character of Tamra. I'm sprinkled all through the book. People who know me will say, "I remember when you tried that recipe or ordered that." *Chesapeake Song* is like a quilt of my life. Not my life exactly, but pieces of it.

How difficult was it for you finding a publisher for this book, since it doesn't fit the mold generally set for the portrayal of Black families?

Actually, that's why the book was purchased. I was working as a journalist when I wrote a piece for the *New York Times* about the difficulty of marriage. I shared how all my single friends assumed I had this perfect life, but that my life had no fewer frustrations than the single woman looking for a man and how I had to work hard to keep the marriage going. I heard from many publishers as a result of this, but everybody wanted me to write nonfiction. Then I met Charles Harris of Amistad Press. I told him I would love to write a book with a positive portrayal of an African-American man, the kind of people I've known all my life but never see in books. He told me if I wrote the first two chapters and gave him an outline in two months, he'd give me a contract. I did that, and three months later had my contract. I had never written fiction in my life, so I had to go to fiction workshops to learn how to do it so I could finish the book. I owe it to Charles, so that's why I named the main character after him.

Some have mistakenly placed *Chesapeake Song* in the romance category. How do you feel about that? Do you think there are any lessons to be learned from romance novels or are they purely for entertainment?

I remember once being introduced to an audience as a romance writer and being horrified at first. Then I thought, *Well, that's okay, because they will expect a romance and get something very different.* It would be like cutting open some exotic piece of fruit. You think it's going to be an orange, and then there are all these little grooves and cells in there. But I like romances, I think they give us hope. And that is what I wanted more than anything with *Chesapeake Song*. I think so many of us have lost hope and are giving up on love. Anyone who's been in love, even for a short while, but particularly if you've been in love for a long while and it's been requited, knows there's nothing else better in life. So how do you attain it? And maintain it? I will spend the rest of my life talking to people about that because I want everyone to know it and experience it.

Brenda Lane Richardson is the 1995 Go On Girl! Author of the Year

CHAPTER SIX

Out of this World
The Science Fiction and Fantasy Genre

Considering the harsh conditions in which nineteenth century Blacks lived, it's no wonder the earliest African-American writers in this genre portrayed distortions of the cruel reality they faced. In Martin R. Delany's *Blake, or Huts of America* (1859), a Black male protagonist leads a slave insurrection in some Southern states and Cuba. Sutton E. Grigg's distorted premise for *Imperium in Imperio* (1899) involves a secret society of Black men planning to take over Texas and form a separate Black government. In the mid-'30s, social satirist and ultraconservative George Schuyler played out his utopian fantasies in weekly installments he wrote for the African-American newspaper *The Pittsburgh Courier*, where he worked as a correspondent. Published as a complete text in 1991, *Black Empire* focuses on a secret organization comprised of the best Black scientists and engineers. While Whites fight among themselves in battles instigated by the secret organization, the Blacks implement a plan to overthrow the government so they can create their own.

This type of literature is best categorized as speculative fiction, since the more widely used term science fiction is too limiting. Coined in the '60s, speculative fiction is an umbrella genre under which utopian, fantasy, science and supernatural fiction all fall.

Supernatural works, like Charles Waddell Chestnutt's stories in *Conjure Woman* (1899), are rooted in Black folklore and magic. Set in the old South, his characters, usually slaves, are transformed into animals and such through hoodoo. This is a theme that stands the test of time. Contemporary novelist Tina McElroy Ansa frequently takes her readers for a walk on the other side via characters with supernatural powers or characters who narrate from the dead. In her most recent work, *The Hand I Fan With*, Lena conjures up Herman (her man), a ghost who teaches the generous community caretaker how to take care of herself. The spirit at the center of Toni Morrison's Pulitzer prize–winning novel *Beloved* (1987) is the ghost for which the novel is named. Seeking revenge for the violent way she died as a child, the spirit taunts her mother Sethe and sister Denver.

Science fiction, meanwhile, refers to works created with a real scientific theory or technique in mind. Despite conventional thinking, science fiction does not always feature creatures from another planet, nor is it always set in the future or in another dimension. The most successful African-American sci-fi writers are Samuel R. Delany and Octavia Butler, both winners of the genre's Nebula and Hugo awards. Delany's first novel, *Jewels of Aptor* (1962), looks at the destructive capabilities of technology. Nineteen seventy-six marked the debut of the talented Octavia Butler, whose *Patternmaster* was the first of a five-novel Patternist saga. Butler has attracted a diverse audience with her exploration of racial and sexual awareness, genetic engineering, advanced alien beings, nature and the proper use of power. In 1995's *Blood Child*, a collection of short stories and essays, Butler offers commentary explaining her inspiration for each story.

THE GO ON GIRL!
Science Fiction and Fantasy
Reading List

Wild Seed / Octavia Butler

Kindred / Octavia Butler

Parable of the Sower / Octavia Butler

Black Empire / George Schuyler

The Hand I Fan With / Tina McElroy Ansa

My Soul to Keep / Tananarive Due

The Literary Work

BOOK PRAISE FROM GO ON GIRLS

"*I'm a sci-fi reader, but Octavia Butler's* Wild Seed *was the first book of this kind that really spoke to me. It's science fiction from an African-American perspective. I love Octavia for bringing this to me. Here's a sister who takes science fiction to a different realm. Her character Anyanwu takes on different life forms in order to protect herself and her family.*"

Willette Hill
Washington, DC

"*I didn't need to seek the world of the supernatural by consulting a psychic hotline or by planting myself in front of the TV to languish over the doings of a soap opera. I found spirit-fullness, as well as a true dramatic presence, in Tina McElroy Ansa's* The Hand I Fan With, *in which the character Lena conjures up the perfect man. McElroy Ansa reveals that life is a cyclical journey . . . much like the seasons. One can often find solace and guidance in the throes of one's own imagination.*"

Shirley D. Hawkins
Chicago, Illinois

"*What an imagination! It's amazing how in* Kindred, *Octavia Butler connects two totally different time periods—slavery and present day—and tells her story. I like that she didn't warn us when Dana was time traveling, but Dana was always prepared. Knowing the future helped Dana survive slavery. After this book, I bought every book Octavia wrote. What a fabulous storyteller!*"

Cherryl Neill
Washington, DC

Parable of the Talents
by Octavia E. Butler

In Octavia Butler's continuation of Parable of the Sower, Parable of the Talents, *she gives us an account of Lauren Oya Olamina's establishment of a new community and a new religion in the year 2032. Octavia, herself, describes it as a first-person narrative of a woman who, after her death, might be thought of as a goddess.*

From ***The Journals of Lauren Oya Olamina***
SUNDAY, SEPTEMBER 26, 2032

Today is Arrival Day, the fifth anniversary of our establishing a community called Acorn here in the mountains of Humboldt County.

In perverse celebration of this, I've just had one of my recurring nightmares. They've become rare in the past few years—old enemies with familiar nasty habits. I know them. They have such soft easy, beginnings. . . . This one was, at first, a visit to the past, a trip home, a chance to spend time with beloved ghosts.

My old home has come back from the ashes. This does not surprise me, somehow, although I saw it burn years ago. I walked through the rubble that was left of it. Yet here it is restored and filled with people—all the people I knew as I was growing up. They sit in our front rooms in rows of old metal folding chairs, wooden kitchen and dining room chairs, and plastic stacking chairs, a silent congregation of the scattered and the dead.

Church service is already going on, and, of course, my father is preaching. He looks as he always has in his church robes: tall, broad, stern, straight—great black wall of a man with a voice you not only hear, but feel on your skin and in your bones. There's no corner of the meeting rooms that my father cannot reach with that voice. We've never had a sound system—never needed one. I hear and feel the voice again.

Yet how many years has it been since my father vanished? Or rather, how many years since he was killed? He must have been killed. He wasn't the kind of man who would abandon his family, his community, and his church. Back when he vanished, dying by violence was even easier than it is today. Living, on the other hand was almost impossible.

He left home one day to go to his office at the college. He taught his classes by computer, and only had to go to the college once a week, but even once a week was too much exposure to danger. He stayed overnight at the college as usual. Early mornings were the safest times for working people to travel. He started for home the next morning, and was never seen again.

We searched. We even paid for a police search. Nothing did any good.

This happened many months before our house burned, before our community was destroyed. I was 17. It was 2026. Now it's 2032, and I'm 23 and several hundred miles from that dead place.

Yet all of a sudden, things have come right again. I'm at home, and my father is preaching. My stepmother is sitting behind him and a little to one side at her piano. The congregation of our neighbors sits before him in the large, not-quite-open area formed by our living room, dining room, and family room. This is a broad L-shaped space into which even more than the usual 30 or 40 people have crammed themselves for Sunday service. These people are too quiet to be a Baptist congregation—or at least, they're too quiet to be the Baptist congregation I grew up in. They're here, but somehow, not here. They're shadow people. Ghosts.

Only my own family feels real to me. They're as dead as most of the others, and yet they're alive! My brothers are there and they look the way they did when I was about 14. Keith, the oldest of them, the worst, and the first to die, was only 11. This means Marcus, my favorite brother and always the best looking in the family, is 10. Ben and Greg, almost as alike as twins, are eight and seven. We're all sitting in the front row, over near my stepmother so she can keep an eye on us. I'm sitting between Keith and Marcus to keep them from killing each other during the service.

When neither of my parents is looking, Keith reaches across me and punches Marcus hard on the thigh. Marcus, a year younger, a lot smaller, but always stubborn, always tough, punches back. I grab each boy's fist and squeeze. I'm bigger and stronger than both of them, and I've always had strong hands.

The boys squirm in pain and try to pull away. After a moment, I let them go. Lesson learned. They let each other alone for at least a minute or two.

In my dream, their pain doesn't hurt me the way it always did when we were growing up. Back then, since I was the oldest, I was held responsible for their behavior. I had to control them even though I couldn't escape their pain. My father and stepmother cut me as little slack as possible when it came to my hyperempathy syndrome. They refused to let me be handicapped. I was the oldest kid, and that was that. I had my responsibilities.

Nevertheless, I used to feel every damned bruise, cut, and burn that my brothers managed to collect. Each time I saw them hurt, I shared their pain as though I had been injured myself. Even pains they pretended to feel, I did feel. Hyperempathy syndrome is a delusional disorder, after all. There's no telepathy, no magic, no deep spiritual awareness. There's just the neurochemically induced delusion that I feel the pain and pleasure that I see others experiencing. Pleasure is rare, pain is plentiful, and, delusional or not, it hurts like hell.

So why do I miss it now?

What a crazy thing to miss. Not feeling it should be like having a toothache vanish away. I should be surprised and happy. Instead, I'm afraid. A part of me is gone. Not being able to feel my brothers' pain is like not being able to hear them when they shout, and I'm afraid.

The dream begins to become a nightmare.

Without warning, my brother Keith is gone. Just gone. He was the first to go—to die—years ago. Now he's vanished again. In his place beside me, there is a tall, beautiful woman, black-brown-skinned and slender with long, crow-black hair, gleaming. She's wearing a soft, silky green dress that flows and twists around her body, wrapping her in some intricate pattern of folds and gathers from neck to feet. She is a stranger.

She is my mother.

She is the woman in the one picture my father gave me of my biological mother. Keith stole it from my bedroom when

he was nine and I was twelve. He wrapped it in an old
a plastic tablecloth and buried it in our garden betwee
of squashes and a mixed row of corn and beans. L
claimed it wasn't his fault that the picture was ruined b
and by being walked on. He only hid it as a joke. How
supposed to know anything would happen to it? Tha
Keith. I beat the hell out of him. I hurt myself too, of co
but it was worth it. That was one beating he never told
parents about.

But the picture was still ruined. All I had left was the me
ory of it. And here was that memory, sitting next to me.

My mother is tall, taller than I am, taller than most peopl
She's not pretty. She's beautiful. I don't look like her. I loo
like my father, which he used to say was a pity. I don't mind.
But she is a stunning woman.

I stare at her, but she does not turn to look at me. That, at
least, was true to life. She never saw me. As I was born, she
died. Before that, for two years, she took the popular "smart
drug" of her time. It was a new prescription medicine called
Paracetco, and it was doing wonders for people who had
Alzheimer's disease. It stopped the deterioration of their intellectual function and enabled them to make excellent use of
whatever memory and thinking ability they had left. It also
boosted the performance of ordinary, healthy young people.
They read faster, retained more, made more rapid, accurate
connections, calculations, and conclusions. As a result,
Paracetco became as popular as coffee among students, and, if
they meant to compete in any of the highly paid professions, it
was as necessary as a knowledge of computers.

My mother's drug taking may have helped to kill her. I
don't know for sure. My father didn't know either. But I do

know that her drug left its unmistakable mark on me—my hyperempathy syndrome. Thanks to the addictive nature of Paracetco—a few thousand people died trying to break the habit—there were once tens of millions of us.

Hyperempaths, we're called, or hyperempathists, or sharers. Those are some of the polite names. And in spite of our vulnerability and our high mortality rate, there are still quite a few of us.

In spite of all that, I want to know my mother. She's the part of me that I don't know. But she won't even look at me. She won't turn her head. And somehow, I can't reach out to her, can't touch her. I try to get up from my chair, but I can't move. My body won't obey me. I can only sit and listen as my father preaches.

Now I begin to know what he is saying. He has been an indistinct background rumble until now, but now I hear him reading from the twenty-fifth chapter of Matthew, quoting the words of Christ:

" . . . For the kingdom of Heaven is as a man traveling into a far country who called his own servants, and delivered unto them his goods. And unto one he gave five talents, to another two, and to another one—to every man according to his several ability—and straightway took his journey."

My father loved parables—stories that taught, stories that presented ideas and morals in ways that made pictures in people's minds. He used the ones he found in the Bible, the ones he plucked from history, or from folk tales, and, of course he used those he saw in his life and the lives of people he knew. He wove stories into his Sunday sermons, his Bible classes, and his computer-delivered history lectures. Because he believed stories were so important as teaching tools, I

learned to pay more attention to them than I might have otherwise. I could quote the parable that he was reading now, the parable of the talents. I could quote several Biblical parables from memory. Maybe that's why I could hear and understand so much now. There is preaching between the bits of the parable, but I can't quite understand it. I hear its rhythms rising and falling, repeating and varying, shouting and whispering. I hear them as I've always heard them, but now I can't catch the words—except for the words of the parable.

"Then he that had received the five talents went and traded with the same and made them another five talents. And likewise he that had received two, he also gained another two. But he that had received one went out and digged in the earth, and hid his Lord's money."

My father was a great believer in education, hard work, and personal responsibility. "Those are our talents," he would say as my brothers' eyes glazed over and even I tried not to sigh. "God has given them to us, and he'll judge us according to how we use them."

The parable continues. To each of the two servants who had traded well and made profit for their Lord, the Lord said, "Well done, thou good and faithful servant; thou hast been faithful over a few things, I will make thee ruler over many things: enter thou into the joy of thy Lord."

But to the servant who had done nothing with his silver talent except bury it in the ground to keep it safe, the Lord said harsher words. "Thou wicked and slothful servant. . . ." he began. And he ordered his men to " . . . Take therefore the talent from him and give it unto him which hath ten talents. For unto everyone that hath shall be given, and he shall have in

OCTAVIA BUTLER, OUR SISTER
FROM ANOTHER PLANET

Published Works: *Patternmaster*, 1976; *Mind of My Mind*, 1977; *Survivor*, 1978; *Kindred*, 1979; *Wild Seed*, 1980; *Clay's Ark*, 1984; Xenogenesis Trilogy: *Dawn*, 1987; *Adulthood Rites*, 1988; *Imago*, 1989; *Parable of the Sower*, 1993; *Bloodchild*, 1995; *Parable of the Talents*, 1999

Home Base: Pasadena, California

Literary Heroes: "I have favorite books like the *Doom* series by D. Hugh and *Perfume* by Peter Suskind and some favorite nonfiction writers like Oliver Sacks, a neurologist who has written some marvelous books on what it means to be human as far as our brain and our perceptions are concerned."

Claim to Fame: "That people are reading my stuff." Science fiction awards include a Nebula, two Hugos, a MacArthur Award and a Locust Award

---

Your work has been described as science fiction or futuristic. How do you interpret those terms?

These are other people's terms. They are marketing gadgets and schoolteacher stuff. I write stories. They [the labels] are not what I'm about. I don't object to them, I just don't care about them.

You write in a genre few authors of color explore. What makes it an interesting base for your story developments?

It is probably the freest genre that exists. In it you can do absolutely anything. There is nothing that you can't deal with, no topic, nothing past, present or future. And people tend not to realize that. They think, *Oh science fiction,* Star Wars. And they tend to want to live in it and turn it into something that is extremely small. The truth is it's all over the place. You *can* be all over the place and still be within it. I've been very comfortable with all the freedom.

With the continuing story of *Parable*, what is it you want your readers to come away with?

A couple of things. *Parable of the Sower* was supposed to be about problems and kind of establishing what the problems are. *Parable of the Talents* is supposed to be about solutions. That's what was supposed to happen; it didn't exactly work out that way. What I came up with was a book about a woman who is so focused on the one thing in the world that she wants. That runs ahead of her, and she's so focused on it that even though everything else might be lost to her, this one thing keeps her going. Something terrible happens early in the book that is really quite devastating. It results in some deaths. It strikes her as terrible and she's upset by it. But she also says look what this person did. This person had absolutely no chance of getting what he believed was important but he managed to get it anyway even though it cost him his life. While other people say, "Oh, how terrible," she's saying, "My God, he did it." And later when things become more terrible for her, she also does it in spite of everything. It's about figuring out what you want and going after it and letting nothing stand in your way. I don't mean she's out using people; she does have a moral sense. She has every reason to curl up and die, forget, give up. But she doesn't do it. She keeps on and finally reaches what she wanted, and it costs her a great deal. But she does it. It's about solutions. The kind of solutions people reach for when they're frightened.

So where do you get your inspiration for your stories?

It takes a lot of things coming together. Generally it will be something that I'm passionate about. Sometimes it will be a character or a particular thing that a character has the matter with her or some kind of an ability she has. Sometimes it will be just an idea. For instance, with the Xenogenesis books, one of my early ideas was that we human beings seem to have characteristics that don't work well together and they seem to put us on the path of self-destruction. It was difficult to come up with a story around that, and I didn't really come up with one. I held onto the idea, and folded other things into it. Like baking a cake. Everyone has an imagination; it's just a matter of what you do with it. Far too many of us take our imaginations and hide them, because we get criticized for them or laughed at for them.

In *Bloodchild,* you did a collection of short stories. How different was writing short stories versus novels for you?

I am essentially a novelist. I don't really enjoy writing short stories. It takes just as much energy to create the characters in the situation. And then you get very little play out of it. I tend to want to create universes and stay in them for a long time. It is one of the things that gives me pleasure about writing. So, short stories are kind of a cheat for me; I'm in and out before I know it.

After each story in *Bloodchild*, you interestingly give commentary about the story. Why did you choose to do that?

A man did an introduction to my book *Kindred* years ago after it had first been published for Beacon, when they reissued it. And I was annoyed because he blows the story for people. I wanted to make certain I didn't do that, yet on the other hand, I wanted to put my two cents in.

Are there any events that have taken place recently that you could explore for future story plots?

That's not the way I do it. There has to be something that catches my attention and other things fold into it. Even though you have all the ingredients to make a cake, if you haven't put them together in the right proportions, you're not going to have a cake. And if you don't bake it at the right temperature for the right period of time, you're not going to have a cake. So it takes a lot more than a new invention for me to begin to have a novel.

As a child, did you read much science fiction?

When I was in my teens, I barely read anything else but science fiction and comics and whatever teachers forced me to read.

Octavia Butler is the 1994 Go On Girl! Author of the Year

CHAPTER SEVEN

Here Today, Here Tomorrow
Classics

———

With the boom of Black books today, one might overlook the treasure trove of African-American literature from our past. That would be a mistake. For a contemporary reader, nothing compares to discovering a gem like Zora Neale Hurston's *Their Eyes Were Watching God* (1937). The Harlem Renaissance writer received critical acclaim for capturing on the page the dialogue of her native Florida. Considered Hurston's masterpiece, the novel charts the growth of teenager Janie Crawford into a self-fulfilled woman.

For a poignant portrayal of a Black single mother living in the big city, today's readers can check out *The Street* (1946). Its author, Ann Petry, was the first African-American female writer to examine the problems faced by Black women in urban environments rather than the Southern locales typically featured at that time. Amazingly, the conditions under which Petry's characters struggled still exist today.

The Souls of Black Folk by W. E. B. DuBois (1903) is another historically significant work. This rich portrait of Black life reveals that DuBois was indeed a man before his time. Many of his opinions and reflections are relevant today. Ralph Ellison's award-winning *Invisible Man* (1952) features the timeless theme of self-discovery. Chronicling a Black youth's search for his identity, Ellison spins a tale of racial repression and betrayal.

Novels from our most recent past, such as *The Color Purple* (1982) and *Sassafras, Cypress and Indigo: A Novel* (1982), will be must-reads for generations to come because of the profound impact these works have had on Black literature, and because they represent the best kind of storytelling—inventive. Ntozake Shange, who's most known for her performance piece *for colored girls who have considered suicide when the rainbow is enuf*, uses narrative, poetry, recipes, magic spells and letters to tell the story of three sisters in *Sassafras*. Womanhood is also a theme in Alice Walker's Pulitzer prize–winning novel *The Color Purple*. Told through letters from one sister to another, the novel explores Black women's relationships with men.

A library of Black literature lacking in classics like these is far from complete.

THE GO ON GIRL!
Classics Reading List

The Measure of Time / Rosa Guy

The Street / Ann Petry

Dust Tracks on a Road / Zora Neale Hurston

Sassafras, Cypress and Indigo / Ntozake Shange

The Souls of Black Folks / W. E. B. DuBois

Incidents in the Life of a Slave Girl / Harriet Jacobs

I Know Why the Caged Bird Sings / Maya Angelou

The Best of Simple / Langston Hughes

Go Tell It on the Mountain / James Baldwin

BOOK PRAISE FROM GO ON GIRLS

"James Baldwin's classic Go Tell It On the Mountain *motivates us to soul search. What struck me most is the passage where John is on the church floor experiencing an emotional bout with the Devil. We all go through a time of reflection when we have to look deep inside ourselves."*

Joanie McClinton
Memphis, Tennessee

*"*Incidents in the Life of a Slave Girl *was a poignant story about a woman's struggle to overcome the daily injustices of being a slave. It was amazing what she went through and that she was still able to keep her sanity. Imagine living in a crawl space for years to protect yourself and children from your slave master."*

Gayle Newell
Mitchellville, Maryland

*"*The Best of Simple *was my introduction to Langston Hughes, and I loved all the characters, especially Simple. He had a way of seeing things the way they really are and explaining it in a simple, straightforward way. Through humor, Hughes delivers powerful messages, such as the need to support our artists. This light, easy collection of conversations strung together reads like one long story you never want to end."*

Lysette Moore
Brooklyn, New York

Dust Tracks on a Road
by Zora Neale Hurston

The Zora Neale Hurtson memoir Dust Tracks on a Road offers a jubilant account of the author's rise from poverty in the rural South to a place of literary prominence as a champion of Black heritage.

FIGURE AND FANCY

Nothing that God ever made is the same thing to more than one person. That is natural. There is no single face in nature, because every eye that looks upon it, sees it from its own angle. So every man's spice-box seasons his own food.

Naturally, I picked up the reflections of life around me with my own instruments, and absorbed what I gathered according to my inside juices.

There were the two churches, Methodist and Baptist, and the school. Most people would say that such institutions are always the great influences in any town. They would say that because it sounds like the thing that ought to be said. But I know that Joe Clarke's store was the heart and spring of the town.

Men sat around the store on boxes and benches and passed this world and the next one through their mouths. The right and the wrong, the who, when and why was passed on, and nobody doubted the conclusions. Women stood around there on Saturday nights and had it proven to the community that

270

their husbands were good providers, put all of their money in their wives' hands and generally glorified them. Or right there before everybody it was revealed that one man was keeping some other woman by the things the other woman was allowed to buy on his account. No doubt a few men found that their wives had a brand new pair of shoes oftener than he could afford it, and wondered what she did with her time while he was off at work. Sometimes he didn't have to wonder. There were no discreet nuances of life on Joe Clarke's porch. There was open kindnesses, anger, hate, love, envy and its kinfolks, but all emotions were naked, and nakedly arrived at. It was a case of "make it and take it." You got what your strengths would bring you. This was not just true of Eatonville. This was the spirit of that whole new part of the state at the time, as it always is where men settle new lands.

For me, the store porch was the most interesting place that I could think of. I was not allowed to sit around there, naturally. But, I could and did drag my feet going in and out, whenever I was sent there for something, to allow whatever was being said to hang in my ear. I would hear an occasional scrap of gossip in what to me was adult double talk, but which I understood at times. There would be, for instance, sly references to the physical condition of women, irregular love affairs, brags on male potency by the parties of the first part, and the like. It did not take me long to know what was meant when a girl was spoken of as "ruint" or "bigged."

For instance, somebody would remark, "Ada Dell is ruint, you know." "Yep, somebody was telling me. A pitcher can go to the well a long time, but it's bound to get broke sooner or later." Or some woman or girl would come switchin past the store porch and some man would call to her, "Hey, Sugar! What's on de rail for de lizard?" Then again I would hear some man say, "I got to have my ground-rations. If one woman can't take care of it, I gits me another one." One man told a woman to hold her ear close, because he had a bug to put in her ear. He was sitting on a box. She stooped over to hear whatever it was he had to whisper to her. Then she straightened up sharply and pulled away from him. "Why, you!" she exclaimed. "The idea of such a thing! Talking like dat to me, when you know I'm a good church-worker, and you a deacon!" He didn't seem to be ashamed at all. "Dat's just de point I'm coming out on, sister. Two clean sheets can't dirty one 'nother, you know." There was general laughter, as the deacon moved his foot so that I could get in the store door. I happened to hear a man talking to another in a chiding manner and say, "To save my soul, I can't see what you fooled with her for. I'd just as soon pick up a old tin can out of the trash pile."

But what I really loved to hear was the menfolks holding a "lying" session. That is, straining against each other in telling folks tales. God, Devil, Brer Rabbit, Brer Fox, Sis Cat, Brer Bear, Lion, Tiger, Buzzard, and all the wood folk walked and talked like natural men. The wives of the story-tellers might yell from backyards for them to come and tote some water, or chop wood for the cook-stove and never get a move out of the men. The usual rejoinder was, "Oh, she's got enough to go on. No matter how much wood you chop, a woman will burn it all up to get a meal. If she got a couple of pieces, she will make it do. If you chop up a whole boxful, she will burn every stick of it. Pay her no mind." So the story-telling would go right on.

I often hung around and listened while Mama waited on

me for the sugar or coffee to finish off dinner, until she lifted her voice over the tree tops in a way to let me know that her patience was gone: "You Zora-a-a! If you don't come here, you better!" That had a promise of peach hickories in it, and I would have to leave. But I would have found out from such story-tellers as Elijah Moseley, better known as "Liege," how and why Sis Snail quit her husband, for instance. You may or may not excuse my lagging feet, if you know the circumstances of the case:

One morning soon, Liege met Sis Snail on the far side of the road. He had passed there several times in the last few years and seen Sis Snail headed towards the road. For the last three years he had stepped over her several times as she crossed the road, always forging straight ahead. But this morning he found her clean across, and she seemed mighty pleased with herself, so he stopped and asked her where she was headed for.

"Going off to travel over the world," she told him. "I done left my husband for good."

"How come, Sis Snail? He didn't ill-treat you in no ways, did he?"

"Can't exactly say he did, Brother Liege, but you take and take just so much and then you can't take no more. Your craw gits full up to de neck. De man gits around too slow to suit me, and look like I just can't break him of it. So I done left him for good. I'm out and gone. I gits around right fast, my ownself, and I just can't put up with nobody dat gits around as slow as he do."

"Oh, don't leave de man too sudden, Sis Snail. Maybe he might come to move round fast like you do. Why don't you sort of reason wid de poor soul and let him know how you feel?"

"I done tried dat until my patience is all wore out. And this last thing he done run my cup over. You know I took sick in de bed—had de misery in my side so bad till I couldn't rest in de bed. He heard me groaning and asked me what was de matter. I told him how sick I was. Told him, 'Lawd, I'm so sick!' So he said, 'If you's sick like dat, I'll go git de doctor for you.' I says, 'I sho would be mighty much obliged if *you* would.' So he took and told me, 'I don't want you laying there and suffering like that. I'll go git de doctor right away. Just lemme go git my hat.'

"So I laid there in de bed and waited for him to go git de doctor. Lawd! I was so sick! I rolled from pillar to post. After seven I heard a noise at de door, and I said, 'Lawd, I'm so glad! I knows dats my husband done come back wid de doctor.' So I hollered out and asked, 'Honey, is dat you done come back wid de doctor?' And he come growling at me and giving me a short answer wid, 'Don't try to rush me. I ain't gone yet.' It had done took him seven years to git his hat and git to de door. So I just up and left him."

Then one late afternoon, a woman called Gold, who had come to town from somewhere else, told the why and how of races that pleased me more than what I learned about race derivations later on in Ethnology. This was her explanation:

God did not make folks all at once. He made folks sort of in His spare time. For instance one day He had a little time on his hands, so He got the clay, seasoned it the way He wanted it, then He laid it by and went on to doing something more important. Another day He had some spare moments, so He rolled it all out, and cut out the human shapes, and stood them all up against His long gold fence to dry while He did some important creating. The human shapes all got dry, and when He found time, He blowed the breath of life in them. After that, from time to time, He would call everybody up, and give them spare parts. For instance, one day He called everybody and gave out feet and eyes. Another time He give out toe-nails that Old Maker figured they could use. Anyhow, they had all that they got up to now. So then one day He said, "Tomorrow morning, at seven o'clock *sharp*, I aim to give out color. Everybody be here on time. I got plenty of creating to do tomorrow, and I want to give out this color and get it over *wid. Everybody* be 'round de throne at seven o'clock tomorrow morning!"

So next morning at seven o'clock, God was sitting on His throne with His big crown on His head and seven suns circling around His head. Great multitudes was standing around the throne waiting to get their color. God sat up there and looked east, and He looked west, and He looked north and He looked Australia, and blazing worlds were falling off His teeth. So He looked over to His left and moved His hands over a crowd and said, "You's yellow people!" They all bowed low and said, "Thank you, God," and they went on off. He looked at another crowd, moved His hands over them and said, "You's red folks!" They made their manners and said, "Thank you, Old Maker," and they went on off. He looked towards the center and moved His hand over another crowd and said, "You's white folks!" They bowed low and said, "Much obliged, Jesus," and they went on off. Then God looked way over to the right and said, "Look here, Gabriel, I miss a lot of multitudes from around the throne this morning." Gabriel looked too, and said, "Yessir, there's a heap of multitudes missing from round de throne this morning." So God sat there an hour and a half and waited. Then He called

Gabriel and said, "Looka here, Gabriel, I'm sick and tired of this waiting. I got plenty of creating to do this morning. You go find them folks and tell 'em they better hurry on up here and they expect to get any color. Fool with me, and I won't give out no more."

So Gabriel run on off and started to hunting around. Way after while, he found the missing multitudes lying around on the grass by the Sea of Life, fast asleep. So Gabriel woke them up and told them, "You better get up from there and come on up to the throne and get your color. Old Maker is might wore out from waiting. Fool with Him and He won't give out no more color."

So as the multitudes heard that, they all jumped up and went running towards the throne hollering, "Give us our color! We want our color! We got just as much right to color as anybody else." So when the first ones got to the throne, they tried to stop and be polite. But the ones coming on behind got to pushing and shoving so till the first ones got shoved all up against the throne so till the throne was careening all over to one side. So God said, "Here! Here! Git back! Git back!" But they was keeping up such a racket that they misunderstood Him, and thought He said, "Git black!" So they just got black, and kept the thing a-going.

In one way or another, I heard dozens more of these tales. My father and his preacher associates told the best stories on the church. Papa, being moderator of the South Florida Baptist Association, had numerous preacher visitors just before the Association met, to get the politics of the thing all cut and dried before the meetings came off. After it was decided who would put such and such a motion before the house, who would second it, and whom my father would recognize first and things like that, a big story-telling session would get under way on our front porch, and very funny stories at the expense of preachers and congregations would be told.

No doubt, these tales of God, the Devil, animals and natural elements seemed ordinary enough to most people in the village. But many of them stirred up fancies in me. It did not surprise me at all to hear that the animals talked. I had suspected it all along. Or let us say, that I wanted to suspect it. Life took on a bigger perimeter by expanding on these things. I picked up glints and gleams out of what I heard and stored it away to turn it to my own uses. The wind would sough through the tops of the tall, long-leaf pines and say things to me. I put in the words that the sounds put into me. Like "Woo woo, you wooo!" The tree was talking to me, even when I did not catch the words. It was talking and telling me things. I have mentioned the tree near our house that got so friendly I named it "the loving pine." Finally all of my playmates called it that too. I used to take a seat at the foot of that tree and play for hours without any toys. We talked about everything in my world. Sometimes we just took it out in singing songs. That tree had a mighty fine bass voice when it really took a notion to let it out.

There was another tree that used to creep up close to the house around sundown and threaten me. It used to put on a skull-head with a crown on it every day at sundown and make motions at me when I had to go out on the back porch to wash my feet after supper before going to bed. It never bothered around during the day. It was just another pine tree about a hundred feet tall then, standing head and shoulders above a grove. But let the dusk begin to fall, and it would put that crown on its skull and creep in close. Nobody else ever seemed to notice what it was up to but me. I used to wish it would go off somewhere and get lost. But every evening I would have to look to see, and every time, it would be right there, sort of shaking and shivering and bowing its head at me.

I used to wonder if sometime it was not going to come in the house.

When I began to make up stories I cannot say. Just from one fancy to another, adding more and more detail until they seemed real. People seldom see themselves changing.

So I was making little stories to myself, and have no memory of how I began. But I do remember some of the earliest ones.

I came in from play one day and told my mother how a bird had talked to me with a tail so long that while he sat up in the top of the pine tree his tail was dragging the ground. It was a soft beautiful bird tail, all blue and pink and red and green. In fact I climbed up the bird's tail and sat up the tree and had a long talk with the bird. He knew my name, but I didn't know how he knew it. In fact, the bird had come a long way just to sit and talk with me.

Another time, I dashed into the kitchen and told Mama how the lake had talked with me, and invited me to walk all over it. I told the lake I was afraid of getting drowned, but the lake assured me it wouldn't think of doing *me* like that. No, indeed! Come right on and have a walk. Well, I stepped out on the lake and walked all over it. It didn't even wet my feet. I could see all the fish and things swimming around under me, and they all said hello, but none of them bothered me. Wasn't that nice?

My mother said that it was. My grandmother glared at me like open-faced hell and snorted.

"Luthee!" (She lisped.) "You hear dat young 'un stand up here and lie like dat? And you ain't doing nothing to break her of it? Grab her! Wring her coat tails over her head and wear out a handful of peach hickories on her back-side! Stomp her guts out! Ruin her!"

"Oh, she's just playing," Mama said indulgently.

"Playing! Why dat lil' heifer is lying just as fast as a horse can trot. Stop her! Wear her back-side out. I bet if I lay my hands on her she'll stop it. I vominates a lying tongue."

Mama never tried to break me. She'd listen sometimes, and sometimes she wouldn't. But she never seemed displeased.

D I S C U S S I O N   G U I D E

1. Zora reportedly made significant parts of herself up. Why do you think she did this? What parts of *Dust Tracks on a Road*, if any, seem suspect?

2. Zora's memoir was considered controversial by many. Why do you think that was the case?

3. In her foreword to the 1991 edition, Maya Angelou notes that Zora makes no reference to the overt White hostility that she surely witnessed growing up in the rural south. Discuss what seems to be a glaring omission.

4. How do you think growing up in an all-Black town influenced Zora?

5. What do you make of Zora's characterizations of the Whites she comes in contact with? Is she implying that the nicest people she met as a child were White?

6. Discuss the differences in the way Zora was treated by her father and her mother.

7. What do you think of Zora's argument *against* race pride and race consciousness? Do you see a contradiction in her point of view and her work as a champion of Black culture?

ZORA NEALE HURSTON, OUR LITERARY *SHE*-RO

Published Works: *Jonah's Gourd Vine*, 1934; *Mules and Men*, 1935; *Their Eyes Were Watching God*, 1937; *Tell My Horse*, 1938; *Moses, Man of the Mountain*, 1939; *Dust Tracks on a Road*, 1942; *Seraph on the Suwanee*, 1948

Home Base: Eatonville, Florida

Claim to Fame: Hurston was the first African-American to publish a volume of Black American folklore (*Mules and Men*). Having published more than 50 short stories, essays and plays, she was the most prolific Black female writer of her time.

Unconventional, spunky, free-thinking, funny, outspoken. Sound like the description of a sister you'd like to meet? Well, while we are no longer blessed with the physical presence of literary genius Zora Neale Hurston, you can get to know her through her work.

Her memoir, *Dust Tracks on a Road*, will shed light on how she was shaped by a childhood in rural Eatonville, Florida, the only incorporated all-Black town in America. Zora was born in 1891, the fifth of eight children to John Hurston, a preacher, town alderman and three-time Eatonville mayor, and Lucy, a former country schoolteacher.

Zora's bold and bodacious spirit shone through even as a child, as evidenced by her clashes with her authoritarian father. *Dust Tracks* offers many examples of this volatile relationship, such as the time her father asked each Hurston child to share over dinner what they wanted Santa Claus to bring them in a few days. Zora's big brothers each wanted a baseball uniform. Ben and Joel wanted air rifles. Her sister wanted patent leather pumps and a belt. Zora writes, "Suddenly a beautiful vision came before me. Two things could work together. My Christmas present could take me to the end of the world," a place about which she had been daydreaming. Zora happily tells her father, "I want a fine black riding horse with white leather saddle and bridles." Her papa gasped and then exploded, "It's a sin and a shame! Lemme tell you something right now, my young lady; you ain't White. Always trying to wear de big hat! I don't know how you got in this family nohow. You ain't like none of de rest of my young 'uns."

Indeed, this uniqueness is reflected in the reported creative license Zora took with this memoir. In the afterword to this controversial account of Zora's life, Henry Louis Gates, Jr., notes that she did make up significant parts of her life "like a masquerader putting on a disguise for the ball." But what's as real as ever in *Dust Tracks,* as well as in most of her other work, is her "mastery of the language and linguistic rituals spoken and written both by the masters of the Western tradition and by ordinary members of the Black community," writes Gates. In the memoir, "she constantly shifts back and forth between her literate narrator's voice and the highly idiomatic Black voice."

Zora takes a similar approach in her critically acclaimed

Their Eyes Were Watching God, which tells the story of a woman coming into her own, finding her own voice. She shifts between first person and a blend of first and third person in this bold, feminist novel.

Zora's skill as an expert translator of Black idiom was born out of years of researching Black folklore. After studying anthropology at Barnard with Franz Boas, who pioneered the discipline in the United States, she obtained a research fellowship from the Association for the Study of Negro Life and History and headed South. When the fellowship money fell short, she enlisted a White patron, who contracted Hurston to "compile and collect the music, poetry, folklore, literature, hoodoo, conjure, manifestations of art and kindred subjects related to and existing among the North American Negro." For a $200 monthly stipend, Zora agreed not to share her findings without the patron's permission. Finding a forum for the lore she had compiled proved to be her biggest challenge. But she soon decided on something she felt would bring the language and experience to life—the stage. Zora collaborated with Langston Hughes for what was to become the best known of her theatrical ventures, *Mule Bone*. While neither lived to see the work performed, Zora enjoyed moderate success with the folklore concerts she produced after leaving the payroll of her benefactor. She was later awarded a Guggenheim Fellowship, which she used to conduct ethnographic research in Haiti. Eventually, Zora's fieldwork found its way onto the written page. Her career as a novelist began with the publication of *Jonah's Gourd Vine* in 1934. Hurston went on to publish six books in eight years and countless stories and essays in important journals and periodicals of the day.

Amazingly, by the mid-'40s, Zora had fallen into relative

obscurity, the protest implicit in her art overlooked as race novels, like those by Richard Wright, emerged. By 1950, Zora was working as a maid in Miami. In 1960, she died penniless in a Florida welfare home.

Her sad ending made her rediscovery in the '70s all the more bittersweet. Generated primarily by Black female authors looking to trace their own literary lineage, the new attention given Zora was significant in that it reflected an appreciation for something that many had once found degrading—our own vernacular speech and rituals. But more than anything, women writers identified with Zora's ahead-of-her-time, feminist stance.

Part III

Insider Tips for Starting and Sustaining a Book Club

CHAPTER ONE

Nothing to It But to Do It
Organizing Your Book Club

We all have a friend, or perhaps it's you yourself, who can always be counted on for a good party: the right number and mix of interesting people, good music, great food, impeccable ambiance, the comfort of familiarity and the excitement of surprise. To top it all off, this entertaining sister makes it look so easy—every little thing in place, including the upsweep of her immaculate dreadlocks. But don't be fooled. It looks effortless because the thought and work have been done beforehand. You too will need to lay the groundwork for your successful book club prior to the first meeting.

First and foremost on your agenda: What do you want the book club to do for you? How you answer this question will heavily impact every decision you make for forming the group. Do you love to read and are looking for a casual exchange among sisterfriends with a book as the jumping-off point for personal sharing? Or are you seeking more academic enrichment, where serious, well-thought-out discussions about the plot and character development, the author's voice and the authenticity of time, place and cultural experience take a front seat to the social chitchat that can easily work its way into the book exchange? You will choose the members you want to join you based on this vision. If you know your time is limited, perhaps you'll only want to meet every two months; and if you have a specific interest in the advancement of the race, maybe you want to start a group that only reads revolutionary books or those that are heavy on social commentary. Groups with these clearly defined goals exist across the country and all are worthy, exciting ventures. So, what's it going to be for you?

When the three of us decided to start the Go On Girl! Book Club, we had a meeting to plan our first meeting. We were clear that we wanted our group to look and feel like anything but work. Relaxed, loosely structured and full of fun was our MO. We also determined that as a group, we only wanted to read books by writers of African descent; whether they were male or female didn't matter. And finally we concluded that the titles we read should be varied—the heavy, cultural stuff that is a favorite of Lynda's, mixed with Tracy's coming-of-age preferences, Monique's human-interest leanings and then everything else in between.

While it's important to establish some basic guidelines for the group you'll start—how many members and what the demographic will be; the attitude of the meetings; the theme, if any, for the books read—don't determine all the directives yourself. Leave room for discussion and decisions amongst the entire group during your first organizing meeting; no one likes to be dictated to. If everyone is part of the planning, then everyone is more likely to buy into the final plan.

15 Reasons to Start or Join a Book Club

1. You welcome a friendly forum for discussing important issues
2. You want to give your critical thinking skills a workout
3. Reading for you is no longer something your grade-school teacher makes you do, it's something you choose to do
4. You realize reading can be emotionally freeing. If you come to a sad part in the story, the book doesn't tell you to stop crying. Likewise, you can laugh to your heart's content
5. You want to broaden your literary experience by being introduced to books you wouldn't necessarily read on your own
6. You need a motivating factor —like the guilt or awkwardness of showing up for a meeting unprepared—to help you make the selfish commitment to yourself to read
7. You just finished a book you love and would like someone other than your disinterested mate to discuss it with
8. You're ready to do the exciting work that leads to an open mind and an open voice
9. You're seeking social release
10. You're looking for a relatively inexpensive hobby
11. You love to entertain and to be entertained
12. Constant "baby talk" with your child has you pining for adult conversation and stimulation
13. You desire networking and nurturing opportunities
14. Your ears are burning from the mere thought of hearing diverse points of view
15. You long for a wholesome feeling of belonging

CHAPTER TWO

The Who
Choosing Your Members

All women, all men. Gen Xers, boomers, sorors, church members. Just plain folk from all walks of life. They're all groups that can work, but it's important to realize that the makeup of your book club will bear heavily on the experience.

A homogeneous group allows you to interact with readers who share many of the same interests and similar goals. As African-American women, Go On Girls, for instance, have in common our interest in works by writers of the African Diaspora, and we also tend to face many of the same issues. Having a circle of sisters who can relate is absolutely affirming, uplifting and satisfying to the soul. A group of new mothers, single women or Southerners recently transplanted up North would be able to forge a similar bond. This shared demographic may or may not influence the titles you read, but it can certainly make your exchanges all the more fulfilling.

Heterogeneous groups, meanwhile, celebrate the differences and expose members to alternate ways of thinking and experiences. Though Go On Girls are all Black women, our membership is not restricted by age, profession or marital status, so we're still a study in variety. We find that this diversity only adds to the book club experience. Imagine a discussion on Langston Hughes' *Best of Simple* between older members,

who can recall how the short stories—first published in the
'40s—were common reference points at Black gatherings of
the day, and twentysomething members who are only just discovering the wisdom of Simple. Belonging to a group comprised of people with different personal, professional,
geographical, spiritual and philosophical backgrounds is
bound to broaden your literary and life perspectives. Just
think of how stimulating a discussion on a book that addresses sexuality issues would be among straight *and* gay book club
members.

Gender makeup ranks high among considerations when
determining a group mix. A desire to regularly carve time out
of our busy schedules and get together with our girlfriends
was a primary goal when we started Go On Girl, so we never
considered including men. Now all-male groups are growing
in popularity. Says one member of a Brooklyn-based group of
brothers, "The book club is one way for us to connect and
reflect on important issues—our families, our constant struggle to hold onto our manhood and dignity in a hostile society
that threatens to take it away, our jobs and our pain—in a safe
environment. If I said, 'Hey guys, let's get together to discuss
these issues,' some would come, but most would do so reluctantly. But if I say, 'Let's get together and talk about Nathan
McCall's new book,' the brothers would come because it
sounds sexier, more enticing, and ultimately we would end up
discussing the important issues raised by the book anyway."

An argument can also be made for coed groups. They hold
great appeal because of the lively discussions gender differences tend to jump-start. Some of our chapters invited the
men in their lives to join them for a discussion of Nathan
McCall's autobiography *Makes Me Wanna Holler*. McCall's

account of growing up Black and male in America and how that perspective influenced his life choices provoked a raucous debate. The women all agreed that the discussion was enhanced by men being present to shed personal insight.

Familiarity among members is also something to consider as you ask people to join. While the founding chapter of the Go On Girls was primarily comprised of friends, some of our newer chapters have formed as a result of informational mixers held in response to the hundreds of letters we get each year from women who've read about us and are seeking an opportunity to connect with other women, a primary goal of some of our sisters in small towns where they feel isolated. These Go On Girls say hooking up with complete strangers hasn't hampered their book-club experience at all. In fact, a lack of familiarity in the beginning may actually enhance group discussions, since it's sometimes easy to lose focus when members know each other so well and have so much more to talk about.

The number of members is key, since it can affect the type of exchange your group will have. To prevent your discussions from feeling like a class lecture, you may want to keep membership below 20: If you have to raise your hand and wait to make a point, then the fun is lost. Besides, some people may be uncomfortable speaking before what may appear to be a large group. An intimate discussion where every member has an opportunity to join in is more likely with even fewer than 20. We do suggest at least six members, so there are enough voices to make the conversation lively. There are, however, some clear advantages to operating as a somewhat larger group, such as never worrying about having enough people for a stimulating discussion should some members be absent.

Our chapters each have no more than 12 because intimacy has always been a priority for us. Since we envisioned having these meetings in our homes, we knew smaller meant more manageable, both in terms of the discussion and the physical comfort level. Providing a cozy yet nonconfining atmosphere should be the goal.

Finding members is not as difficult as one may expect, even in towns where few of us live. If word of mouth isn't generating enough interest from the right type of members you seek, post notices in places that book lovers frequent, such as bookstores and libraries. Or take out a small ad in a local paper. And if you're looking for members who share your interests in books and other concerns, put the word out among groups in which you or they may already be a member, say, a professional organization, church auxiliary or community coalition.

Choosing a good member shouldn't be based on the number of books someone has read. More important is what have they read and what do they want to read? Are they as enthusiastic and committed about the reading group as you? Will they bring something to the discussion? Be probing now or be prepared to pay later. Nearly every Go On Girl chapter has their own torrid tale of truants, tardys and ticks, those who rarely read the books but feed off of the opinions of the more conscientious members.

It's not too much of an exaggeration to say choosing your fellow book-club members can be as tricky as choosing a mate. It's all about the right fit. Conflicting points of view can make for a stimulating session, but conflicting personalities may create tension, and that could impede group unity. Since you can't possibly predict exactly how each member will respond to one another, the best you can do is assemble a group that at least has the potential to get along. As you consider members, keep in mind the personality types that complement each other. You wouldn't want, for example, a group made up of all the quiet and reserved people you know, nor would you want a group bursting with big egos. Knowing how to manage different personality types will help your group as well. Listed here are a few of the more challenging types you may encounter and suggestions on how to handle them.

Long-winded Leslie

Members who love to talk are certainly an asset to any discussion group, but if they don't know how to share the floor, like Leslie, they take away from the discourse. Everyone should have ample opportunity to take part in the discussion.

You may find it necessary to come up with a policy that specifically addresses the more verbose among you. See Chapter 8 for details on handling this potential discussion buster.

Silent Sondra

Sondra is at the other end of the spectrum. Here's the member whose voice you'd never recognize. She attends every meeting but skips out on the discussion. Her reasons for not joining in could run the gamut from shyness to low self-esteem. Whatever her reasons, an attempt should be made to draw her in. First, create a forum where everyone can feel comfortable sharing their thoughts without fear of being shot down. Secondly, ask questions throughout the discussion of *all* group members, including her. If you don't direct questions to the others, but ask her in an effort to get her talking, she may feel like she's being put on the spot.

Rambling Renee

This enthusiastic member has a lot to say, but just isn't very good at organizing her thoughts. Asking pointed questions of her and redirecting her when she moves ahead to a point not yet being discussed should help keep her on track. Members like this would best benefit from a discussion driven by a set of questions, which would help them stay focused.

Diane the Drifter

Diane is a distant cousin of Renee the Rambler. While both have difficulty staying focused, at least Renee sticks to the subject at hand. Diane, meanwhile, drifts off to matters that are meaningless to the discussion. An interruption is the only sure way to bring this girl back to shore.

Danitra the Devil's Advocate

There's one in every group. If you say the sky is blue, she'll argue the opposite for no apparent reason other than to stir things up. Sometimes playing the Devil's advocate can be a conversation stimulant. After all, if everyone held the same opinion there would not be much to talk about.

Righteous Robin

This sister is always right, and you, of course, are always wrong. There really is no place in a group discussion for this trying type. There is no wrong or right interpretation of literature. How a reader responds to a work is most often determined by her life experience. And since there are bound to be differences in our lives, there will be different assessments of what is being discussed. Make it clear right from the start that members who can't respect the opinions of others should just move on.

CHAPTER THREE

You're Invited
Planning Your First Meeting

─────────

CREATE EXCITEMENT!

It's true. You only get one chance to make a first impression—make it count. Now that you've decided who to invite to the initial planning meeting, get them revved up about the idea from the moment go.

• Send a brief note explaining your concept for a reading group, along with a formal invitation to attend the inaugural gathering.

• Be creative in the design and wording of the invite. There's a lot you can do on the computer, and you can even use popular book titles to cleverly deliver the information—i.e., "Are You *Waiting to Exhale*? Then on Saturday, June 22, perform a *Disappearing Act* and *Get Your Groove Back* with 12 other sisters who share your love of reading."

• Send your invitation out in plenty of time for everyone to clear their schedules—about four to six weeks in advance is suggested (any earlier and folks are liable to forget). Choose a meeting place that's convenient for everyone, and include directions to be on the safe side.

• Enclose one or two articles about the popularity and benefits of reading groups. No doubt, book clubs are hot—help your new members get on fire!

• You'll have a lot of ground to cover in the first meeting, but limit the time to two or three hours. You don't want to scare people right out of the box by requiring an overwhelming time commitment.

• Because it's important not to leave the first meeting without sound ground rules covered, it may be advisable not to plan on actually discussing a book at the first meeting. If, however, you like the idea of whetting everyone's appetite with an actual book discussion, limit the exchange to one hour, and go all out to select a provocative title with far-reaching appeal (we highly recommend any of the books excerpted in Part II of this book). If the book is available in paperback, buying copies of it and sending it out as a gift with the invitation is a generous act that will go a long way to getting your group off to a great start. A local Black bookstore you do regular business with may be willing to give you a nice discount on the cost, especially if club members plan to buy their books there.

• If the gathering will be the first time many of the potential members meet, plan an ice-breaker. In the invitation, you can ask each guest to bring a favorite book to briefly share with the group. Or you can prepare an interactive, getting-to-know-you activity, like the one the St. Louis Go On Girls greeted us with when we visited their city for the club's annual awards weekend. A typed list of questions required us to ask each other about one another for the answers. For example, one question was: "Who has more than five signed Black books in their library?" while another one asked us to identify two people in the room originally from the South. The one who answered all the questions first received a prize.

CREATE STRUCTURE

Even the most free-form group needs some organizational guidelines. Consensus on the general purpose of the group, the tone of the meetings and the types of books to be read is essential. Then there are the additional operating procedures to be decided on: Will your group collect dues and how will they be used? Who will lead the discussions? How often will you meet and what will be your attendance requirements?

Here's a general checklist of issues to discuss and some considerations to take into account when deciding on the club's format:

WHO'S THE BOSS?

A group gets started usually because someone wants it. Unable to find an existing book club to join, they do the groundwork of getting a new one off and running. In many cases, the group already has a leader in this person, someone in charge or who is willing to set things in motion to form a successful reading group. But once the group is formed, this same person isn't necessarily still involved in running things.

Most groups try to keep it simple, and they shy away from titles with responsibilities attached to them. In fact, very few groups that we know of have a president, secretary, treasurer. Many do, however, have a facilitator, someone in charge of the housekeeping part of the meeting. Go On Girl! chapters tend to rotate this duty yearly. As for leading the book discussions, this can be one person particularly adept at keeping the conversation going and inviting everyone's participation, or you can rotate the responsibility. Because as a group we write letters of feedback and encouragement to the authors of the books we read, we take notes on our book discussions. A questionnaire with about 15 standard points is completed for each book, and someone in the group simply volunteers to fill it out for the month. A secretary to send out meeting notices isn't really necessary for our groups, because we like to set a standard meeting date and time for each month—say the second Sunday every month at 3 P.M.—and we make a calendar for the year of who's hosting where. It's given to each member at the beginning of the year, and no reminders are expected, although some hosts like to send a postcard or make "don't forget" telephone calls. People in book clubs are generally busy, so, again, everything is best streamlined.

WHAT'S THE GROUP'S ATTITUDE?

Most book clubs we know of like to keep things informal. The discussion is free-form but focused, and everyone feels comfortable sharing in no particular order. If the group gets too off track in its discussion, by osmosis someone always speaks up to get us back on course. The operating rules are usually discussed and understood by members of a reading group but seldom written down. Of course the Go On Girl! Book Club is another animal entirely. While our chapters are small—no more than 12 members—our guidelines or bylaws are extensive, largely because we've tried to offer our new chapters the kind of extensive blueprint this book now provides you with. The local founding chapter the three of us belong to structures its meeting in three parts: discussion of any business, general announcements and personal update exchange; discussion of the book; then sharing of the meal.

WHAT BOOKS WILL BE READ?

The one who pulled the group together may have already clearly defined what kinds of books the group will read, but this might still be open for discussion. Will the group only read works written by women? By persons of African descent, African-Americans only, any person of color, or any work about people of color regardless of the author's race? Are only books written in the last two years up for consideration or will the book club begin with works from the Harlem Renaissance and work its way up to contemporary writings? Will the group lock in on one specific genre, say novels or mysteries, or will it seek to choose a book in a different genre for each meeting? Once these questions are answered, then the group must decide how the reading list will be formed. Will a few in-the-know members make the list? Will each person hosting the meeting select the book for that meeting (the most common method)? Or will the group adopt a list from Blackboard's best-seller list or form it based on established critics' choices? All can work, but you have to decide on which to implement.

HOW OFTEN AND WHERE WILL WE MEET?

This is nuts-and-bolts stuff that must be nailed down, and we get into it in detail in the next chapter. The main thing to remember is to try to take each member's lifestyle and time constraints into consideration, but once the group has decided on the meeting schedule, you need to stay with specific dates unless the group decides to revisit its entire meeting schedule. If you get into changing a meeting date because it's one person's anniversary or because someone has a business trip that week, you're asking for trouble.

WILL DUES BE COLLECTED, AND IF SO, HOW MUCH AND HOW WILL THEY BE SPENT?

Most small reading groups don't bother to collect dues, because basically they have no expenses. If $25 or so is collected from each member each year, it is usually used for postage and photocopying or for goodwill causes, like sending a birthday card from the group to a member. If the group meets anywhere other than in one another's homes, dues may be collected to pay space rental fees. One of our chapters considered collecting dues to be equally divided as funds to cover the hostesses' food costs, but they decided to continue with the common practice of leaving it up to the hostess to provide refreshments according to what she is willing and able to spend.

WILL FOOD BE SERVED?

We personally feel food can be the icing on the cake of a successful meeting—we look forward each year to the hearty, homemade soup we know we're going to get at Debbie's annual autumn meeting. The food doesn't have to be elaborate, nor does it have to be an all-out meal, but a little something to wet your whistle after all that talking and a few snacks are usually appreciated by all. But you don't want the food to get in the way of your central purpose—coming together to discuss books. See Chapter Five to learn how to avoid this.

WHAT WILL THE MEMBERS IN THE GROUP BE RESPONSIBLE FOR?

Few of us need another job. If anything, we need an escape, the kind of release that naturally happens when the sharing and discussion begins at a book-club meeting. The Go On Girls, like most members of reading groups, have two primary duties: obtain and read the book each month and come to the monthly meeting prepared to actively discuss it. The following additional responsibilities might also be required, depending on how you structure your group:

• Host one or more meetings each year, and provide refreshments.

• Pay any dues the group may set.

• Pitch in and help with occasional mailings or planning for any special activities, like inviting an author to attend a meeting.

Just how your group has defined its mission may require a little more of a commitment. Some of our chapters have pledged to attend at least one book-related event or reading as a group per year. Others take on even more ambitious projects that require more time and energy, like sponsoring junior chapters for young girls. One Go On Girl summed it up this way: "The members of your group have to decide whether they're coming together to save the world or to save themselves, or both."

WILL THE GROUP HAVE A NAME?

We wouldn't bring a new life into the world without bestowing a name upon it, and though certainly a less magnanimous thing, an infant book club still warrants a special name so its family members can intimately refer to it and even be reminded of its mission. What you name your club says something about you and your hopes and dreams for it, not terribly unlike the thinking that goes into naming a child. The author Benilde Little chose to christen her daughter Baldwin in honor of the genius of her literary favorite James Baldwin. "I didn't want her to have a name from Africa but one grounded in America, because we've made a contribution here. Baldwin is my hero. He lived his truth, which is what I'm trying to do," says Little. The fact that we chose the name "Go On Girl! Book Club" speaks to the self-affirming attitude of our group. A close runner-up for our name was "Black and Read," for its play on color and meaning—for sure our logo would have made the most of ebony and crimson! The African-American Women's Literary Guild was also suggested but later voted down, because it sounded too serious. We wanted to keep the attitude of our group light; again, nothing that reflected the stodginess of work for us. The only work we wanted to do when we formed was work of the inner kind, though the national organization now accepts the challenge of external work, like turning others on to the joy of reading and encouraging the writings of those of African descent.

YOUR CHECKLIST FOR PLANNING AND
RUNNING THE FIRST MEETING

❏ Be clear about what you want the book club to do for you.

❏ Seek out members who will be committed and share the same objectives.

❏ Send out a brief note about your idea for the book club, along with invitations, to prospective members.

❏ Prepare a suggested reading list or ask potential members to bring ideas about what to read with them.

❏ Make a mental agenda or jot down notes for yourself, so you can be sure to cover all the basics at this important meeting. No need to pass out an agenda to everyone; it seems too formal.

❏ Plan to serve light refreshments.

❏ Open the meeting by describing the vision for the club, and ask for feedback. Then confirm that everyone is on board and committed to the mission.

❏ Engage in an ice-breaker activity.

❏ Establish your book selection process.

❏ Set the meeting calendar.

❏ Create and distribute a member list with telephone numbers and addresses.

❏ Decide who will be the group facilitator or the one responsible for housekeeping duties, like informing members of changed meetings. Select any additional officers or persons to carry out specific tasks, like taking the notes on book discussions if you plan to communicate with authors and publishers.

❑ Provide take-home materials for each member (optional), such as a list of phone numbers for area bookstores, libraries or other helpful contacts, and any reminders. Copies of articles about book clubs, new literary works, Black authors and literary events are also a good idea.

❑ Have fun! There will be no midterm, final or pop quiz!

THE BOTTOM LINE OF BEING
IN A BOOK CLUB

Participating in a book club might well be one of the least expensive hobbies you can take up. For as little as the price of a paperback book each month, you can have a stimulating and enjoyable exchange with others who share your love of reading. In some cases, you can get off even cheaper if the book is available at your local library! Additional minimal costs may be as follows:

- The price of food you serve when you're the hostess

- Postage fees for mailings (meeting reminders, etc.)

- The small rental fee you may have to pay for your meeting location if you don't get together in one another's homes

- If most of your members have children, you may want to chip in and hire a babysitter to engage the kids in the yard or in another part of the house while you're meeting.

- If your group plans to take part in additional activities, like hosting a holiday party for the members and their mates, or if it has a charitable agenda, such as financially contributing to a reading program at a homeless shelter, there may be some added costs involved.

- To be a stickler, one might include the cost of getting to the meetings.

CHAPTER FOUR

Same Place, Same Time?
Deciding Where and When to Meet

———

SET A MEETING SCHEDULE EARLY AND STICK TO IT

Go On Girls can't wait to meet each month; for many, it's the only time they regularly etch out for themselves. Most reading groups, in fact, meet monthly, though there are no set-in-stone rules. So if you and your friends can only get together quarterly, go for it! No matter how frequently you meet or the day and time of the week you choose, maximize your chances for a successful group by setting the meeting calendar early on and not deviating from it. If the group decides that the third Saturday of every month at 3 P.M. is the meeting date and time, then the third Saturday at three it is. That little bit of structure isn't much to ask, and it establishes the meeting—indeed, the group—as a priority for one day each month. Plus, you eliminate the nuisance of having to call around and check if the meeting is this week or next, or if the date works for everybody. Spacing the meetings a full month apart—instead of on the second Wednesday in March, then the first Wednesday in April, for instance—is also a good idea. It allows members ample time to read.

While most groups, including the Go On Girls, meet year-round, some book clubs, who have suffered from poor attendance during the summer months when many travel, do not meet in July and August. That doesn't mean, however, that they don't read during this time. One group we know of takes the summer off but selects a weighty, thick tome to read over these two months, and they discuss it when the group reconvenes in September. The members express a great sense of accomplishment having read every page of a 910-page anthology like *Brotherman: The Odyssey of Black Men in America.*

HAVE A TIME FRAME FOR YOUR MEETING

Decide how long your meetings will last, and start and finish on time. Not to do so is inconsiderate of the hostess and of members who may have family obligations waiting for them at home. Once members see you're going to move ahead with the meeting at the appointed hour, they will make the effort to be on time. Book clubs tend to meet for two to three hours, and if some want to hang around after the meeting and the hostess is game, ain't nobody's business if they do.

It also helps to establish a format for your meetings, so everyone knows what to expect, something like book discussion the first hour, eating and socializing the second. Our own group allows for arrival chitchat the first 15 minutes, then we discuss housekeeping business, which usually takes about ten minutes, followed by about an hour of book discussion, then the meal.

HOME IS USUALLY WHERE THE HEART IS

Most book clubs take turns meeting in the members' homes. The Go On Girls like this idea because we feel we can best relax, reflect and let loose in our book discussions. We have held a few meetings at restaurants, but if you're not seated in a private dining room or in a quiet corner of the restaurant on one of its slow days, you run the risk of disturbing others or having them disturb you. We also like the home experience because sharing our homes has become a way of sharing ourselves. Of course, if you meet at homes, the space and comfort factor may limit the number of people who can be in the club. With the help of a few folding chairs, none of our members has had difficulty hosting the 12 of us. If other reasons prevent the hostess from holding the meeting at her home (in transition from one apartment to another or other members in the household would make a successful meeting difficult), all she need do is ask if someone else in the group would be willing to make their home available, and she would still provide the refreshments. There's always a way to work it out.

If your group is too large to do the home thing, or your members simply choose not to meet at one another's houses, there are several possible sites for meeting on the cheap—community rooms in apartment buildings, libraries and schools; meeting rooms at churches; the conference room at one of the members' place of employment; the local bookstore your club patronizes. If you choose to meet in a restaurant, aside from reserving the most private area, it's best to discuss housekeeping business after the meal has been ordered, socialize while dining, and discuss the book after the table has been cleared and while you're waiting on and enjoying after-the-meal tea or coffee. With all of the meeting locales mentioned, make sure the space is conducive to having an effective book discussion (see the next chapter for more on creating the right atmosphere).

DEALING WITH ABSENCES AND TARDINESS

It's a fact of life that not everyone will make every meeting, and there's likely to be someone late to every meeting as well. But do establish at the outset that members are expected to be on time and to attend all sessions, except for emergencies, business trips and family obligations that can't be postponed. A reading group, like any other organization, has its own dynamic, which is seriously disturbed when the configuration changes because several people are absent or because it's constantly interrupted by late arrivals.

If attendance is not a chronic problem for your group, then a simple call to the hostess as early as possible that you can't make it or that you're running late should suffice. We must admit, however, that absences and tardiness have been cancerous, affecting most of our chapters at some point or another. We decided to set guidelines: Four absences in a year (whether with warning or not) and the group will politely ask you to withdraw your membership. A member can request a leave of absence for circumstances like a medical condition or a temporary relocation for work, if they plan to be away for no more than six months and no less than four months. We've also made provisions for lateness: Tardy by more than 30 minutes and it counts as a half absence. With these rules in place, our attendance has improved dramatically, and those who can't make the commitment leave with no hard feelings.

ABOUT GUESTS, CHILDREN AND NEWCOMERS

After a few meetings of your book club, the group dynamics will shape itself, with members feeling very comfortable with one another. That feeling of "family," a reason why many will join in the first place, may be lost with a revolving door of visiting guests. You can handle guests in a number of ways, but what you almost certainly don't want are folks popping in at random who haven't even read the book. Consider these options:

Simply do not allow guests. It's all right to view your monthly meeting as a sacred time for its "family" members. Outsiders can create issues of confidentiality and the comfort level can be threatened.

Decide who will be welcomed. If you plan to allow guests, should only those who meet the demographics of the group be allowed to visit? Should only potential members be invited? Should a community person or professional who has special relevance to the book's theme be invited? How many times can the same person come as a guest?

Determine when guests will be allowed to attend. Some groups designate one meeting a year as the time when each member can invite a guest. Others allow the meeting's hostess to invite a guest. Whenever a guest will be joining the group, do inform the hostess well in advance so space and food provisions can be made. It's a good idea to inform the other members too, so they won't be caught off guard. When possible, all guests should read the selected book and participate in the discussion. A fresh perspective can be a very good thing.

As for children, the group should decide at the onset whether members will be allowed to bring their kids or not. Don't wait to deal with this after someone has already brought along little Shelley; the member almost definitely will take it personally if it's decided not to allow kids. Most of the Go On Girl! chapters shy away from kids at meetings. Again, this is sister-bonding time. If your child needs your attention, then you can't fully be engaged in the book discussion. And if your baby has a crying spell, as they are understandably known to do, or your five-year-old becomes fidgety because he's bored, this can create a disturbance that you and the group will be uncomfortable with. If a slightly older child sits in on a meeting, that might have consequences too—members may be reluctant to discuss or share certain topics if they think the subject matter is not suitable for young ears.

Some members in a group with kids make arrangements for a babysitter to engage their children in the yard or in a part of the house where they won't present a disturbance. Of course, the hostess should be consulted first if children will be present. Not everyone's home is child- or soundproof.

Any group with some longevity is likely to experience loss of members due to job transfers, conflicting work schedules or other personal priorities. If your group drops in membership and you can't have the kind of discussions you want, then invite newcomers. The same considerations used to form the initial group should be applied, and members can suggest people they think might be a complement. It's best not to invite a perspective member to a meeting to be "screened" or to see if they measure up. If someone in the group is recommending them, you can question your member, but ultimately you should take her word that the person will be an asset. If your book club has a ceiling on the number of members it allows, you can decide who gets to invite a new member in several ways: by randomly putting the names of members interested in bringing in a new person into a hat and drawing for the chance; by seniority based on your membership; or by attendance record, creating another incentive for members to be present and on time.

Most groups welcome new members any time the club's not

at its membership capacity, but this can mean the group is in constant flux. The argument can also be made, however, that welcoming members year-round can add new interest and excitement to the group dynamic. Regardless of when a new person joins, make sure she knows exactly what's expected of her.

CHAPTER FIVE

Let Me Entertain You
Hosting a Memorable Meeting

Most book-club meetings are held in a member's home, and great pride and delight is taken in being the hostess with the mostess. Attention should be given to the room's readiness for a productive discussion; the environment needs to be free of disruptions; and if food is to be served, let it be a delectable, unobtrusive asset to the meeting.

Some book clubs don't include food at their meetings—the Go On Girl! Book Club, to our personal taste, isn't one of them! Our members enjoy making low-fuss dishes like vegetable-and-cheese lasagna with a tossed salad for the group. Those too busy to shop and prepare a meal simply order up a smorgasbord of Chinese delights or some such other inexpensive, deliverable fare. Book clubs that choose not to have food do so because they say food often gets too much attention and takes away from the main objective of discussing books. Food, they argue, is just not essential to the goal of literary analysis and/or social camaraderie. In truth, they are right. You don't *need* food for a great meeting. An overwhelming majority of book clubs, however, do serve something, whether it be as simple as coffee and tea served with cookies after the discussion or wine with cheese and crackers. For sisters with down-home roots, in particular, our tradition of Southern hospitality may make it unthinkable to have folks over for several hours without something to wet their whistle or tantalize their taste buds. Besides, food can be emotionally bonding. Whenever we celebrate something special in our lives, food is almost always there.

If you will serve food, keep in mind the following points:

• **Don't let company catch you unprepared.** Some groups start with eating; that way the meal can already be prepared and the hostess can fully participate in the book discussion to follow.

• **If you will serve food after the discussion,** prepare it in advance and make sure that final preparations won't require you to miss more than the last five minutes of the book exchange. Remember, you're a valued member first, then the hostess. No one will be happy if you spend the entire meeting in the kitchen, not the least of all you.

• **Be mindful of your group's guidelines** for the types of foods to be served and their place in the meeting: light snacks or full-blown meals, eaten before, during or after the book discussion?

• **If you plan to serve snacks or finger foods** during the meeting, it may be better to place them in several small containers spread out around the room and easily accessible for all members. Using one big bowl or platter and placing it in one part of the room may create annoying disturbances with people getting up and down.

• **Sodas, juice, water and wine make fine beverages** for serving, but refrain from hard liquor. Things could get ugly.

• **Consider members' dietary needs** when preparing the menu.

• **Serve what's within your financial means,** unless your group has established a price range to spend on food. This is not a B. Smith contest to see who can serve the most elaborate meal.

NOTE: If your book club will meet in public or community spaces instead of in one another's homes, be sure to check the facility's rules for food and drink. They are not always allowed.

Aside from issues of food, there are several other ways to ensure a successful meeting.

• **Send out reminders** a week or so before you host. It is always appreciated, though not always mandated.

• **Surprise members with a special book-related treat,** like playing the music of the '70s during the meal to tie into a discussion of April Sinclair's *Ain't Gonna Be the Same Fool Twice*, which is set in this period. Remember, this kind of extra or any special activity at the meeting should be strictly optional. (See "Don't Just Read the Books, Bring Them to Life" in Chapter Nine for more creative ideas.)

• **Give thought to seating.** Everyone needs to be comfortable in order to fully engage in the book discussion. It also helps if everyone can see each other. That's why we personally like a circle seating arrangement. Body language and facial expression can be especially useful when trying to grasp a member's views on a book. If the furniture in your room isn't laid out this way, folding chairs or large, comfy sitting pillows can be the answer.

- **Provide proper lighting.** Save the candles or mood lighting for some other time. Adequate lighting in every part of the room where members will sit is essential. People often like to refer back to a specific part of the book when discussing it, and they need to be able to read from it or from their notes.

- **Eliminate any noise or disturbance.** If possible, plan an outing for your kids when it's your turn to host, so the members won't be disturbed by their frolic, and so the children won't be asked to do unrealistic things like be still and stay quiet. If you have a roommate—partners count here too—let them know far in advance that it's your time to host and encourage them to engage in an out-of-the-house activity. A loud stereo or TV or someone clanging pots in the kitchen can impede on one's train of thought when discussing a book.

Be mindful of other noises that can also prove to be a nuisance. For example, turn the ringer off on your phone, and turn on the answering machine. Thank your sweetie for finally cutting the grass, but ask him to put it off just a few hours longer so the power lawn mower won't be a disturbance.

- **Pet your pet later.** Your beloved cat or dog may be the source of allergy, fear or aggravation for a club member—we won't even mention the possibility of your fluffy friend getting into the main food dish! During the meeting, put your pet in an isolated area. If your cat is a whiner or your dog a barker when you close him up in a room, this can also be a disturbance if the meeting is just on the other side of the door. It may be best to conveniently schedule a grooming appointment that coincides with the time you'll be having your meeting. Be sure too that there are no stray hairs around to stimulate allergic reactions. Of course, members should never bring pets to someone else's meeting. Don't even think about asking.

CHAPTER SIX

Making a List and Checking It Twice

Selecting the Books

───────

YOU ARE WHAT YOU READ

Novels aren't the only game in town, but, more often than not, they dominate a reading group's book list. Some clubs, however, form with the express purpose of reading a specific genre, like mysteries or revolutionary works. When we founded the Go On Girl! Book Club, we knew we wanted to read broadly. We came up with 12 different genres for the year, ranging from science fiction/fantasy to social commentary, and filled in the specific book blanks by allowing the hosting member for a scheduled meeting to decide. Because we too were heavily drawn to novels, especially since they tend to get the most reviews, we set some guidelines for the three or four novels that made our list: One had to be written by a brother, another had to be penned by a new author, and the other one or two could just be. We strongly encourage your group to compose a list featuring a variety of literary forms. One of the true benefits of being in a book club is the exposure to books you wouldn't necessarily read on your own.

The Go On Girls exclusively read books by writers of

African descent, and we avail ourselves to work by both sisters and brothers. Recently, we had a debate about whether we should broaden our parameters to include nonfiction work about Blacks written by those not of the African Diaspora. The dilemma centered around Michael D'Orso's book *Like Judgment Day: The Ruin and Redemption of a Town Called Rosewood*. The book made the list but was later dropped as a required read because the author's ethnicity is not compatible with our bylaws. We strongly suggested that our members read it, however; and many of them did and were moved.

WHEN AND HOW TO SELECT THE BOOKS

In the beginning, the first Go On Girl! chapter drafted its monthly reading list for the year in December. This worked well, because the 12 of us placed our entire book order as a group, which meant purchasing nearly 150 books and amounted to a heavy price discount. While it required an up-front investment, buying our books early kept us from scampering around at the last minute to find the book of the month, and those eager beavers in the group, who seem to devour books, could get started whenever they wanted. There was a downside, however. We felt a little boxed in and unable to react to a hot, new book released after the list had been made up. We attempted to lessen this problem by coming up with an ancillary book each month that members could discuss amongst themselves outside of the meeting. That didn't completely work, because some members whose lifestyle precluded them from reading more than one book a month still missed out on reading the more current titles. Ultimately we changed our process. We now select books twice a year, each time for six months. This allows us to get newer titles on the list and be a part of the buzz about a current release.

Your book club will need to decide who chooses the books. As stated before, initially each Go On Girl! member had a chance to pick the book for the meeting she hosted. Occasionally, some in the group weren't enthusiastic about a member's choice, like when a die-hard sports fan in the club selected Jim Brown's *Out of Bounds*. But she had to read Frances Cress Welsing's heady *The Isis Papers*, which didn't particularly call her. Aside from fair being fair, a few of us were surprised by how much we enjoyed books we initially didn't want to read.

When new chapters joined our network, this "each-one-pick-one" strategy no longer worked. We wanted members in all chapters to read from the same list, and the only way to do that was to put it to a vote. Currently, each chapter nominates six books in the specified genres for the reading period. The books receiving the most nominations make the list. We are now discovering that this process too has flaws. Some of our chapters are confused about what genre to place a title in, and a book may not make the list because the vote was split in several categories. Also, some chapters aren't as privy to new book release information, so their nominations are considered too dated by other, more in-the-know chapters. To make members of all chapters aware of the many book options, we've formed a book review committee that receives updates from publishing houses and is constantly on the lookout for books to recommend. They write synopses—which appear in the club's quarterly newsletter and on our Web site—for ten or more new books each quarter. The premise? Armed with these synopses, chapters can make more informed choices when nominating books.

The idea of a book selection committee to actually choose the books for the list has been bandied about for some time. While some members don't like this approach, because they want to retain some say about what is read, others argue that with so many chapters voting—32 now—individuals really don't have that much say anyhow. The list would be a lot stronger and more current, they contend, if a committee of well-informed members, who talk to authors, receive mailings from publishers and religiously read reviews, simply made the list. Stay tuned!

PURCHASING THE BOOKS

Once the list has been settled on, consider how the books will be purchased. Some of our chapters, like the one we belong to, order as a group from a Black bookstore to get generous discounts and to keep the business in the family. Other chapters choose to do their buying individually, because some want to purchase paperbacks (they cost less and fit easier in a work bag), while others want to invest in hardcovers (they are more expensive, but they stand the test of time better, and if you're establishing a library or collecting, they are the way to go). When possible, some members prefer to check the book out of the library and decide after reading it if it's a keeper. Not buying your books in bulk also allows you to take advantage of drastically reduced books at one of the larger retail chains or a used bookstore, and sometimes a signed copy is sitting on the shelf.

Five Book Truths

• If you're a gambler, bet on the fact that each book selection will not appeal to every member. Still, respect and honor the decision of the member who recommends the book.

• Best-sellers are not always the best choices for discussion.

• If you vary the selections, you're bound to hit upon titles during the course of the year that will make each member happy.

• Books that weren't really a favorite often lead to the most provocative discussions.

• No book is a bad book, so long as you learned something, even if it's that you just can't get with a particular author's writing style.

CHAPTER SEVEN

Between the Lines
Reading the Books

Those who learn early on that reading purely for pleasure is decidedly different from reading in preparation for discussion will probably be your club's most satisfied members. We Go On Girls vary in our approach to the read of the month. First there are the very well-read among us—the ones who probably purchased the book when it was first released and had finished it even before it showed up on our reading list. For them, the selection of the month will be a luxurious second read, a more reflective read.

Then there are those of us who are still tracking down the book on Saturday, the day before we meet. These latecomers find themselves forced to read on two levels at once—to gain a basic understanding of the plot, characters, themes and structure, as well as to determine the author's purpose, interpret the characters' actions, evaluate the author's style and consider their own emotional response to the book.

Somewhere in between are those who read the selection within the month and simply leave enough time to pick up the book again for a skim just before the meeting, taking care to note their questions and key points and passages they liked.

Whatever your approach, you must at some point read with concentration and record key details, something you're not likely to do if you are reading just for enjoyment. Some find it helpful to use stickie notes to mark important points, particularly poignant passages and elements they questioned. Some members even write directly in the margins of their books.

You must have an understanding of the book's main idea to be able to discuss it effectively and be familiar with enough aspects of the story to have a discussion of any real length and quality. The times our busy schedules have kept us from finishing—or even starting—the book are a testament to that. But while we can't claim to have been intellectually stimulated that month, we do walk away with some emotional satisfaction. For unlike in some groups, Go On Girls don't let not finishing a book keep us from coming to a meeting. While we recognize that we are first and foremost a book club, we still place a high value on connecting with one another. For many of us, the monthly book-club meeting is one of the few opportunities we have to just hang with the girls. Besides, even if you haven't read the book, listening in and asking questions can often enhance a future read.

Again, remember, as you read, you should:

• Gain a basic understanding of the plot, characters, themes and structure

• Determine the author's purpose

• Interpret the characters' actions

• Evaluate the author's style

• Consider your emotional response to the book

LITERARY LEXICON

Keep these literary terms in mind while you read. Being able to discuss the works on an emotional level—how you respond to the given story—is wonderful, but it is equally enriching to have a dialogue that examines the creative merits of the book. The following glossary will be helpful in an exchange on this level.

allegory: Figurative treatment of one subject, under the guise of another; symbolic narrative

anachronism: Representation of someone as existing or something as happening in other than the chronological, proper or historical order

anecdote: A short account of an interesting or humorous incident

antagonist: The principal character in opposition to the protagonist or hero of a narrative or drama

anticlimax: A decline viewed in disappointing contrast with a previous rise

antihero: A character (usually the main character) who is distinguished by a lack of traditional heroic qualities, such as idealism or courage

archetype: An ideal example of a type

climax: The turning point in a plot: there can be several climaxes before the final denoument

dialect: A regional variety of a language distinguished by pronunciation, grammar or vocabulary, especially a variety of speech differing from the standard literary language or speech pattern of the culture in which it exists

epilogue: A short addition or concluding section at the end of a literary work, often dealing with the future of its characters. In this sense, also called an afterword

essay: A short literary composition on a single subject, usually presenting the personal view of the author

figurative language: Lyrical language used in a nonliteral way (hyperbole, metaphors, similes, etc.)

folklore: The traditional beliefs, myths, tales and practices of a people

foreshadowing: To present an indication or a suggestion of an action or situation before it actually happens

genre: A category of artistic composition in literature marked by a distinctive style, form or content (mystery, science fiction, romance, etc.)

hyperbole: A figure of speech in which exaggeration is used for emphasis or effect, as in *I could sleep for a year* or *This book weighs a ton*

idiom: A speech form or an expression of a given language that is peculiar to itself grammatically or cannot be understood from the individual meanings of its elements, as in *keep tabs on*

imagery: The use of vivid language to represent objects, actions or ideas

irony: Incongruity between what might be expected and what actually occurs

metaphor: A figure of speech in which a word or phrase that ordinarily designates one thing is used to designate another, thus making an implicit comparison, as in *a sea of troubles*

motif: A dominant theme or central idea

narrative: A narrated account; a story

parody: A literary or artistic work that imitates the characteristic style of another author or work for comic effect or ridicule

plot: The plan of events or main story in a narrative or drama

point of view: The attitude or outlook of a narrator or character in a piece of literature

protagonist: The main character in a drama or other literary work

realism: The representation in literature of objects, actions or social conditions as they actually are, without idealization or presentation in abstract form

satire: A literary work in which human vice or folly is attacked through irony, derision or wit

setting: The time, place and circumstances in which a story takes place

simile: A figure of speech in which two essentially unlike things are compared, often in a phrase introduced by "like" or "as," for example, "His mind is like a sponge"

stream of consciousness: A narrative technique revealing the workings of a character's mind. Conventional syntax and punctuation is usually abandoned

surreal: Having an odd, dreamlike quality

symbolism: Attributing symbolic meanings or significance to objects, events or relationships

verisimilitude: Something that has the appearance of being true or real

voice: The distinctive style or manner of expression of an author or a character

*Definitions adapted from the *American Heritage Dictionary*

CHAPTER EIGHT

Can We Talk?
Having a Discussion That Works

Before you can begin discussing the books, your group must decide how it wants to structure the discussion. It can be informal, with everyone just jumping in, or formal, with a take-turns approach. You also must determine if a particular member will act as the discussion facilitator for every meeting or if the role will rotate. Whatever you decide, a consistent structure that all members are comfortable with should be established.

While each of the Go On Girl! chapters have a facilitator or person who oversees the group's housekeeping business, this person is not necessarily the member who leads the discussion. Our facilitators operate more as presidents of the chapters, representing her club on the organization's national board of directors and disseminating information from the national level to the local members.

Most of our chapters rotate the role of leading the discussion. That way each person gets a chance to sharpen her leadership and communications skills. In some chapters, the person hosting the meeting leads the discussion. Other groups say anybody but the hostess should lead. The thinking is she's got enough on her plate preparing the house and refreshments.

Though not widely practiced by the book clubs we know of, some groups with many members, like a community book club, solicit a professional facilitator to lead the exchange. You can check your local library, bookstore or community college to find someone to fit the expert facilitator bill.

Our discussion leader usually begins with the first of the 15 questions on our standard form. Other clubs do it differently. When New York Chapter #1 held a joint meeting with the Women's Literary Society, also of New York, we were treated to a summary of the book before the questions began. In other reading groups, the discussion leader offers a brief bio of the author, sometimes highlighted by juicy tidbits that may shed new light on the work being discussed.

While the Go On Girl! Book Club chapters fill out the club's form when discussing the book, we've never let it restrict us; we simply use it as a jumping-off point. As our chapters have grown in number, this questionnaire has become even more useful, since it allows us to have a consistent means for recording opinions of members all across the country. We even include a few questionnaires in the letters we send to authors so they can get a sampling of the often divergent opinions held by our membership. When we meet annually at our national conference, the binder full of author letters and corresponding questionnaires is always a highlight, as members look forward to reading the opinions of their sisters near and far and finding out which chapters' forms got an audience with the authors.

Go On Girls start each book discussion by examining our emotional response to the book. We ask members for an overall rating of the book, akin to four hearts (Loved It!), three hearts, two hearts, one heart (Hated It!). After recording that tally, we ask for reasons why a book worked or didn't work for members.

The next series of questions focuses on the book's content. Members discuss their impressions of the plot, memorable and favorite characters, important themes and the significance of the book's title. We then address the author's writing style and whether they left any unanswered questions. We end the discussion with a tally of how many members would recommend this book to others, how the book rates with others we've read so far in that year, and even whether we think the book cover is attractive.

In most Go On Girl! chapters, the conversation flow is very free form and rather informal. If you have something to say, you just say it. We're pretty good at letting each other finish a thought before jumping into the discussion. But this is not always the case with book clubs. It depends on the makeup of your membership. If, for example, you have more than your fair share of "Long-winded Leslies" and "Rambling Renees," it may be difficult for other members to get a word in edgewise. A number of groups, and even a few of our chapters, have had to come up with ways to give everyone a chance to participate in the discussion. We've heard of the "Talking Stick," which is held by a member while they are speaking. The discussion doesn't move on until the stick gets passed. Another group uses "The Chair." When members sit in the designated seat, they can let loose with their thoughts. When they rise, another member takes a turn.

10 Tips to Being a Good Discussion Leader

1. Even if you use a list of standard questions, come up with questions specific to the book being discussed to add depth to the dialogue.

2. Ask questions that are open-ended rather than those that generate a simple yes or no answer.

3. Pose questions that go deeper rather than broader.

4. Encourage conversation about ideas, not the plot.

5. Be a good listener by maintaining eye contact with the respondent and resisting the urge to interrupt unless they stray off course or monopolize the discussion.

6. Become adept at engaging shier types.

7. Become a master at penning in discussion hogs.

8. Clarify ambiguous responses. If you don't understand a member's comments, it's likely others feel the same way but are hesitant to speak up.

9. Recognize when the group has become too fixed on one aspect and move the discussion along to another point.

10. Know when to wrap things up.

CHAPTER NINE

What's Next?
Moving Beyond the Books

At the very first meeting of the Go On Girl! Book Club, we never imagined doing more than just reading the books and responding to authors and their publishers with letters of support. But as we've discovered, reading and discussing the books can be just the beginning. There are a number of activities your group can engage in to further expand its literary horizons. We are still in awe at how much we've grown in scope since we started. Yet there was never a blueprint; things just started happening. Through it all, we've kept an open mind. And that just may be the secret to our success.

Expanding geographically, for example, was a natural progression when members from the original chapter either relocated or were corralled by family and friends outside of New York to help them duplicate the Go On Girl! vibe in their own special circle.

Honoring our favorite authors is something our book club decided to do on a whim during our second year. Whoever thought the likes of Gloria Naylor and barbaraneely would not only acknowledge the honor, but actually come to our first awards ceremony to accept it?

Going en masse to author readings has gone from being an occasional outing for us to something we—and the authors we visit—regularly look forward to. Authors of note, especially our award winners, know they will cross paths with Go On Girls as they canvass the country.

Arranging an intimate audience with a favorite author may prove difficult, but it's not impossible. Authors actually love coming face-to-face with their readers. Of course, it helps to get a personal audience with a writer if someone in the group knows or has connections to an author. A member in one of our Brooklyn chapters is a neighbor of Donna Grant's, and she invited Grant and her writing partner, Virginia DeBerry, to attend the meeting when they discussed *Tryin' to Sleep in the Bed You've Made*. In other instances, such as the author dinners our Chicago chapters have attended with *Tumbling*'s Diane McKinney-Whetstone and *Twice I've Wished for Heaven*'s Dawn Turner Trice, author contact has come about as a result of alliances forged between local chapters and the Black bookstores in their area. Other times, our strong reputation for supporting authors has prompted them to ask for an audience with us.

Getting behind a worthy literary cause just made good sense to the progressive sisters in the Go On Girl! Book Club. Locally, members have, among other things, invested in a self-publishing project that produced an Afrocentric children's book, donated books to women's penitentiaries, collected Afrocentric children's books for a church-run day-care center and an elementary school library, supported a group of teen orators with financial and time investments, and recognized young writing talent with a student essay contest.

Collecting works by African-American authors has become an obsession for many book-club members. They not only buy hardcovers of selections on our reading list, but look to get them autographed as well. Some of us seek out first editions, which are identifiable by a date on the title page that corresponds with the copyright date. Those of us really bitten by the collecting bug have extended our search to valuable titles from the past. A few have started specialized collections, such as Black cookbooks and Black children's books.

TIP: If you're collecting books with the purpose of selling for a profit later, it's best not to have an author sign your name to a message. The book will have more value to others if it just has the author's signature.

DON'T JUST READ THE BOOKS, BRING THEM TO LIFE!

Creative ways to add excitement to the book-club experience.

• If a book is set in a particular country, why not serve the cuisine of the region? With Akosua Busia's book *Seasons of Beento Blackbird*, for example, you could present a dish native to the places the main character visits each season. Guests could be treated to foufou from Africa, conch fritters from the Caribbean and a dessert of cheesecake from New York.

• Make the setting of the book your setting. A beach meeting to talk about Terry McMillan's *How Stella Got Her Groove Back* is the next best thing to being in Jamaica.

• Take a field trip relevant to the book being discussed. Go On Girl! members in the Washington, D.C., area visited nearby Monticello, the home of Thomas Jefferson, after reading *Sally Hemings*. The historical novel by Barbara Chase-Riboud tells the story of the lifelong liaison between Jefferson and his quadroon slave. In New York, after reading *Having Our Say:*

What's Next?

The Delany Sisters' First 100 Years, members attended the Broadway production of the autobiographical novel.

- Since some of the books we've read have been produced for the big screen, a book discussion could be complemented by a video clip shown at the meeting.

- Put yourself in the story by sharing personal memorabilia relevant to the book's theme. When *Doublestitch: Black Women Write About Mothers and Daughters* was discussed by our chapter, members brought in photographs of their mothers and shared a special memory.

- Open your discussion to others who can share a unique perspective. The conversation is bound to be provocative if a Black women's reading group joined with a Jewish women's group in discussing James McBride's *The Color of Water*, which deals with him growing up as the son of an African-American man and a Jewish woman.

- To capture the period of a book, play the music of the time during refreshments or ask members to come dressed for the era.